Slap and Tickle

Also by Tom Cutler

A Gentleman's Bedside Book
The Gentleman's Instant Genius Guide

Slap and Tickle

Tom Cutler

Constable • London

Constable & Robinson Ltd
55–56 Russell Square
London WC1B 4HP
www.constablerobinson.com

First published in the UK by Constable,
an imprint of Constable & Robinson Ltd, 2012

A copy of the British Library Cataloguing in
Publication Data is available from the British Library

ISBN: 978-1-78033-611-4 (hardback)
ISBN: 978-1-78033-836-1 (ebook)

Printed and bound in the UK

1 3 5 7 9 10 8 6 4 2

MIX
Paper from
responsible sources
FSC® C018072
FSC
www.fsc.org

To the very dear and well-beloved friend
of my prosperous and evil days –

To the friend who, though in the early stages of our
acquaintanceship did ofttimes scream and howl at me, has since
become to be my most harmonious comrade –

To the friend who, however often I may wring his neck,
is never (now) discordant in revenge –

To the friend
who, marked with coolness by all the female
members of my household, and regarded with suspicion
by my very cat, nevertheless seems day by day
to be more drawn by me, and in return to
more and more impregnate me with the
resonance of his friendship –

To the friend who never tells me of my faults, never wants to
borrow money, and never talks about himself –

To the companion of my idle hours,
the soother of my sorrows,
the confidant of my joys and hopes –

My finest and sweetest guitar,
this little volume is
gratefully and affectionately
dedicated.

WITH APOLOGIES TO JEROME K. JEROME

I like my sex the way I play football, one on one with as little dribbling as possible.

LESLIE NIELSEN

Acknowledgements

Let's keep this short.

Several people who helped me with their true-life stories for this book have, understandably, asked me to camouflage their identities. Others, who didn't care, I've mentioned in the text. But who else should I thank? My parents, who wish I would grow up? My wife, Marianne, who wishes I would get a proper job? My son, Jed, who thinks I am an old fart? My friends, who wonder why I never call? My barber, Charlie, who creates the look of hair from the twelve remaining strands? My agent, Laura Morris, who looks at me kindly, but askance? My editors, Leo Hollis and Andreas Campomar, who sighed a lot? All the other guys at Constable, who turned my rambling shambles into a book? The tea, the Lagavulin and the toast, which stopped me going bonkers while I wrote? Or those ladies – they know who they are – who taught me all I know, on the practical side, anyway, about the delightful subject of this book?

No, mainly I thank myself, for my patience, hard work and exquisite good taste, for my hours of research in dusty libraries and my superb interviewing skills. I have found myself so easy to work with, and always such fun; so witty, wise, thoughtful, kind and handsome.

Who do I think I am kidding? *Nobody*. But if you can't flatter yourself in your own acknowledgements, where can you?

CONTENTS

Introduction 1

The History of Sex, 1: From the Rude Giant to stone
phalluses 3

Titbits: A quick look at breasts 20

The History of Sex, 2: From lizard tails to 'gross indecency' 29

Cock of the Walk: A quick look at the penis 48

The History of Sex, 3: From Krafft-Ebing to the
Sexual Revolution 56

Stuffed and Mounted: A penetrating look at sexual
intercourse 72

Sexuality Under the Microscope: From monkey
glands to the 'copulating machine' 88

Wash Your Mouth Out! A concise glossary of filthy
language 105

The Spice of Life: The sexual spectrum, from vanilla
to kinky 114

Fetish Me Sideways! Unusual desires, from rubber
to robots 139

Caught With Their Pants Down: Four front-page
sex scandals 148

A Helping Hand: Dildos, vibrators and sundry sex
aids down the years 170

Fancy That: The science of sexual attraction 187

Your Sex Life as a Film Title: A diversion for wet
    Wednesdays   205

When Things Go Wrong: Sexual dysfunction in
    a nutshell   209

Dirty Books, 1: A history of sexual literature   224

Cut That Out! Censorship – a brief unexpurgated history   241

Dirty Books, 2: An anthology of sexual literature   248

Glossary   272

Further Reading   288

Index   291

INTRODUCTION

This book is about sex, but it is not a how-to book, it is a cheerful history of the subject. There again, it is not exhaustive, though it may be exhausting because it's such a gigantic field. If you don't believe me, try putting the word 'sex' into an internet search engine. You will find that it brings up about 2,830,000,000 (two billion eight hundred and thirty million) results in less than a twentieth of a second. Near the top comes the female deep-sea anglerfish, a monstrously ugly cross between Vincent Price and a huge and hideous screwed-up paper bag. The only job the female anglerfish's tiny husband has in life is to attach himself to her body and dissolve, leaving nothing sticking out but his testicles, a single – or rather *double* – doleful reminder that he ever existed at all. Luckily, human sexual relations are more equitable, and it is these with which *Slap and Tickle* is chiefly concerned.

Here you will find the unusual history of sex in all its variety as practised by various human cultures down the years: the Ancient Egyptians, the Greeks and Romans, the Puritans, the Regency sex maniacs and those hypocritical naughty Victorians. The book goes right up to, and beyond, the Sexual Revolution and the freedom-soaked grooviness of the recent past, before the rise of HIV/AIDS put the kibosh on all that. Stirred into the mix is the science of sex, from the basic biology to what it is that makes us fancy certain people and not others. You can discover why women encourage promiscuity in men, find out all about 'monkey-gland' transplants, read about curious and incredible sexual maladies and, for good

1

measure, learn about Ulysses, the stupendous-sounding, first ever, 'copulating machine'.

Slap and Tickle covers the sexual spectrum from 'vanilla' to 'fetishistic', looking also at sundry sex aids down the years. There is an investigation of some hilarious front-page sex scandals and a peek at dirty books and filthy language. At the back, for aficionados, you will find some choice unexpurgated excerpts from the decidedly saucy erotica of yesteryear.

The volume is arranged in chapters, and the history is chronological, but you can read it in any order you like without missing anything. In that way it is more like *Midsomer Murders* than *EastEnders*. There is a bit of technical vocabulary sprinkled about and a few old-fashioned short words that one is not supposed to shout out in the library, but I'm sure you are sophisticated enough not to have an attack of the vapours when you read these terms in context. In case you are puzzled by any of them, there is a brief glossary at the back of the book.

Digging the golden nuggets from the rich seam of sex has been a labour of lust and I was obliged to consult a small mountain of books, some of which you will find mentioned in the 'Further Reading' table. My library researches have been augmented by the stories of various sex-havers, professional and amateur, who kindly answered my questions on the nitty-gritty. Talking to them has been a breath of fresh air. As sex worker Kitty Stryker put it to me, 'We get so much bullshit in this work I decided I'm gonna tell it like it is.'

I hope you find it all educational, informative and entertaining. I know I have.

Tom Cutler

1
THE HISTORY OF SEX, 1
FROM THE RUDE GIANT TO STONE PHALLUSES

*

'Remember, if you smoke after sex
you're doing it too fast.'
WOODY ALLEN

Cut into a chalk hillside near the village of Cerne Abbas in Dorset stands the biggest and most famous 'dirty postcard' in Britain, the Cerne Abbas Giant, which was once, but is no longer, supposed to be prehistoric. The figure is a 180-foot naked person (unmistakably male), holding a knobbed club. He is sometimes referred to as the Rude Man because of his stupefying erection, his thing being 120 feet long. His *club*, I mean. His penis is much smaller – though, scaled down, it is equivalent to a 10-incher on your average chap.

Many people still believe the Giant to be prehistoric but the earliest written reference to him was made in 1694. In *The History and Antiquities of the County of Dorset* (1774), Revd John Hutchins writes that the giant had only been carved the previous century. So it is most likely that the Rude Man is a pretty modern earthwork and not an ancient fertility symbol after all. Still, barren couples traditionally used to dance around a maypole on the white giant's thigh in an effort to evoke ancient pagan magic and encourage conception. Even today hopeful youngsters copulate on the site, points being awarded for performance by people with binoculars in the nearby National Trust car park. Not really; I made that up about points. But being what it is, the Cerne Abbas giant remains a magnetic tourist attraction, pulling in not only the long-lensed Japanese but also the occasional oddball. In August 2007 the *Dorset Echo* reported that a chap visiting the Giant, calling himself the 'Purple Phantom', had painted his penis purple (the *Giant's* penis).

Body of evidence

Few modern people go through life without sex. I mean, if they aren't actually getting any, they are probably thinking about it much of the time – especially if they are men. Indeed, Aldous Huxley characterized chastity – what people often now call 'celibacy' – as 'the most unnatural of the sexual perversions'. I think he put his finger on it there, if you will pardon the rude picture that conjures up.

Although it's as old as the hills, sex isn't the method used by all living creatures to reproduce their genes. Simple organisms like bacteria don't bother with it: they just divide, making identical copies of themselves for ever. This might save on expensive dinners and the fear of sexually transmitted infections but if humans reproduced non-sexually it would be a disaster. Just imagine endless identical copies of Piers Morgan or the

Duchess of York replicating down the generations. Absolutely frightful! No, the chief biological benefit of sexual reproduction is variety of offspring. But more important, to most of us, is that while you're propagating your genes you can have an enormous amount of fun – which people have known since long before recorded history.

About four million years ago, which isn't long in evolutionary time – some African chimpanzee-like creatures stopped walking on all fours and began wandering about on their hind legs instead. The sexual organs of these newly upright walkers (our distant ancestors) now became hard to spot. The vertical female of the species had no breasts to speak of and the male's penis was vanishingly small.

As the creatures evolved, the forest of body hair began to disappear and breasts took up residence on the female chest. The prominence of these sex organs indicated a female's suitability as a mate, but males learned, over hundreds of thousands of years, that staring at a woman's breasts was as dangerous as staring at the sun and could damage your eyes, in the sense that you could end up with black ones.

Likewise, much larger and more obvious genitalia developed on the male. Modern men may boast about their small mobile phones and large penises, but size, it seems, was already becoming important a couple of million years ago.

Charles Darwin pointed out that losing body hair and walking upright would be hard to explain from a natural-selection (survival of the fittest) point of view – you'd be colder and slower – but that they both had 'sexual-selection' (survival of the sexiest) advantages. In essence, our distant ancestors were finding less hairy partners 'sexier', and preferring mates with larger sexual organs. These upright partners could now use their hands more easily too, a significant evolutionary (not to say *sexual*) advantage.

One of the first things the less hairy upstanding male of the species did was to give the female some prehistoric chocolates and take her out to a romantic Stone Age restaurant. After the cheese and coffee he banged her on the head with his club, and dragged her back to his cave for a bit of postprandial monkey business.

It is of course conjecture just how much fun our sex-having antecedents were getting from sexual intercourse, but possibly it was a great deal. There are some primates today who spend much of their time in a kind of sex-maniacal non-stop orgy which has no reproductive function. For example, bonobos, so-called 'pygmy chimpanzees', have sex a lot. They indulge in 'French kissing' and oral sex too, neither of which makes babies. After a big fight, two bonobo males are inclined to defuse the situation by rubbing their scrotums together in an apish version of that Truth and Reconciliation Commission which Archbishop Desmond Tutu (a different kind of primate) was involved with. Perhaps British pub punch-ups and football riots could be resolved in the same way.

Modern man and his women

Anyway, as the upright-walking sex-havers reproduced down the generations they continued to evolve. Modern humans (Homo sapiens, meaning 'wise human being') are believed to have emerged in Africa about 195,000 years ago. The earliest known human art – a sign of intelligence – doesn't appear until the Upper Palaeolithic period (Late Stone Age), roughly between 40,000 and 10,000 years ago, give or take 30,000 years, but when it does, surprise surprise, sex seems to be one of the major preoccupations.

Of the few remaining examples of early human art, the Venus of Laussel, a Stone Age carving, has frankly sexual subject matter, being a naked woman with the horn – or at least with *a* horn. This voluptuous (fat) lady also has prominent sex organs. The Venus of Willendorf, a small stone-carved female figure from some time between 22,000 and 20,000 years ago shares the fat figure and large breasts of other 'Venuses' of the period, of which hundreds have been discovered. Although, like the others, her head is present, her features, interestingly, are not. Political correctness doesn't seem to have bothered the artists of the time.

Sexual subject matter is indisputably visible in cave paintings dating from around 5,000 years ago in the Val Camonica, in northern Italy. These works clearly depict a man copulating with what looks like a donkey. Similar odd scenes are also visible in Siberian rock paintings. Quite what these images of bestiality mean is the subject of vigorous dispute among archaeological academics with beards. Anyway, sex was quite clearly all over the place and it looked the same then as it does now – donkeys aside. Some of the sexual depictions resemble modern-day porn. In a fascinating piece of Mongolian rock art a lady is to be seen effecting fellatio on one gentleman while having sexual intercourse with another – one of the earliest examples of multi-tasking, a skill for which women are now famous.

The carving of small figurines like the 'Venuses' lasted into the Mesolithic period (Middle Stone Age), while huge upright stones from the Neolithic period (New Stone Age) are still visible today in parts of Britain and France. These can be suggestively phallic, especially with the sun behind them. Le Grand Menhir Brisé is a huge one of these, and at some sixty feet in height was once the largest known standing stone in Europe. Today it is broken into huge pieces which lie where they fell, possibly at the moment of unsuccessful erection, if you understand me.

Early sex books

As civilization progressed, sex remained, along with the weather, a main topic of conversation amongst gentlemen around the globe, as well as a few ladies. Ancient Indian, Greek, and Roman texts overflow with sex, and some were lavishly illustrated. The Bible is famously stuffed with sex, and violence too, and the subject was clearly on everybody's mind, as well as in nearly everybody's bedroom. Indeed, since our forebears started walking upright, sex and hunger have been the two vital motivating forces. Things haven't changed much either: food and sex continue to sell very well. I was in Wardour Street recently and I saw a man selling hot dogs outside a porn cinema.

Although examples of sex books are fairly few before the Classical period, India has long had a reputation in this area, taking a practical approach to sex education through literature as well as art. Among the oldest books in the world are the Vedas, a large body of Sanskrit texts from Ancient India, dating from around 1500–1000 BCE, roughly the period of the Late Bronze Age and Iron Age. These Hindu writings show that in Ancient India sex was regarded as a marital duty. They also reveal differences in moral attitudes and sexual practices between the rich and powerful and the man in the street. Polygamy, for example, was practised by the rich but not by the poor, which is interesting as I find few men survive one wife, let alone two, three or more.

The *Kama Sutra*, the best known of the old Indian sex books, contains practical advice on sexual intercourse in many different positions. Its separate parts were written between about 400 BCE and 200 CE, though many of the sex positions look to me like recipes for slipped discs and twisted quadriceps. After doing some of the more acrobatic ones I think a large tin of Ralgex would be on the cards, though care would be required. A rugby-playing friend of mind once sprayed his thigh with the stuff but overshot the runway, liberally squirting his nether regions. He told me he suddenly felt as if his scrotum was on fire and found himself performing an involuntary dance – with noises – around the changing room.

In case you are wondering, 'Kama' means sensual pleasure, and 'Sutra' may be translated as 'a collection of aphorisms in the shape of a manual'. It's not just about sex, though; it also concerns thoughts on virtue, the nature of love, family life and how to start your car on a cold morning. (Not really.) The *Kama Sutra* was first translated into English in 1883 by the exotic not to say Byronic Sir Richard Burton, an intrepid explorer and fan of sex and sex books. Burton was a funny chap, who recorded the length of the natives' penises in the various places he went to and then put them down in his travel books – a sort of *Hitchhiker's Guide to Knobs*. He was helped in the translation of the *Kama Sutra* by his chum F. F. Arbuthnot, an orientalist and phallus expert. The book was privately printed by the Kama Shastra Society, an entirely made-up body consisting only of the strange couple, Burton and Arbuthnot. By this sleight of hand the pair dodged the obscenity laws of the time.

In China the *I Ching*, an ancient and rather inscrutable text, deals surprisingly straightforwardly with sex, at one point describing heaven metaphorically copulating with earth. The size of the condom required for that one boggles the mind. The Chinese Taoist tradition, beginning some time around the sixth century BCE, extolled something called 'The Joining of the Essences'. The theory was that by practising this, you would do your 'energetic substances' a world of good and be healthy and possibly even immortal. But the cost seems to have been high. For example, one of the Taoist 'energetic substances' is *jing*, and once this has all been used up, say through the loss of body fluids, the body dies, or so they reckon. The fluid claimed to contain the most *jing* is, wait for it, yes, semen, so Taoists recommended decreasing the frequency of, or complete avoidance of, ejaculation so as to conserve 'life essence'. Assuming, for argument's sake, the truth of the Taoist assumptions (which are plainly crackers), there can't be many chaps who would sign up to have their assets frozen in this way.

The Chinese thinker Confucius (551–479 BCE), who had a thing or two to say about sex, prefigured the thinking that developed later in the Christian church, proposing for example that marriage should be a monogamous relationship. But in works from the Tang dynasty (618–907) and from the much later Qing dynasty (1644–1912), a broad spectrum of sexual practices is recorded, including homosexual as well as heterosexual goings on.

Confucius's monogamy idea was certainly not taken up by the Japanese, whose attitudes were much more relaxed. Married men often dallied with courtesans, and the Japanese novel *The Tale of Genji*, written in the early eleventh century, treats eroticism as an important part of life, not just a duty. Prostitution too has a long tradition in Japan, with ladies of questionable virtue becoming especially popular during the 'Japanese economic miracle' following the Second World War – mainly because evening entertainments were tax-deductible. This is an example of having your tart and eating it too.

Japanese pornography has acquired an international reputation in modern times owing partly to their technical nous, and partly also to the diversity of the subject matter. The Japanese fetish scene flourishes today, reminding me of a man I once worked with who had been a sailor in the Far East during the Second World War. 'Those Japanese girls,' he said to me one day as he scrubbed a plate, 'will do *anything*.' It was an idea to conjure with as a young chap, and I did.

The sex-mad Egyptians
The Ancient Egyptians have been a bit left out of the story of sex, partly because the Greeks and Romans cast rather a long shadow. We normally think of the Egyptians either as desiccated mummies with their guts in jars or as haughty pharaohs ordering slaves about in another pyramid-building project. But they were not so different from the rest of us. Hidden away in Ancient Egyptian temples you can today find all kinds of rude religious iconography.

In several temples religious images of gods with stupendous erections are to be found, including a cracking one of Geb, the god of the Earth, indulging in a bit of auto-fellatio. This is not the kind of religious picture the Archbishop of Canterbury would be likely to commission for the wall of Lambeth Palace. We have become more puritanical in the modern age.

Pith-helmeted archaeologists have discovered several fascinating sexual illustrations which show that Ancient Egyptian party makers behaved very much as modern party makers do. For instance, enthusiastic sex-havers often appear in the same pictures as people making music and drinking alcohol. It's the old story of wine, women and song all over again.

The rudest of all known Egyptian artefacts can be seen in the Museo Egizio in Turin. Evasively known as Papyrus 55001, or more informatively as the Turin Erotic Papyrus, it is well over 1,000 years old, dating from the twentieth dynasty of Ancient Egypt 1186–1069 BCE. Though damaged, the Bronze Age artwork remains intact enough for scholars – or just men in raincoats – to make out a number of supernaturally endowed and acrobatic old fellows giving a few young ladies the benefit of their experience. So graphic are the illustrations that the papyrus has been described as 'the world's first porn mag', and, 'the filthiest book in all of ancient history'.

The papyrus is long and skinny and full of holes, and owing to the ravages of time it has had to be preserved between glass sheets. According to Ancient Egyptian porn experts, the girls in the pictures are under the influence of the narcotic lotus flower, which is painted above their heads (*drugs* now). In between the illustrations of the ladies sitting stark naked on pointy things, and couples having explicit and enthusiastic sex, two of them in a rather spiffing chariot, the papyrus is sprinkled with dirty talk. This is not a religious piece; it is an ancient example of that modern phenomenon: the dirty book, just much more elegant,

and it makes the Egyptians seem a lot less remote and more like us than those chilly, if gorgeous, sarcophagi.

The first record of a possibly homosexual couple in history is an Egyptian relief from 2400 BCE showing a male pair, Khnumhotep and Niankhkhnum. They are pictured in a nose-kissing position, the most intimate pose in Egyptian art.

Those Greeks
For their part, the Ancient Greeks left behind them a cornucopia of rude writing and sexual imagery and are particularly well known for their relaxed, not to say encouraging, attitude to homosexual relationships, which are even depicted on vases and whatnot. Greek writers, including Plato, have filled us in a bit on the detail of male homosexual relations. In his *Symposium*, Plato also mentions female homosexuality. Sappho, a lady poet from the now famous island of Lesbos, wrote many love poems addressed to the female sex, thereby accidentally lending her island's name to the love that used not dare to speak its name but, as Robertson Davies

put it, now won't shut up. Male same-sex relations were openly practised, and officially sanctioned, from the seventh century BCE. Known as 'pederasty' or *paiderastia*, meaning 'love of boys', these relationships, which went on all over the place, including in the military just as today, were subject to an elaborate social code and were intimately entwined with Greek culture and philosophy. The spiritual and erotic relationships between men and boys were thought superior to the bluntly sexual sort, being a kind of Carpentry-and-Media-Studies apprenticeship, maybe with a bit of sex on the side, just as in the English public school system.

The first Athenian pederasts were aristocrats whose role was to educate, protect and provide a model for their *eromenoi* ('loved ones'). Their payment, intellectually anyway, was supposedly the boys' beauty, youth and promise, so there was more to it than just jumping too low in the leapfrog, which is what it looks like on those vases. These relationships were not quite what we would term 'homosexual' today, because the men involved would commonly also have wives, and/or 'girlfriends'. And, in any case, the ancient concept of 'homosexuality' was much vaguer than the modern one.

Marriage was not the same then, either. Marriage today is based on ancient cultural practices and on the doctrines of the medieval Christian church. Until modern times marriage had been a practical business transaction between two families, who often arranged the deal. The British royal family only stopped doing it this way fairly recently.

Greek husbands in their thirties commonly took very young teenagers as their wives. Moreover, they regarded them as little more than commodities: baby factories whose function was to put aside their supposed envy of the male sex organ and get on with having children. Neither were these unlucky wives mistresses in their own boudoirs, being obliged to compete sexually with their husbands' *eromenoi*, and with courtesans too. These courtesans were not just good-time girls, they were sophisticated and well-educated female 'companions', though they often did have sexual relations with their bosses, rather in the style of today's more enthusiastic au pair girls. So being a Greek wife wasn't necessarily a load of fun.

Not surprisingly, modern Greeks are very touchy about all this, especially the gay thing. In 2002 a conference paper on the subject of Alexander the Great's homosexuality caused such outrage that the meeting was invaded by protesters, and when a film, *Alexander*, came out two years later, spluttering Greek lawyers threatened to sue the film's makers.

The first properly recorded stirrings of medico-sexual science began in Greek times with Aristotle (384 BCE–322 BCE), one of the fathers of Western philosophy. Unfortunately, old Aristotle was a beginner in the subject of female sexual anatomy, believing that the uterus moved around a woman's body during the month, changing her mood according to where it was. When her womb was in her heart she cried more and when it was in her head she would go bonkers (the first recorded identification of PMS). Indeed, the word 'hysteria' comes from the Greek *hystera*, meaning 'womb'. I'd better get off this subject or I'll get letters.

The other thing the Greeks are famous for is their celebration of the phallus, sometimes in the shape of a herm, a statue in the form of a square stone pillar surmounted by a bust or head, especially of the phallic god Hermes. Hermes' name comes from the pillar (*herma*), not the other way round. Anyway, these pillars had erect penises eye-catchingly carved in just the right spot, and passers-by would rub them with olive oil for good luck. You might like to try that yourself on the beach next summer. Just get yourself a bottle of cooking oil and a sign saying, 'Roll up, roll up for free good luck.' Let me know how you get on.

Amongst the other gods worshipped by the Ancient Greeks was Eros, who gave his name to 'eroticism', and whose statue you can see in Piccadilly Circus, firing one of his arrows at the Japanese tourists. He was the god of love, lust and sexual intercourse, who bestowed the gifts of sexual desire and pleasure, while driving people mad.

Roman scandals

Hard on the heels of the Ancient Greeks came the rude Romans, who have since acquired an unrivalled reputation for excess and sexual licence. Although the Romans didn't take wholeheartedly to the Greeks' sexual philosophy, culture and practices, they did worship a similar love god, Cupid by name. They also adopted the famous herm. Sexual variety was big with them and the sex orgies of Ancient Rome have become something of a cliché.

The ancient festival of Lupercalia, observed in February, included an archaic fertility rite, and the Floralia festival saw Roman temples decked with flowers, as citizens donned bright clothes and stood around watching nude dancing. While this was all going on, Roman prostitutes did a brisk trade. Sex was not a separate behind-closed-doors thing for the ancients; it was a celebratory part of everyday life.

When the Roman Republic ended in some annoying civil wars and was replaced by the Roman Empire, Rome's first emperor, Augustus, oversaw the introduction of legislation to try to control adultery. For example, married women who had affairs were now to be punished, though not the men, which you might think was a naughty boys' charter, seeing as how they could get off scot-free.

When Pompeii was excavated in the 1860s, much Roman erotic art saw the light of day for the first time in 2,000 years. The Obscene Publications Act of 1857 had already prohibited the publishing of much of the jolly, cheerful and life-affirming rudery that people had been turning out around the globe since Palaeolithic times, and the Victorians, who were alleged (quite falsely, actually) to cover their piano legs for fear of alarming the servants, went white with shock when they saw the Roman 'porn'. So they just hid the rude images in a cupboard (after having a good look themselves) and the only people then allowed access were 'scholars', members, naturally enough, of the rich-and-powerful brigade. The working classes were kept well away, in case they might be turned into werewolves by the sight of a chap in a toga rogering a lady, a goat or even another chap.

The Romans were flexible about sex labels and there are no Latin words for 'homosexual' or 'heterosexual'. Just like the Greeks, they saw nothing wrong with men being attracted to teenage boys, and girls too, and the Greek practice of pederasty was continued, though *effeminacy* was frowned upon. Remaining masculine and dominant was important.

In Ancient Greece and Rome the modern concept of 'sexual orientation' was unknown. Sex between men was considered part of normal, 'straight' behaviour, although chaps who took the passive role were regarded as being of a 'different' and inferior 'gender'. Modern non-Western concepts of male sexuality are comparable to this view, as any fellow who has visited the Arab world, say Tangier, Algiers or Morocco, will tell you, sometimes through gritted teeth, especially if he's been propositioned up the Casbah.

The idea of a more 'plastic' male sexual identity seems to have a universal history, and exists in animals too. Sheep and monkeys who swing both ways are ten a penny, or so I understand, and I recently read of an apparently gay penguin who, when a female was introduced into the pen he shared with his boyfriend, turned out to be bisexual when he 'left' him. Alexander Selkirk, who was the real-life model for Robinson Crusoe, and who first went to sea at fifteen to escape a formal charge of 'undecent beaiviar', wrote about the goats on his island, with whom he used to *dance*, in terms that one might find rather off-putting. But what was he to do? There weren't any humans on there and he was a red-blooded man, just possibly exploiting the plastic nature of his sexuality. As he might have said to his rescuers, 'If God had not meant man to have sex with a goat, why did he put the horns in such a handy position?' It is the same in prisons, on ships and in single-sex boarding schools, where you take advantage of what's available. After all, as Churchill said of Lord Boothby, buggers can't be choosers (see chapter XI).

The Roman aristocracy was unabashed about sex and much explicit erotic art survives from the ruined buildings of Pompeii and Herculaneum. A series of paintings from the Suburban Baths at Pompeii depicts a variety of activities including oral sex (let's hope those aristocratic ladies weren't speaking with their mouths full) and group sex with partners of both sexes in combinations of all kinds.

Prostitution was legal, public and widespread throughout the Roman Empire and the discovery of Roman coins with a very rude picture on one side and a Roman numeral on the other (called spintriae) led archaeologists to pronounce them 'brothel tokens'. However, in his 2007 paper, 'Is That A Spintria In Your Pocket, Or Are You Just Pleased To See Me?', Geoffrey Fishburn of the University of South Wales argued that the tokens might actually have been used for admission to the theatre, and bang went another theory.

Roman literature gives us an insight into the place of the golden weft of sex in the Roman robe of life. The comic playwright Plautus (died 184 BCE) wrote a number of successful sex comedies, and Ovid (died 17 CE) also presented a variety of sexual doings in his writings. The poet Horace is said to have had a mirrored room in his home, which he used to get an all-round perspective when a prostitute came calling, while Emperor Tiberius's bedrooms were adorned with 'lascivious' paintings and sculptures. Tiberius also kept a notorious sex manual by the renowned Greek poetess Elephantis.

As usual, sex and social class went hand in hand. If you were an alpha male, you got the lion's share, while the ideal Roman marriage was seen to be an affectionate partnership, in which behaving properly and having babies were important. The intertwining of the interests of the State with human sexuality and reproduction was exemplified in the Roman cult of Venus, the goddess of love, beauty, sex, seduction and fertility. No wonder her arms fell off.

While the Greeks had been keen on naked men in their art, keeping women for the most part clothed, the Romans began to show ladies like Venus with their clothes off. By the first century CE, the female nude was depicted doing all kinds of things, including sexual things. In contrast, Roman men increasingly kept their genitalia covered and were less often shown starkers, in the manner of Greek art.

The phallus

The phallus was another big thing for the Romans. The penis amulet (fascinum), meaning both *phallus* and *magical spirit*, was so common that many still survive, especially in the form of phallic wind chimes (tintinnabula). Like the modern smiley, the fascinum hung on everything from jewellery to lamps, a bell dangling from the tips of a multitude of penises.

Keeping the theme going, the Romans had a god called Priapus, whose chief attribute was his outsize erect member. You can see him and it for yourself today in Roman frescoes. If you upset Priapus he might punish you by causing a state of permanent erection in your own member, without means of relief. This was and is no laughing matter and Priapus has leant his name to the uncomfortable condition of 'priapism', an eye-watering medical emergency to this day (see chapter XV).

The phallus was worshipped worldwide, in Babylon, Egypt, Europe, India – where the god Shiva is represented by a penis –

Italy, Mexico, Persia, Scandinavia, Spain, Syria, as well as Greece and Rome. There are some huge stone phalluses to be seen cocking a snook at passers-by on various Pacific islands too. Even today in Bhutan your host will dip a wooden one in your cup before offering you tea, and possibly a custard cream.

The penis having evolved as a 'badge' of masculinity, it is no surprise that it should have been celebrated for so long, and so graphically, by men and boys. Indeed, the stylized depiction of the male genitalia engraved into the top of his school desk is the first graffito a boy is likely to encounter. But nearly equal in popularity to this tuberous pictogram is its female equivalent, the pair of gigantic breasts. Generally these are sprayed onto an underpass wall in gargantuan parabolic curves, a pair of monstrous nipples added – Rolf Harris-like – with a single squirt of the aerosol paint can. The preoccupation with this double-barrelled badge of femininity is as vigorous today as it was in the time of the Venus of Willendorf. So in the next chapter we examine breasts in more detail, to see what all the fuss is about.

11
Titbits
A QUICK LOOK AT BREASTS

*

*'Scientists now believe that the primary biological
function of breasts is to make men stupid.'*

DAVE BARRY

Breasts are the round things on a lady's chest that contain the milk-producing mammary glands. Sometimes, if oestrogen and testosterone hormone levels go wrong, they can also grow on boys and men, a condition known as gynecomastia, or, more rudely, 'moobs' (man boobs).

Apart from their brief use as convenient milk bottles, breasts play a large part in human sexual behaviour. For example, on sexual arousal, breasts get bigger and the nipples harden (the well-known 'peanut smuggling' look). But let's be honest, if it weren't for their sexual purpose they would be in the way just sitting there most of the time.

Beyond what they look like, few men know much about these cuddly glands, so it's good to know about a groundbreaking German study which reported that staring at women's breasts for ten minutes a day has the health-promoting benefits of a thirty-minute bike ride, adding five years to a man's life by exercising the heart and improving circulation.

Some comparable research from Victoria University of Wellington uncovered the related and not very surprising fact that men often look longer and harder at a woman's breasts than at other parts of her body. The researchers observed that, 'Men may be looking more often at the breasts because they are simply aesthetically pleasing, regardless of the size.' Which is a kind of 'never mind the width, feel the quality' approach. This shows not only that men make excellent art critics, but also highlights the pointlessness of Breast Awareness Week as far as men are concerned. Chaps are perfectly well aware of those things, thanks very much, sometimes painfully so.

Many hills and mountains have been named after their resemblance to breasts. The delightful sounding Maiden Paps in Scotland, and the Irish Paps of Anu sound good for a brisk hike. The US Teton Range is named after the old word for 'tit' or 'nipple', which is shared by various European languages, as in the Tetica de Bacares in Spain, and the Cerro Las Tetas in Puerto Rico.

As we all know, human knockers vary pleasingly in size and shape, and it is common for a woman's left breast to be slightly larger than the right. Symmetrical breasts are a signal of a woman in tip-top breeding condition, which might account for the male fondness for close examination of a lady's credentials. This reminds me of the limerick about a lady from Wiltshire.

> There was a young girl of Devizes
> Whose breasts were of different sizes.
> The one that was small
> Was no use at all,
> But the other won several prizes.

Pretty obviously, girls don't have breasts until puberty, when female sex hormones trigger sexual development and the boobs start to make their presence felt. Their shape depends mainly on support provided by the suspensory ligaments of Cooper, on which they are hung from the collarbone.

But ladies continue to change shape and size over time,

sometimes dramatically. In her twenties, a woman's breasts are made of fat, milk glands and connective tissue, which keeps them looking pert. But over the years the Cooper ligaments become slack, and fat replaces much of the other stuff. The breasts then sag and fall forwards like bread dough on the edge of a table under the inexorable influence of the Earth's gravitational pull.

Sizing up the competition

Even before her boobs head south and start getting under a lady's feet, size variations are remarkable, with everything from the fried-egg look to the appearance of having been shot in the back by two torpedoes. In 2009, *The Guinness Book of World Records* recognized fifty-year-old Norma Stitz, who has a non-standard bra size of 72ZZZ, as the unrivalled owner of the world's biggest unadulterated hooters. Each of Norma's un-augmented breasts weighed in at a not-to-be-trifled-with two stone.

The cliché that big breasts are a compensatory function of reduced intellect may be politically incorrect but one scientist thinks there's some truth to it. Dr Erwin O. Strassman, of Houston, Texas, surveyed more than 700 childless women and found that, on average, bigger breasts meant lower IQ scores.

But it is not only size in which nature is occasionally over-generous. When the goddess of boobs is handing out the breasts and nipples some women – and some men too – get given an extra one or two. So-called 'supernumerary nipples' are fairly common, with about one in eighteen chaps and one in fifty ladies having a spare one. West Ham footballer Jonathan Spector claims to intimidate opponents by judicious use of his third nipple, which he keeps up his sleeve – metaphorically speaking, obviously.

In 2005, Radio 1's Jo Whiley reported that a doctor had told her that a 'mole' near her breast was actually an 'accessory nipple'. Swiftly nicknamed Scaramanga by her husband, after the James Bond baddy who not only had an extra nipple but was a bit of an all-round tit, she had it removed. Like supernumerary nipples, multiple breast syndrome can also be treated with surgery – for those who believe you can have too much of a good thing.

The over-shoulder boulder holder

Holding the things up has been a bit of a task for centuries. The bra is a pretty modern invention, and even now it is a somewhat inflexible and less-than-perfect tool.

The most popular bra size in the world is B but in 2004 market research from Mintel revealed that between 1998 and 2004 British breasts had got bigger, even allowing for people's increasing girth. Bra maker Triumph discovered that the biggest breasts in all of Europe now belong to the British, with more than half of Britain's women wearing a D cup. Second place in the Triumph survey went to Denmark, followed by third-place Netherlands, but the smallest knockers belonged to the Italians, with sixty-eight per cent of Italian ladies wearing a B cup, despite all that spaghetti. In 2010 the most common bra size sold in the UK was 36D but by 2011 the biggest bra available in the shops was a whopping KK. This size increase has been attributed to all kinds of things, including the growing popularity of boob jobs, and 'better nourishment'.

In his delightful book about bra history, *Bust-Up: The Uplifting Tale of Otto Titzling* (1972), Wallace Reyburn tells how his hero loses a legal bra fight with one Phillip de Brassiere. Unfortunately, this story is entirely made up, as the fellow's name ought to indicate. After all, 'tit sling' is playground slang for a bra.

Bra-like garments appear in Minoan images from the fourteenth century BCE, and during the Ming Dynasty a cloth with cups and shoulder straps was used to support the Chinese bosom. Prototype Roman bras dating back to 62 CE can also be seen depicted in the art of Pompeii.

The word 'bra' is short for 'brassière', not to be confused with 'brasserie', which is a sort of French bar or restaurant, or 'brazier' which is a kind of metal bucket of holes, full of fire, that builders warm their hands around. 'Brassière' comes from bracière, an Old French word meaning 'arm protector' (*bras* in French means 'arm'). Over time the word changed to refer to a military breastplate, and later to a corset.

Before modern bras, ladies wore corsets to hold things in place. The corset developed from the sixteenth century until, by the nineteenth century, nifty gizmos for hanging the breasts from the shoulder were being played around with. *Vogue* magazine first used the term 'bra' in 1907, and a bra patent was issued in the 1930s. Large-scale commercial production of what look like modern bras did not begin until the 1930s, about the time 'The Star-Spangled Banner' became the US national anthem.

The word 'cup' was first recorded in 1916, when stretchable cups were used to fit the wide variety of breast sizes. Fixed cup sizes themselves were only invented in 1932.

But bra design is not an absolute science and, unfortunately, cup sizes have never been very consistent, or uniformly comfortable – I'm told. I don't know for sure because I've never had to wear a bra. Bra-fitting methods, also invented in the thirties, don't work beyond a 38D and exasperated ladies with especially big ones are advised to match any bra they wish to buy with a good one they already own. This makes you wonder how they are ever going to find out what size they really are other than by endless trial and error. In many cases it's error: apparently more than eighty per cent of women wear the wrong size bra for their bosom. The commonest reported bra faults are: 1) straps that cut into shoulders, 2) cups that are too small and, 3) narrow side panels that cause 'bulging'. Maybe there's a niche here for a new breast-sizing consultancy. You'd just need a pair of callipers, chaps, and a notebook for home visits.

In an effort to get bras to fit better, adjustable bands with hook-

and-eye fastenings were introduced, and by the end of the Second World War most with-it European women were wearing a bra. The adoption of this new technology was accounted for partly because corsets, which is what ladies had been wearing till then, contained rather a lot of metal, which was needed during the war to make guns and aeroplanes.

Early bras were stiffened with bone but metal was introduced after the end of hostilities, such that today the US Transportation Security Administration recommends that women flying by plane should avoid wearing bras containing metal because they set off the detectors. Sensing a gap in the market, Triumph unveiled its 'Frequent Flyer Bra' in 2001. It has non-metallic clasps, and underwires made of resin.

But not all ladies took bras to their bosom. In 1968, during the Miss America contest, some four hundred women protested by throwing false eyelashes, stiletto shoes, make-up, corsets and bras into rubbish bins. In an effort to make a better newspaper picture they decided to burn the contents but were forbidden. Undaunted, newspapers nonetheless began referring to the 'bra-burning' stunt, conjuring up in their readers' fevered imaginations a mental picture of flaming brassières being waved about by humourless bare-breasted feminists. As one wit put it at the time, 'I bet it was a small fire.'

As the bra had encircled the bust, it now encircled the world, lifting the bosoms of Asia, Latin America and parts of Africa. Indeed, the bra racket is now a multi-billion-dollar industry. Hong Kong Polytechnic University even offers a degree in Bra Studies, which focuses on the nitty-gritty of design and manufacture, including modules such as 'underband tension', 'bottomband pressure', 'loop density', 'elastic yarn tension' and 'cup strain'.

For nearly half a century, the Queen has taken a lively interest in the subject. In 1960, while granting Somalia its independence, Her Majesty bestowed on Rigby & Peller – the famous

Knightsbridge bra and pants firm – the Royal Warrant of Appointment, making them her official 'Corsetières', and, at the same time, augmenting her own role as the country's titular head. Rigby & Peller are big on proper, personalized measurements, taken by a professional. They believe that the tape measure alone leaves a great deal to be desired because so much hangs on the measurements, and because women are all different.

Guessing a woman's bust size
There's even a delightful game that men, and women, if they like, can play to entertain themselves and their friends: it's called 'Guessing a woman's bust size'. The bust size is the distance around the fullest part of a woman's breasts and is governed by rib-cage size. In guessing this, you need to begin with a bit of trial and error, a few game ladies and a tape measure. You should start getting the hang of things before too long. But beware, it's easy to underestimate a circumference.

Anyway, let's suppose, for practice, that you've guessed a bust size of 38 inches. *Remember this.*

Next estimate the circumference around the chest *under* the hooters. If you guess an even number, add four; if odd, add five. Your final figure is the lady's hypothetical band size. Suppose you guess 32 (even) and add four, you get a theoretical band size of 36.

To get the cup size, compare the band size with the bust size. If the numbers are the same, then she's an A cup; if the bust is an inch larger than the band, then she is a B cup; two inches larger, a C; and so forth, spasmodically through the alphabet. In our example the bust size (38) is two inches larger than the band (36), so she is a C cup. But beware: funny cup sizes like DD at the Mae West end of the scale can confuse the novice. Whatever happens, though, you'll have a lot of fun weighing the evidence and working it all out. It's better than telly, anyway.

At the present time there is a certain amount of confusion how rude a lady's breasts actually are. In some cultures, notably in African countries, women are customarily bare breasted. But in Britain, much of continental Europe and the USA a lady might well find herself being chucked out of one restaurant for discreetly feeding an infant, especially, one suspects, if she shoots an involuntary jet of milk up to three feet in response to her child's cry, as it is possible to do. In other restaurants, however, she might be welcomed to carry on suckling. It all depends on where you are and which side of bed the manager got out of.

In most developed Western cultures breasts tend to be kept under wraps in public unless a lady is on the beach, in which case people hardly bat an eye these days. Few women, though, would go shopping in Harrods with their knockers out, and no television journalist worth her salt would turn up to read out the news with her breasts exposed. Having said that, I remember a Russian television station which used to broadcast a rubbishy but popular news programme called *Naked Truth*. This low-budget show featured a pretty presenter by the name of Svetlana Pesotskaya, who took off her clothes as she read out the news. There were practical disadvantages, of course. For example, the 'journalist' was obliged to wear her microphone in her hair because there was nowhere else comfortable to stick it. But, mixing coyness with prurience, the managers at M1 TV made sure Svetlana was never fully exposed. There was always a prop, a hand or a bit of foliage to cover her embarrassment, in typical tabloid style.

Exposés
Which I suppose leads us on to Page Three girls. 'Page Three' and 'Page 3' are both registered trademarks of News International Ltd., the British news division of Rupert Murdoch's News Corporation, which, according to recent figures, was, maybe not coincidentally, the world's second-largest media conglomerate. The reason these

terms are trademarked is partly because of their profound value to the *Sun* newspaper.

The *Sun* was first published as a broadsheet in 1964 but was bought and relaunched as a tabloid by Rupert Murdoch in 1969. Photographs of glamour models immediately began to appear on Page 3, the most prominent page after the front page. In the beginning these models had their clothes on but in November 1970 the first nude appeared. She was a young model named Stephanie Rahn, who had been snapped sitting tastefully in a field. Significantly, though, one of her breasts was visible. And that was it. Over time, more fleshy real estate was gradually revealed and it wasn't long before nipples became frequent visitors to Page 3. The *Sun*'s circulation duly soared, until it was selling more papers than any other British daily.

The bare breast facts
1. The preference of the *Sun* is for round and upward-pointing young breasts. This contrasts with East Africa where they prefer them long and pendulous.
2. Breasts are the most sun-sensitive part of the female body. The skin is thin and contains few melanocytes, the cells that produce melanin, the skin's protective pigment.)
3. In some countries, women spread garlic, soot or pepper on their nipples to encourage babies to move on to solid food.
4. Breasts can grow up to a quarter during sexual arousal. This does not happen to women who have breastfed their offspring.
5. Some of the advantages of breastmilk: 1) it's sterile, 2) it's warm, 3) it contains antibodies, 4) it's cheap, 5) the cat can't get at it.

III
THE HISTORY OF SEX, 2
FROM LIZARD TAILS TO 'GROSS INDECENCY'
*

'The body is meant to be seen, not all covered up.'
MARILYN MONROE

Sexual science has tended to stagger along, rather than progressing smoothly over the ages, and the Church has often objected to progress, and to sex in general. Non-science sex books really took off during the second century CE, but this boom in Greek and Latin smut was not to last. By now, Christianity was gaining a strong foothold and straightforward descriptions of sex soon began to disappear from books, being reserved solely for theological or medical texts. Some of the classical ideas for sexual medicine might strike the urologist of today as rather unlikely. One theory recommended limiting semen production in men with cooling, drying and astringent therapies. These included the famous 'cold bath', along with advice to avoid flatulence-causing foods, which can only have been a good thing. In his book, the *De medicamentis*, Marcellus Empiricus, a Latin medical writer from Gaul, described more than seventy treatments for erectile dysfunction and growths or lesions on the genitals, as well as the best way to ensure a woman's fidelity. His recipe for this is not so much conventional as complementary:

> If you've had a woman, and you don't want another man to get inside her, cut the tail off a green lizard with your left hand and release it while still alive. Keep the tail closed in

the palm of this same hand until it dies, and touch the woman and her private parts when you have intercourse.

Let me know how you get on with this one.

The amazing Elagabalus

In 218, while still a teenager, a chap called Elagabalus (c. 203–222) became emperor of Rome, taking the name Marcus Aurelius Antoninus Augustus. His youthful exuberance was demonstrated by his fondness for an early form of whoopee cushion, which he used to blow off at cocktail parties, ruffling a few togas. But Elagabalus became infamous mainly for his unbridled sexual inhibition. He married five times, at one point taking a Vestal Virgin as his wife. This was an ostentatious breach of tradition, which insisted that any Vestal Virgin who had intercourse must be buried alive. Thank goodness modern society is more relaxed about this sort of thing otherwise the whole place would be continually dug up.

Despite sex with all these girls, Elagabalus painted his eyes and dressed in wigs before prostituting himself in taverns and brothels, and even the imperial palace. According to Roman historian Cassius Dio, he was wont to shimmer behind a curtain and flutter his lashes at passers-by, and was known for enthusiastically buttering up a string of male courtiers, who seem to have been common-or-garden 'trade'. Elagabalus is also said to have publicly 'married' an athlete called Zoticus, though his closest relationship was with a blond chariot driver named Hierocles, who he called his husband.

As if this weren't enough, Elagabalus reputedly offered money to any doctor who could furnish him with female genitalia, in what may be the first recorded case of attempted sex reassignment surgery.

It is perhaps unsurprising that Elagabalus, who offended

politicians and people alike, was assassinated in 222 in a plot involving his guards. He was only about eighteen years old.

The Good Book

The Hebrew Bible, what Christians call the Old Testament, prescribed harsh punishment for male homosexuality; it was the death penalty for both chaps (Leviticus 18:22 and Leviticus 20:13). The Old Testament has much to say on the subject of sex, all round – 'Thou shalt not commit adultery' (commandment number seven) being one of the more famous prohibitions. Unfortunately for one bible printer, a compositor's error in 1631 resulted in the word *not* being omitted, thus changing the sentence to 'Thou shalt commit adultery'. He was fined and had to pulp the books. In 2010 a rare remaining copy of this so-called *Wicked Bible* was being offered for sale for $89,500.

Another sex commandment is that one about not coveting thy neighbour's wife (number ten), which I have to confess I once broke when I lived next door to a most attractive Swedish lady, who used to dress up as an elf at Christmas, and her husband, who was away a lot. What's worse, when he accused me I bore false witness (number nine).

Deuteronomy has a whole list of sexual prohibitions, some of which carry the death penalty:

* Pre-marital sex: death by stoning for any girl not a virgin at the time of marriage (Deuteronomy 22:13–21)
* Adultery: death penalty for both partners (Deuteronomy 22:22)
* Rape of a betrothed virgin in a town: death by stoning for both partners (Deuteronomy 22:23–24). The same done *in the countryside*: death penalty for the man only (Deuteronomy 25:27)

The English translators of the Bible were a bit squeamish about some things though. In Genesis 47:29 it says,

> And the time drew nigh that Israel must die: and he called his son Joseph, and said unto him, If now I have found grace in thy sight, put, I pray thee, thy hand under my thigh, and deal kindly and truly with me; bury me not, I pray thee, in Egypt.

The translators had cleaned things up a bit, turning 'penis' into 'thigh'. The idea then being that if you were making a solemn oath your testicles would be in jeopardy if you bore false witness. When your lawyer next uses the words 'testament', and 'testify', remember that he or she is using words with the same root as, 'testicle'. Just so long as you are not asked to put your hand there . . .

Orthodox Judaism forbade, amongst other things, staring at members of the opposite sex, and wearing their clothing. It also required men and women to be separated while dancing. So any woman wearing jeans and boogying with a man while staring into his eyes would have been for it. No wonder the Orthodox disco never took off. Another rule, and one which I must say I totally agree with, is the prohibition on sex with animals and corpses. I think the no-sex-with-corpses rule is probably more important than the commandments about not working on Sundays.

For some reason, the authors of the Bible seem to have had an unhealthy preoccupation with circumcision and foreskins. According to infidels.org, the words 'circumcise', 'circumcised', 'circumcising', 'circumcision', 'uncircumcised', 'uncircumcision', 'foreskin' and 'foreskins' appear 157 times in the King James Bible, which ought to be enough for anyone.

It's not all warnings and rules, though. Proverbs 5:19 says, 'Let her be as the loving hind and pleasant roe; let her breasts satisfy thee at all times; and be thou ravished always with her love.' I certainly think that one has a lot to be said for it.

New Testament ideas about sex

Christianity became established in the first century but the New Testament has less to say on the subject of sex. Nonetheless, over the years there have always been those who wanted to pour cold water on everybody else's fun and sometimes they use the Bible as an excuse. Prudes have been pretty much against sex since the beginning of recorded time. In the British Museum you can find a statue of the Ancient Egyptian god of fertility, whose name is Min. The Egyptians gave him a large and impressive symbol of his fertile potency in the shape of a gigantic horizontal erection, but at some time in the fairly recent past some spoilsport has mutilated it by pulling it off (if you'll pardon the expression), leaving him holding nothing but fresh air. These vandals are people of the sort who procreate by Morse code and who look on a glimpse of stocking as something shocking even now, when anything goes. For many of these sackcloth personalities religious zeal is the twin trait of censoriousness. Mercifully, though, like those who hang dangly dice from their car mirrors, these Mrs Grundies warn you of their uncongenial personalities by their actions, so the moment you see one of them covering a piano leg or pursing her lips at a snogging couple, you can be grateful you've been given a clear warning; clamber out of a window and run away to a nice pub up the road somewhere.

Augustine of Hippo (354–430), also known as St Augustine, was Bishop of the interestingly named town of Hippo Regius, which today would be in Algeria, and a theologian whose writings were very influential in the development of Western Christianity.

Augustine had been a follower of the weird religion of Manichaeism but in 382 CE the Roman Emperor Theodosius I decreed that Manichaeans would be put to death. For some reason Augustine converted to Christianity, leaving his mistress and children. He embraced chastity and became more Christian than Jesus. Writing later about his conversion in his *Confessions*, he included details of his own long-standing sexual compulsions. He admitted having lived a wild life in his youth, with erotic obsessions. 'I defiled, therefore, the spring of friendship,' he wrote, 'with the filth of concupiscence [a favourite biblical word for "lust"], and I beclouded its brightness with the hell of lustfulness.' So, just like an ex-smoker who hates to see other people enjoying a fag, he pronounced the body wicked, flawed and sinful. How sad, and somewhat ironic, that a man who admitted to having major sex problems himself should end up condemning Christians to centuries of guilt and shame as part of his therapy, by making sexual desire sinful. The lunatic was not only running, but *building* the asylum.

Augustine considered lust to be one of the most grievous sins, and, having been an enthusiastic practitioner of extra-marital sex himself, he naturally forbade such relationships for others, pronouncing them unlawful and unbiblical. In the *Confessions*, he admitted to begging in his sex-addict days for 'chastity and continence', but with the qualifier, 'only not yet'. His curious answer to unbridled desire was prostitution. 'If you expel prostitution from society,' he wrote, 'you will unsettle everything on account of lusts.' A strong flavour of Augustine's harsh views on sex persists in the Christian psyche to this day, though on his last point the Church now differs from him.

Another big influence on Christian attitudes to sex came from St Thomas Aquinas (1224/25–75), who is commonly referred to as the greatest Western philosopher of the period. Like Augustine before him, Aquinas felt that though sexual temperance was virtuous, prostitution was a necessary evil. Writing about chastity in his *Summa Theologiae* he wondered whether fornication and 'nocturnal pollution' (wet dreams) were mortal sins. The wet-dream question can't have taken long to work out, since 'nocturnal emission' is about as voluntary as a sneeze. Aquinas was also quite big on 'unnatural sex' by which he meant such diverse things as homosexuality, bestiality and masturbation.

Throughout most of the Middle Ages, marriage, into which the Christian Church increasingly poked its nose, remained a romance-free economic arrangement. As the role of celibate priests became cemented in the church, ordinary church-goers found themselves getting advice on what they were, and were not, allowed to do between the sheets from people who ought to have known nothing about it. Sex advice from a chaste priest is about as useful as arse-kicking tips from a one-legged man.

The Christian position
Anyway, the things that the Church found improper about sex – now as well as then – sound a bit weird. Early religious laws were highly restrictive, insisting for example on the 'missionary position' as the only proper one for intercourse. A married couple caught (how?) having sex with the woman on top, in the 'jackhammer', 'cowgirl' or 'reverse cowgirl' positions, could be burned at the stake, which you might think is a bit of an extreme punishment for forgetting to shut your curtains. In any case, the lady-on-top position had a grand pedigree, having been popular in Ancient Rome, where it was called the *mulier equitans* ('woman riding') position.

The Church stipulated that sex was for conceiving children only. It was pronounced sinful for people, especially women, to enjoy sex and you could end up going to hell. Cynics might say that the priests, who weren't getting any, were getting their own back by making sure that anyone who was (getting any, I mean) was jolly well going to be terrified of punishment. This kind of thing is known by psychologists as 'messing with people's heads'.

Anyway, you can bet it didn't stop people enjoying sex. After all, the forbidden is always exciting.

The Church's obsession with sex is, some might say, a bit suspect. It is rather like the anorexic's obsession with food and if you don't believe that the baleful influence of the Church's ideas about sexual relations has lasted, you should see what the young vicar's wife says next time you try asking her to join you and your partner for a threesome. It's not going to happen, is it?

As the Catholic Church continued its busybodying through history, your ordinary working man and lady took little notice, and their disregard for the niceties of proper conduct has been celebrated in literature and art down the centuries. During the Renaissance, the cultural movement that ran roughly from the fourteenth century to the seventeenth century, paintings and sculpture became an orgy of human nudity. A good place to see this is on the ceiling of the Sistine Chapel, which is chock-a-block with nakedness that would never have been allowed in the medieval period.

Fourteenth-century filth

Geoffrey Chaucer's *The Canterbury Tales*, a collection of earthy stories written in Middle English at the end of the fourteenth century, concerns a group of pilgrims travelling from Southwark to Canterbury Cathedral. The tales contain a liberal sprinkling of fourteenth-century filth. *The Miller's Tale*, for example, never fails to raise the eyebrows of GCSE-English-exam question-setters with its reference to a chap called Nicholas who says he will die if he does not have his end away with a babe called Alisoun, before smartly grabbing her 'queynte', which, if you say it out loud – or under your breath if you are in church – sounds very like the short word much used by ruffians to this day to refer to the female genitalia:

And prively he caughte hire by the queynte,
And seyde, 'Y-wis, but if ich have my wille,
For derne love of thee, lemman, I spille.'

Roughly translated into polite, though ill-scanning, English this means,

And unnoticed he caught her by the whisker biscuit,
Saying, 'Indeed, unless I have my will,
For secret love of you, sweetheart, I'll spill.'

French letters

De morbo gallico ('On the French disease', which is to say, syphilis) was a work by the Italian anatomist Gabriello Fallopio (1523–62). Often known by his Latin name, Fallopius, he was one of the most important anatomists and physicians of his age. He studied the reproductive system in both sexes and described the Fallopian tube which now bears his name. In his treatise, published after his death, he advocated the prophylactic use of condoms, and set up the first French-letter clinical trial. His condoms were not like the modern sort you get out of the bubblegum machines in the pub gents', but rather a linen sheath, which he claimed to have designed. These weren't exactly comfy, being put on over the glans but under the foreskin, or even inserted into the Jap's eye, a slang term, which, like others, pays no heed to possible ethnic offence. Any man still standing to attention after that rigmarole deserves a medal.

Fallopius found himself in competition with a contemporary, Realdo Colombo, or Renaldus Columbus, (c. 1516–59), an Italian professor of anatomy and a surgeon at the University of Padua. Shortly before his death Colombo published his only work, a book of anatomy entitled *De Re Anatomica*, which contained a lot of stuff that overlapped with the discoveries of

Gabriel Fallopio. The most interesting of these was his claimed discovery of the clitoris, which he called 'the love or sweetness of Venus'. Fallopius didn't think much of this and said *he'd* discovered it, down the back of his sofa, possibly. In any case, both claims were later questioned by a Danish anatomist called Caspar Bartholin the Younger, who said the clitoris had been known to anatomists since the second century. It only goes to show that egos were big even then.

But it wasn't long before Puritanism descended, not on Italy but on England, with the establishment of the Commonwealth (1649–60) and the arrival of Oliver Cromwell (1599–1658). H. L. Mencken amusingly defined Puritanism as 'the haunting fear that someone, somewhere, may be happy'. Cromwell's regime certainly seemed a bit like that, frowning on wine, women and Christmas carols, let alone the clitoris, and put paid to the tradition of English bawdiness by instituting a long and dreary ban on public stage performances. We will draw a veil over this glum period because much more fun was just round the corner.

Not long after Cromwell's death there came a delightful resurgence of unrespectable English drama, officially sanctioned by the newly restored monarchy in the shape of King Charles II. The famous Restoration comedies, written and performed in England between 1660 and 1710 marked a return to rudeness.

Casanova

The Enlightenment of the eighteenth century encouraged a more adult look at the vagaries of sex. Giacomo Girolamo Casanova de Seingalt (1725–98) is the most famous sex maniac of the period. Casanova's Italian name translates as Jim Newhouse, which doesn't sound romantic enough for this legendary seducer. By his own accounts he was a satyromaniac – the male equivalent of a nymphomaniac – reputedly breakfasting off forty-eight oysters every morning, served on a lady's naked breasts. All I can say is

that he must have been perkier at cockcrow than I am; it's all I can do to swallow a charcoal biscuit and a cup of Tetley.

In his book, *Histoire de ma vie* (*My Life Story*), Casanova endlessly reported how brilliant he was in the seduction department. The occupational hazard of this was, unfortunately, sexually transmitted infections, and the pox (syphilis), gonorrhoea and other venereal diseases dogged him throughout his life. In later years he sometimes dressed as a woman (don't ask me why) before dying in bed – *on his own* – in 1798.

By the eighteenth century sexual science was beginning to be treated seriously. Samuel Auguste André David Tissot (1728–97) was a Swiss physician and medical adviser to the Pope who, in 1760, published *L'Onanisme*, a monograph on the subject of masturbation and its putative ill effects, thus influencing the unfavourable view of hand shandies that would prevail for centuries to come.

Tissot's exposition was named after Onan, a biblical character who when his brother died, was told by his dad to fulfil his duty by giving his sister-in-law children. After going through the preliminaries, though, Onan 'withdrew', 'spilling his seed on the ground', and was sentenced to death by God.

As you will have spotted, the *Bible* story does not refer to 'weasel greasing' at all but to coitus interruptus, so Tissot, and maybe the Catholic Church, was a bit confused on this point. Nonetheless, Tissot argued, like the Taoists, that semen was an 'essential oil', which, if lost from the body in large amounts, would cause weakness, blurred vision, nervous disorders, gout, rheumatism, enfeeblement of the genitals, poor appetite, headaches and bad memory. There were other symptoms – but I can't remember what they were.

Frog pants
Another interesting sex-related discovery of the early eighteenth century came from the work of Lazzaro Spallanzani (1729–99), an Italian Catholic priest and biologist who in 1777 did the first IVF experiment. He debunked the popular idea that life just sprang from nowhere, and refused to believe, as others did, that a piece of cheese could give birth to mice. In a series of rather hilarious but efficient experiments, he put little pairs of taffeta pants on male frogs. This proved that they were unable to father tadpoles with their clothes on, and demonstrated that sperm are not there just for fun. Of course it could also have been that those frogs were too embarrassed by their very un-masculine frilly knickers to perform, but he forgot to test this.

The other big name around this time was Donatien Alphonse François, Marquis de Sade (1740–1814), who was a bit younger than Casanova, and a French libertine aristocrat into the bargain. De Sade is best known for his pornographic writings, which, unusually, mixed philosophy with violent sex fantasies and rude abuse of the Catholic Church. In 1801 Napoleon Bonaparte, who didn't like his books, ordered his arrest and he was picked up at his publishers and imprisoned without trial. After his family got involved, he was declared insane in 1803. Much of de Sade's writing was done in prison, but after his death his son destroyed all his unpublished manuscripts.

The sex-mad prince

In 1811, a couple of years before de Sade's death, the Regency period, which lasted until 1820, had begun in England. The name of the period resulted from King George III going a bit bananas and his sex-mad, boozy, profligate, vain, gluttonous, adulterous and mistress-mad son, the Prince of Wales, taking over as Prince Regent: a sort of proxy – not to say *poxy* – monarch. He was an unpopular man and an unpopular Prince Regent, *The Times* writing that he preferred 'a girl and a bottle to politics and a sermon'. But though he led a decadent life, he contributed greatly to the romance of the period.

Bawdy art flourished during the Regency, too, while a host of delightfully rude songs and ballads kept people chuckling, a tradition that continued into the Victorian and Edwardian music hall. Three eighteenth-century artists, George Cruikshank, James Gillray and Thomas Rowlandson, published many satirical cartoons during the period. Rowlandson's were particularly juicy. All the new sexual licence did nothing to put the hat on venereal disease and pregnancy, and both continued to be a nuisance – sometimes a deadly one.

Oh, no! It's the Victorians

Naturally there was a backlash against the sexual freedom of the Regency, and it came with the development of a *new* Puritanism during the reign (1837–1901) of the dour and un-sexy Queen Victoria. This pendulum-swing back to sexual repression was enthusiastically enforced by black-suited officials of the increasingly powerful middle classes, and its squeamish influence lasted well into the first half of the twentieth century.

Nonetheless, the stereotype of prudish Victorians covering their piano legs for shame is well debunked by academic Lesley Hall, on her website lesleyahall.net. She says that the piano-leg story originated in an 1839 book, *Diary in America*, by the resoundingly named Captain Frederick Marryatis, and that the author intended it to poke fun at prissy *Americans*. The other famous story, about Queen Victoria declining to outlaw lesbianism in the Criminal Law Amendment Act of 1885 because she couldn't believe it was physically possible, Hall simply describes as 'a myth'.

The Victorians' attitude looks a bit confused, or hypocritical, today. They regarded masturbation, homosexuality and female sexuality as mental illnesses, yet there was plenty of pornography and prostitution around if only you went looking for it, and plenty of venereal disease too. The theory has long been that while polite and upright Victorian chaps with magnificent beards were being told by experts in the science of moral panic that they must limit sex within marriage, and shun fornication, masturbation and nocturnal emissions, they were secretly having a high old time availing themselves of Victorian prostitutes. All the while their demure wives are supposed to have shuddered over their sewing at the very thought of 'intimacy'. The idea that women found the whole business repulsive is exemplified in the much-repeated sex advice of a concerned mother to her anxious virgin daughter, 'Lie back and think of England.' Lesley Hall has found no persuasive evidence that this was ever really said by anybody, amusingly adding, 'It sounds most unlike anything the dear Queen would have said herself.'

Despite the prevalent misconception that they had sex only by telegraph, the inhabitants of the British Empire seem to have been perfectly normal in their sexual behaviour, though somewhat twee in their professed or official attitudes. There is no reason to believe that Victorian women hated sex then any more than women do now. No, much like the Palaeolithic Venuses, the Greeks, Romans and everyone else of years gone by, your typical Victorian lady had as much fun in bed as people always have had. They just weren't supposed to talk about it in the knitting circle, that was all.

The trouble was that all the whispering and pretending were likely to lead to social discomfiture, shame and mechanical ignorance. Although Victorian men had an excellent under-standing of the way a mill wheel works, or how to shove a boy up a chimney to clean it, many were in the dark when it came to the mechanics of sex, the female anatomy being as foreign to them as the exotic flora of an Antarctic ice shelf. They would have been more confident, these chaps, taking apart a lawnmower than trying to have sexual intercourse with their wives. Indeed, sex education for some Victorian men was often just a lesson in the basics from a boy with a bottle and stick in the playground. For women, it was pretty much nothing, and they were left ignorant of the alarming conundrum of sex until their wedding night, when it became a case of suck it and see.

Dirty photographs
Nonetheless, being an entrepreneurial society, the Victorians, for whom the daguerreotype – the first high-quality photographic process – was the latest thing, quickly established a vigorous industry in 'dirty' photographs, under the noses of the finger-wagging and elevated detachment of the authorities.

But the camera didn't put paid to old-fashioned penmanship. In France Édouard Manet was painting perfectly respectable nudes, using photographs as a source, while Edgar Degas and Henri de Toulouse-Lautrec were producing a number of fairly raunchy ones too. A French commercial artist of the time, Édouard-Henri Avril (1843–1928), was churning out illustrations for explicitly pornographic books. Having studied at the École des Beaux Arts in Paris, Avril was commissioned to illustrate Théophile Gautier's novel *Fortunio* (1836) and did so, adopting the pseudonym Paul Avril. He went on to illustrate John Cleland's notorious *Memoirs of a Woman of Pleasure* (1748), better known as *Fanny Hill*. *Fanny Hill* is not a picnic site in Surrey but a rip-roaring dirty book: arguably the prototype English pornographic novel.

Among Paul Avril's other works are his pictures for the anonymous lesbian novel *Gamiani* and some for Hector France's exciting-sounding *Musk, Hashish and Blood*, which could be the nineteenth-century equivalent of a Harold Robbins book. But his major project was to provide illustrations for the French translation of *De figuris Veneris* (*On the figures of Venus*), an anthology of Ancient Greek and Roman erotic writings, classified by subject.

First published in Latin and Greek in 1824, it was later translated into English, French and German. The work concludes with a heroic list of ninety-five sexual positions, the illustrations of which would have made Queen Victoria's crown go wonky if she'd seen them. Reproduced above is a typical one, showing an office-party scene. We've all been to dos like that, haven't we?

Along with its healthy trade in dirty books, the nineteenth century was also a time of new scholarly investigation into sexual psychology, when science began catching up with art in its interest in sex. One of the Victorians' chief medical preoccupations was masturbation, for the preclusion of which a number of terrifying mechanical devices were devised. Masturbators were said to be identifiable by their flabby, pale and tubercular appearance and their withdrawn demeanour – a pronouncement that must have made every Victorian schoolboy rather self-conscious.

'Fallen' women

Paternalistic consternation over 'fallen women' reached its pinnacle in the 1850s and 1860s and moves were made to drive these supposedly verminous, depraved and dangerous members of the oldest profession from the streets, or to 'save them'. Even the future prime minister W.E. Gladstone trolled the pavements at night, seeking out girls he could persuade to give up their well-paid business, and their autonomy, and be 'looked after'. I don't wish to appear cynical but I can't help wondering about Mr Gladstone's subconscious motivations.

As Matt Groening said, 'When authorities warn you of the sinfulness of sex, there is an important lesson to be learned: do not have sex with the authorities.' For more than forty years, from the 1860s on, the social (*read* 'sexual') purity movement, consisting mainly of do-gooding women, sought to abolish prostitution and other 'immoral' activities. Dry as a stick, the movement was chiefly opposed to legalization of prostitution, but soon, having tasted blood, became interested in opposing 'indecent' theatrical displays, nudes in art galleries, contraception, and then got all interested in censorship.

The deliciously named Laura Ormiston Chant (1848–1923) was an active member of the Gospel Purity Association, the Ladies' National Association, and editor of the *Vigilance Record*, the journal of the National Vigilance Association. She wrote hymns, poetry and pamphlets, and lectured in Britain and America on 'social purity', temperance and women's rights. In 1894 Chant accused the Empire Theatre of Varieties in Leicester Square of dressing its ballet dancers in grossly indecent costumes. Having myself seen a photograph of Rudolf Nureyev in a pair of tights, I can see her point, much as she could see the points of some of the dancers.

But, by the 1890s the spinsterish pouts and lemon-faced tutting of the purity people seem to have troubled people less and artists continued to depict sex in the same way as they had always done. The illustrator and author Aubrey Beardsley (1872–98) was a leading figure in the Aesthetic movement, which was concerned with decadence, and which, naturally enough, also included Oscar Wilde (1854–1900). Beardsley's illustrations frequently included frankly sexual subjects, covering all the bases, though the nature of his own sexuality remains somewhat mysterious.

Acts of buggery and the Buggery Act

Oscar Wilde ended up as the most public casualty of an 1885 change to the English law, and was imprisoned under it in 1896. In England and Wales, 'sodomy', or 'buggery', had been made a criminal offence during the reign of Henry VIII, by the Buggery Act of 1533, and until 1861 was punishable by death. But in 1885 Parliament enacted the Labouchere Amendment prohibiting 'gross indecency' between males, a broad waffly term which was meant to cover most or all male homosexual acts. One suspects that this vagueness of terminology was because the prohibitors either didn't like to think about the acts, or *did* like to think about them and were covering their traces. As Christopher Hitchens once pointed out, 'Nothing optional – from homosexuality to adultery – is ever made punishable unless those who do the prohibiting (and exact the fierce punishments) have a repressed desire to participate.'

It was the best part of a century before sexual acts between two consenting men, with no other people present, were legalized on the UK mainland. It was longer for Northern Ireland (1982) and Guernsey (1983), and more than a hundred years for Jersey (1990) and the Isle of Man (1992). In the United States it was 1973 before the American Psychiatric Association finally declassified homosexuality as a mental illness by removing it from the *Diagnostic and Statistical Manual of Mental Disorder.*

By contrast, some nineteenth-century English laws governing sexual behaviour have never been repealed. In Birmingham, for example, an old byelaw makes it illegal to have sexual intercourse on church steps after sundown – though nothing is said about *before* sundown. In the United States, a few laws passed by the various colonial parliaments during the nineteenth century remain accidentally in force. Sex with a porcupine is still illegal, not to say extremely hazardous, in Florida, where it is also against the law to handle a woman's breasts. I should think well over fifty per cent of the population must have committed this crime at some stage. In the town of Conorsville, Wisconsin, it is an offence (an unlikely sounding one) for a man to fire his gun while his wife is having an orgasm. Prostitutes in South Dakota may not ply their trade from a covered wagon and in Minnesota it is illegal to hang male and female underwear from the same washing line. In Tremonton, Utah – one of the states in which it is illegal for a man to have an erection that can be seen through his clothing – a lady is not allowed to have sexual intercourse with a gentleman in an ambulance, while in Kingsville, Texas, pigs are not permitted to have intercourse on airport property, though the cops are going to have their work cut out taking a statement from a rutting boar. Many American states continue to outlaw what Rhode Island calls an 'abominable, detestable crime against nature', and what South Dakota more succinctly calls 'copulation by means of mouth'. But, let's face it, this is going to be another tough problem for the overworked police force to lick.

IV
COCK OF THE WALK
A QUICK LOOK AT THE PENIS

*

'My friend Billy had a ten-foot willy,
He showed it to the girl next door.
She thought it was a snake
So she hit it with a rake,
And now it's only five-foot-four.'

PLAYGROUND RHYME

Voted the best restaurant in the world three years running, from 2010 to 2012, the Copenhagen-based Noma sounds remarkable. On its varied menu are such delicacies as live ants, wriggling prawn and fried moss. But this is nothing compared to Guo-li-zhuang (literally 'the strength inside the pot'), a Chinese restaurant nestling on the interestingly named Dongsishitiao Street, in Beijing.

This is the country's first penis restaurant. But *Why?* you might ask. Well, according to Chinese 'experts', eating penises is good for a man's sexual potency, and at Guo-li-zhuang you can treat yourself to mouth-watering horse, snake, ox and duck dick, amongst other delicacies. Women need not feel left out either, because eating penis improves a lady's complexion. Or so they claim.

This is all fair enough, I suppose, if you forget the phrase, 'You are what you eat', and I must say the 'fried and flambéed steamed yak penis' sounds good to me, as does 'sheep's testicles on a bed of curry'. You can get *boiled* testicles too, not by spending too long in a hot bath, but by asking the waitress to cook them for you in a tasty broth.

For the truly inquisitive, Guo-li-zhuang offers a hotpot of penises of ten different kinds, and if you're after something less challenging, there's always penis-on-a-stick. Called 'Henry's whip', this is a sheep-derived dish that comes coated with sweet cheese and mayonnaise, allegedly in the Western style.

As Shakespeare said in his *Sonnets to Sundry Notes of Music, IV*, 'Were kisses all the joys in bed, One woman would another wed', and since his day we have had time to study the male copulatory organ at length, and have learned a great deal about it.

The human penis is the largest among the primates, both in proportion to body size and absolutely. An adult chimp's erect penis is, for example, only about 3 inches (8 centimetres) in length and a gorilla's is just half that.

Although the blue whale has an impressive popular reputation, having a penis you can drive a car along, the barnacle holds the world-beating penis-to-body-size record. A barnacle's willy can grow to up to forty times its body length, and Mr Barnacle can reach females who live round the corner of the rock, without having to get up off the sofa. For a six-foot-tall man this would be the equivalent of a 240-footer, about the length of the perimeter of a basketball court. Imagine that – you'd need a low loader to drive it round on.

Perhaps surprisingly, there are two types of todger in the human male. The first (called a grower) gets a lot bigger during erection, while the second (called a shower – rhymes with mower not power) looks big most of the time but doesn't increase in size all that much during arousal. Reportedly, seventy-nine per cent of men have growers, while twenty-one per cent have showers.

Excluding the world-beaters, penises tend to be pretty much the same size as one another when erect, though a small flaccid tool can double its length, while a larger one will get only about a third longer.

According to Wardell Pomeroy, one of Alfred Kinsey's sex research team (see chapter VII), the longest penis they found was ten inches (about 25 centimetres). Surely this must have been erect, otherwise it would have been hanging out the bottom of the chap's plus fours. In any case *erect* penises – for the most part, anyway – measure 6–7 inches (15–17.8 centimetres) in length, with the average being about 6.5 inches (16.5 centimetres). At the other end of the size scale, Pomeroy says that the smallest penis that Kinsey recorded was a trifling 1 inch long. In some extreme cases penises have been reported that are no more than 1 centimetre, when erect. But even these 'micropenises' are bigger than the shortest recorded organs, which occur in a condition known as congenital hypoplasia, which we needn't dwell upon.

Stretching the truth
Alfred Kinsey's technique for measuring the penis has been roundly criticized. What he did was give 3,500 men a blank card, which they were supposed to put alongside their erection and record its length with a black mark before sending it back. Well, guess what: people added a bit for luck. A 1996 *Journal of Urology* study found that your typical erect penis was just 5.08 inches long when measured by somebody else, but 6.1 inches when measured by the men themselves.

In her introduction to *The Big Penis Book,* published by Taschen in 2008, also available in a 3-D edition with special glasses, Dian Hanson discusses penis size. The largest penis, apparently, was recorded in the early twentieth century by Dr Robert L. Dickinsons, coming in at 13.5 inches in length and 6.25 inches around.

For women, penis size is only the ninth most important attribute in the man of their dreams. For men, the size of their member comes third in importance. Cashing in on this male obsession, one of the world's most successful media pranksters, Alan Abel, decided to act when he saw an ad from HBO, who were preparing a documentary on male genitalia called *Private Dicks Exposed*. The ad said, 'If you are interested in talking about your private parts, call us.' Abel did just that, telling the programme makers that his name was Bruce. He explained to *Esquire* what happened: 'I figured all these guys were going to call in to brag about their size. So I said I was the smallest in the world. One inch, erect. And they said: "You're on the show!"' At one point during the shoot, the director asked 'Bruce' why he was the only contributor not to have taken his underpants off. 'The director said, "Everyone's taken their clothes off except you, Bruce,"' remembered Abel, as the director asked him to disrobe. 'There were about twenty-five people on the crew, including some very attractive ladies, and I said, "Only if we can have group sex after the wrap." They said no. So I didn't have to take off my shorts.' The show went out before HBO realized they'd been had, but they used Abel's name on the cover of the DVD, which you can still get.

Pulling a fast one

This tale reminded me of Australia's Walibri tribesmen, whom I stumbled upon in my research. Instead of shaking hands when they meet, the Walibri are said to shake each other's penises. I went in search of more but poring over dusty tomes in the London Library I drew a complete blank on this tribe. Unless they have been muddled with the *Warlpiri*, an indigenous group scattered throughout Australia's Northern Territory, who do *not* indulge in this practice, I think this is a leg-pull.

Possibly the most interesting penis survey was one done by Dr Robert Chartham, a fascinating chap whose real name was Ronald Seth (1911–85). After training as a chorister, Seth went to the

Sorbonne and Cambridge and was at various times a BBC staffer and a member of the Special Operations Executive (SOE) who was parachuted into Estonia but captured by the Germans. His later careers included lecturing to British university students on 'How to Enjoy Sex', which must take the prize for the most ludicrous case of teaching your grandmother to suck eggs. Finally he settled down to write about sex, travel and spying, including *Sex Manners for Advanced Lovers* (1969). Chartham was also editorial consultant to *Forum: The International Journal of Human Relations*. In a detailed survey into penis size published in 1970 the largest erect penis *Forum* found was 9.5 inches (21 centimetres). The shortest was 4.75 inches (12 centimetres).

Anyway, Chartham did his own survey into international penis size, measuring erect penises of various nationalities (with permission, obviously). In this he was rather like Sir Richard Francis Burton (see chapter XVIII). Here are the results of his survey, which I present in descending order of length: English, 10.5 inches [well done, chaps]; West German, 8.5 inches; Danish, 8 inches; French, 7.75 inches; Swedish, 7.75 inches; American, 7.75 inches; and Negro [sic], 7.5 inches. With English at the top and 'Negro' at the bottom, this study seems to go against the popular stereotype. Or was this a case of finding what he wanted to find?

From tip to root, a *flaccid* human member generally measures between 3 and 4 inches (8.5 to 10.5 centimetres). In *L'ethnologie du sens genitale* (*The Ethnology of Genitals*), 1935, by somebody who called himself Dr Jacobus X, penises measuring nearly a foot in length are recorded.

Dr 'Jacobus X' was the pen name of one Jacobus Sutor, a nineteenth-century French military surgeon who experimented on the natives in the countries he visited, reporting the results in his book, *Untrodden Fields of Anthropology* (1898). Dr Jacobus recorded big Arab penises of between 8 and 10 inches and a footlong one in the Malinkes tribe in Senegal. This specimen had a diameter of two inches and he calls it, 'a terrific machine . . . more like the yard of a donkey than that of a man'. He claimed rather oddly that this would be sufficient to 'produce serious mischief in the rectum of any poor wretch who consented to suffer its terrible attacks'.

The erect African penis resembled, Jacobus said, 'an India rubber tube filled with liquid'. Which seems rather a subjective claim. He also made the bold assertion that, 'the "Sudanese Negro" possesses the largest genital organ of all the races of mankind'. The English don't get a mention, which would seem to contradict Dr Chartham's findings.

More recently, Jonah Falcon has won the prize for the biggest (known) nudger in the world. It measures an impressive 13.5 inches when off duty. This is about 35 centimetres and too big for most office rulers to measure. In 2010, Mr Falcon announced the interesting fact that he can envelop a doorknob with his foreskin. I read recently that he is unemployed and living with his mother.

The most comprehensive report of penis sizes ever was published in 2007 in the *British Journal of Urology International*, combining the findings of twelve studies of more than 11,000 men. The authors, Dr Kevan Wylie of the Royal Hallamshire Hospital, Sheffield, and Ian Eardly of St James Hospital in Leeds conclude that the average (Caucasian) penis is between 5.5 and 6.2 inches (14 and 16 centimetres) in length and between 4.7 and 5.1 inches (12 to 13 centimetres) in circumference.

The codpiece
An interesting method of size enhancement was the medieval codpiece, which was introduced into men's clothing in the early fifteenth century. The word comes from *cod*, meaning 'scrotum'. Trousers had yet to be invented so as doublets shortened with

fashion, the lines of a gentleman's wedding tackle became visible, barely concealed under his figure-hugging hose, which had a large opening at the front. To cover gentlemen's embarrassment, tailors designed a triangular pouch, tied across the opening to conceal the genitals.

As fashions changed over the next hundred years or so, this cloth was remodelled to project boldly from the body, held closed by string ties or buttons. Sometimes it was made of metal – a wise choice if you were wearing armour. In time, enough padding had been added to exaggerate the look until the upward-pointing bulge stuck out from the body to resemble something like a curved fireman's helmet or the end of a large black pudding. Now the codpiece greatly emphasised rather than concealed a gentleman's equipment. It reached its zenith during the 1540s but had dropped out of fashion by the 1590s.

Lifting

Of course, it's not what you've got that matters; it's what you do with it. In 1995, a Hong Kong master of the ancient Chinese art of Chi Kung named Mo Ka Wang is said to have lifted more than 253 pounds, about 18 stone (115 kilograms), two feet off the floor with his penis, which must have made his eyes water.

But keeping the penis up for a bit is going to be a good idea too. The typical attitude of the erect penis is slightly above the horizontal, rather like the near end of an oar at rest in a rower's hand, though up to a fifth of chaps can manage an angle of about 45 degrees above the horizontal, or below the vertical, if you prefer. Some young bucks can keep it up for an hour, or even much longer under the onslaught of incessant stimulation. The angle decreases with age, like many things, and after fifty you're over the hill and heading downwards. Kinsey reported that men in their late sixties wither after about seven minutes, which would hardly get you from Victoria to Piccadilly Circus on the Tube.

According to German researchers the average 'giggling pin' takes a mere two minutes and fifty seconds to complete a typical intercourse session. On the receiving end, women, the researchers discovered, perceive it as lasting five minutes and thirty seconds. That sounds like the opposite of time flying while one is enjoying oneself. Suppose a chap lives to be seventy-five and ejaculates at least three times a week from the age of about sixteen (these are all rough figures), he will have about 6,000 or 7,000 orgasms, and produce enough semen to fill the petrol tank of a big car, with plenty left over for papering a wall or something.

Most men ejaculate within six minutes of penetration and the average male orgasm lasts six seconds, which is seventeen seconds shy of a woman's twenty-three seconds. That's effectively four times the amount of orgasming (if that is a word) for the ladies than the gentlemen. There are 50 million sperm in the average emission and there can be as many as 300 million, though it would be a tedious job counting them.

V

THE HISTORY OF SEX, 3

FROM KRAFFT-EBING TO THE SEXUAL REVOLUTION

*

'There is no remedy for sex but more sex.'

ANON.

Richard Fridolin Joseph Freiherr Krafft von Festenberg auf Frohnberg, genannt von Ebing, better known, for understandable reasons, as Krafft-Ebing (1840–1902) was an Austro–German psychiatrist who worked in psychiatric asylums and also in academia, though how anyone could tell the difference beats me. He was also the author of an influential mouthful of a book, *Psychopathia Sexualis: eine Klinisch–Forensische Studie* (*Sexual Psychopathy: A Clinical–Forensic Study*). First published in 1886, it went into twelve editions, the last, on which he was working when he died, containing 238 case studies of 'abnormal' human sexual behaviour.

The author said he had given the book a scientific-sounding name so as 'to discourage lay readers'. He had also written parts of it in Latin to keep the eyes of the non-Latin-educated masses away from the lurid stories of sexual deviation, much, though not all, of which we would today regard as well within the broad spectrum of normal practice.

The first edition of the book covered, amongst other things, such diverse subjects as, impotence, sadism, masochism, paedophilia, necrophilia and handkerchief fetishism. Though not universally admired, *Psychopathia Sexualis* was one of the first books to study homosexuality and became highly influential. But, believing that sex for fun, instead of for having children, was perverted (he was Catholic), Krafft-Ebing was obliged to classify homosexuals as perverts, though he opposed criminalizing them. Which was jolly nice of him.

'Inversion'

Homosexuality was further examined in 1897 in *Sexual Inversion*, the first English textbook devoted to the subject. The book was co-authored by a straight chap, Henry Havelock Ellis, better known just as Havelock Ellis (1859–1939), and a bisexual poet, John Addington Symonds (1840–93), who had a penchant for gondoliers. Havelock Ellis was a doctor, psychologist, writer, reformer and what we would now call 'sexologist', who published works on a variety of sexual practices, introducing novel concepts such as autoeroticism and narcissism that were soon taken up by psychoanalysis. He attempted to classify 'normal' and 'perverse' sexual practices in an objective way, leading him to identify a 'third' or 'intermediate' sexual orientation for which he used the term 'sexual inversion'.

'Inversion' was just another word for homosexuality, which everybody had known about since long before tin openers, though the terms 'homosexual' and 'heterosexual' had been invented only in 1869 by Austrian-born writer and campaigner Karl-Maria Kertbeny (1824–82). 'Homosexual' had been coined as a replacement for the disparaging terms 'sodomite' and 'pederast'. Krafft-Ebing had used these new words in *Psychopathia Sexualis* and they soon became part of the standard vocabulary, along with terms such as 'lesbian' and 'Sapphic'. The new field of sexual science was certainly a fertile breeding ground for new words. John Addington Symonds was fond of another term for homosexuals. This was the word 'Uranian', which just went to show that while men were from Mars and women were from Venus, gays were homing in on Uranus.

Havelock Ellis followed up *Sexual Inversion* with *Studies in the Psychology of Sex,* a monster book published in seven volumes between 1899 and 1918. Two decades seems a long time to spend on a book, especially when you are writing obvious things like, 'The corset may thus be regarded as the chief instrument of sexual allurement which the armory of costume supplies to a woman, for it furnishes her with a method of heightening at once her two chief sexual secondary characters, the bosom above, the hips and buttocks below.'

In any case, Havelock Ellis made an odd sex expert. Still a virgin at twenty-two, he married the suffragette Edith Lees, who was a bit of a rum duck as a wife, being openly lesbian. He remained impotent until old age (are you surprised?), when he discovered that the only thing that would get him going was urinating women. He didn't hide the fact at dinner parties, either. Oh, well, we all have different hobbies, I suppose.

Freud
Once the blue touch-paper of sex research had been lit there followed a firework display of new ideas. French neurologist Jean-Martin Charcot (1825–93) resurrected the idea of hysteria, and one of his students, Sigmund Freud (1856–1939) took his ideas further. Freud was a Jewish-Austrian neurologist, and grandfather of the artist Lucian Freud and his brother Clement (the Minced Morsels and *Just a Minute* man). He was also great-grandfather-in-law of Richard Curtis, who wrote *Four Weddings and a Funeral,* and invented the technique of psychoanalysis (Sigmund Freud, not Richard Curtis). Unlike Charcot, Freud focused on sexual desire as the chief human motivation (no brain surgery there, then), and maintained that sexual appetite developed in five stages, which he termed oral, anal, phallic, latent and genital.

Some of Freud's ideas about the sexual subconscious occa-sionally came back to bite him. An addicted cigar smoker, he was never seen without a fat one between his lips, and once, while giving a talk on oral fixation, he was asked by some wag if he was aware of the phallic obviousness of the thing he was sucking, to which he impatiently replied, 'Sometimes a cigar is just a cigar.' This illustrated beautifully that when it comes to Freudianism, you can pick and choose. At one point he did begin to wonder whether his addiction to smoking might be relieving him of 'withdrawal symptoms' from addictive masturbation in childhood, saying, 'I owe to the cigar a great intensification of my capacity to work *and a facilitation of my self-control.*' Though suggestive, neither this, nor any of his other guesses and theories, could be disproved, making the whole Freudian edifice unscientific.

In one curious self-analysis Freud said of his childhood, 'I found in myself a constant love for my mother and jealousy of my father. I now consider this to be a universal event in childhood.' Like many of his pronouncements, the idea that his own peculiar childhood experience was a universal event seems unlikely, though Freud appears to have built the whole notion of the Oedipus complex upon it.

There is a popular misconception that doctors of the period were forever getting their neurotic/randy lady patients to lie down, while they 'massaged' them back to normality. The Greek idea of female sexuality as a mental disorder has still not entirely gone away, even today. On a strange website recently, I read this: 'For centuries, doctors had treated women suffering from "womb fury" or "female hysteria" by performing "medicinal massage", leading to a sudden outburst or "paroxysm". This is now recognized as masturbation leading to orgasm.'

There is precious little evidence presented to back up this assertion, which I keep coming across. And it doesn't ring true. After all, although there were charlatans then, as there are now, normal Victorian doctors presumably had no desire to be struck off for behaving improperly with their lady patients, just as they don't want that today, so the popular picture of GPs servicing a daily quota of randy housewives queuing round the corner is probably an inaccurate one.

'Beastliness'

One of the most prominent men of the new century – a fellow with strong views on sexual behaviour – was Robert Stephenson Smyth Baden-Powell (1857–1941), 1st Baron Baden-Powell, Bt, OM, GCMG, GCVO, KCB. Baden-Powell was a lieutenant-general in the British Army and in August 1907 he organized a camp for twenty-two boys to test out his ideas on scouting. He incorporated some of his findings into *Scouting for Boys*, published the following year. The book has so far sold about 150 million copies and is the fourth bestselling book of the twentieth century, though I have always thought that its title would have benefited from a dash, or colon, or comma, just to avoid any ambiguity.

Baden-Powell's writing contains words of advice to boys on the ticklish subject of homosexuality, which he must have encountered rather frequently in the male-oriented environments he insisted on hanging around in. Indeed, using the if-it-looks-and-sounds-like-a-duck theory, some have suggested that the uniform- and youth-admiring chap who spent his life in the company of men might well have been batting for the other side himself.

In his advice about homosexuality he says: 'It is called in our schools "beastliness", and this is about the best name for it.' In his opinion, the perpetrator of such beastly practices becomes 'feeble in body and mind, and often ends in a lunatic asylum'. In light of this, one cannot help attaching new significance to Baden-Powell's famous advice to scouts to, 'Be Prepared!' A scout, he says, 'is never taken by surprise; he knows exactly what to do when anything unexpected happens . . . he smiles and whistles under all circumstances'. Personally, I think this would be unlikely if, while working towards his camp cook badge behind the scout hut, the unfortunate young scout suddenly found Akela roughly polishing his woggle.

Baden-Powell's relationships with young men certainly seem to have been more successful in some ways than his relationship with his wife. Upon his marriage, he began to suffer persistent 'headaches', which his doctor thought were psychosomatic. The headaches went away as soon as he moved out of his marital bedroom into one set up on his balcony. He seems to have suffered no headaches at all in the company of his bosom friend, Kenneth McLaren, DSO, a major in the 13th Hussars, who had been to Harrow and Sandhurst, two oppressively monosexual setups. McLaren first met Baden-Powell in 1881, when he was just twenty, and Baden-Powell quickly nicknamed him 'the Boy', asking the young man to help him with his scouting endeavours. One can imagine the pair cross-legged in their shorts, seated around the campfire with the boys, roasting their chipolatas.

But the sour-faced prudery, the official tutting and the sexual unworldliness of the man and woman in the street was about to be swept away in a new era of unparalleled sexual invention and creativity.

Flappers not slappers

As the twentieth century got into its stride, flappers made their appearance. Not to be confused with slappers (a modern phenomenon, chiefly visible amongst members of the Adidas community), flappers were modern, jazz-loving, confident and sexy young women who flouted 1920s convention with their bobbed hairdos, short skirts, bold make-up and hard drinking. In *The Great Gatsby*, F. Scott Fitzgerald writes about such ladies, who often expressed their opinions robustly, sometimes while driving cars and smoking cigarettes from holders – not to mention the shameless casual sex they also went in for. I must say I've always thought flappers were a nicer lot than the Victorian purity women.

As the diversity and inventiveness of modern sexual practice accelerated away, there was also an explosion in sex education, which developed an openness and straightforwardness that refreshed or startled, depending on your personality. A pioneer in the field was Dr Marie Stopes (1880–1958), a palaeobotanist and pioneer of birth control and women's rights. Stopes was the editor of *Birth Control News*, which did much to sweep away the Victorian cobwebs of ignorance by giving explicit anatomical advice to women. One wonders if this magazine was delivered in a plain envelope, as many husbands of the period might have choked on their kippers, had they known of its contents.

Stopes also wrote a sex manual, *Married Love or Love in Marriage* (1918). She later claimed that she was still a virgin when she wrote it, which is a bit like having a volume on beer written by a teetotaller. The book was turned down by several large publishers, and with such alacrity that you'd have thought it had been typed on a leper's discarded wound dressings. But it was finally brought out by a small publisher who, I daresay, crossed his fingers rather hard. Doubtless to his great delight, it sold so fast that within two weeks it was already in its sixth impression.

There was now no stopping Stopes, who opened the UK's first family planning clinic in London in 1921, and the organization that bears her name is still going today. Marie Stopes was a pivotal figure in the promotion of a better, less fearful understanding of human reproduction amongst the ordinary women on the Clapham omnibus. *Married Love* remained controversial, influential and bestselling for many years, a trend that would continue with other such books to be published later in the century.

At the same time, the field of sexual relations – that is to say, sex for fun rather than for making children – became better understood, allowing women for the first time to take the bull by the horns. Stopes's advice might have been couched in the terms of 'married love' but marriage tended, then, to be a more enduring institution than the fragile meringue nest it is today, and since anything else would have outraged the authorities – some of whom were already feeling decidedly uneasy – the euphemism was understandable. In any case, many women, armed with this knowledge as they now were, found themselves free to relax, just a bit. By planning what they did in bed, and when they did it, they managed to chop one leg off the terrifying ogre of late periods. At the same time, sexual taboos began to melt under the hot-lamp of increased understanding and the questioning of so-called 'proper' attitudes.

While Stopes was doing her stuff in England and America, the German Weimar Republic was emerging from the wreckage of the First World War. This period was one of Germanic liberalism and sexual decadence – amongst other things – about which Christopher Isherwood wrote a couple of cracking novels, based on his own experiences. These books, *Mr Norris Changes Trains* (1935) and *Goodbye to Berlin* (1939), went on to inspire the poorly received play *I am a Camera* – damned by Broadway theatre critic Walter Kerr with the withering, 'Me no Leica' – and also the well-received musical and film *Cabaret*, which was a feast of fetishistic campery. With the rise of fascism in the early 1930s the Weimar Republic fizzled out, making way for the famously uni-testicular Adolf Hitler, who, one suspects, didn't really like sex much, though he did have a thing for uniforms, and the military in general.

Veni, vici, VD

Naturally enough, the armed services had always been particularly badly hit by sexually transmitted infections. These are recorded as far back as the European outbreak of syphilis in 1494, when 'the French disease', as it has been called since the sixteenth century (except by the French), infected French troops who were trying to besiege Naples. It was a case of, 'See Naples and die of the pox.' Things were little different during the First World War, some 400 years later, when sexually raddled allied troops were so widely infected with venereal diseases that nigh on half a million of them ended up in hospital. A War Office-sponsored silent drama entitled *Whatever a Man Soweth*, a VD health film aimed at servicemen, was made in 1917 but it is so patronizing and dull that I nodded off halfway through. The 'prostitutes' it depicts seem well past their best, but perhaps they were meant to. The best thing about it is that it shows what Piccadilly Circus and Trafalgar Square looked like before they were ruined by advertising hoardings and traffic – that and the inadvertently amusing name of the lead character: Dick.

During the Second World War, steps were taken to prevent VD once more sending vast swathes of combatants on visits to 'Rose Cottage', a military term for the VD clinic. The government funded euphemistic as well as more plain-speaking items of propaganda to drum the dangers of VD into the heads of the troops. Leaflets were passed out, posters mentioning the unmentionable became visible in the streets and many thousands of squirming soldiers, sailors and airmen were made to sit through excruciating films and lectures on the subject. They let off steam in the time-honoured way with witty – but often incorrectly spelt – graffiti like, 'What's green and eats nuts? Answer: Gonorrhoea!', and, 'Women and seamen don't mix.' Nonetheless, despite all the warnings and the near-ubiquity of French letters (condoms) – a favourite talisman tucked inside military wallets at the time – infection rates refused to budge – owing presumably to the age-old tradition of servicemen having an awful lot of casual sex. It was only the widespread distribution of penicillin in the latter years of the war that seriously slowed down the spread of venereal disease.

Lonely wives at a loose end while their husbands were shooting

Germans could also become victims of VD. Sometimes this was the result of drawing a stocking seam up their legs with an eyebrow pencil and having liaisons with, say, visiting US troops, whom British men sullenly regarded as being 'overpaid, oversexed, and over here'.

In 1949 the Crown Film Unit, sponsored by the Central Office of Information, made a sex education film about the dangers of syphilis and the importance of early treatment. Entitled *The People at No. 19*, this melodrama was directed by J.B. Holmes for the Ministry of Health and starts with moody black-and-white titles superimposed in beautiful roman type over a working-class terrace. Expressionistically lit throughout, the film stars Tilsa Page as Joan, a haunted-looking young wife sans eye makeup and with hair like she's just come out of a wind tunnel. She discovers that she is not only pregnant but has contracted syphilis on a night out with a good-time boy. Her husband, Ken, who has dialogue such as, 'Strike me up a gum tree!' is played by a young Desmond Carrington, best known today for his comforting light-music programme on Radio 2. His mother-in-law is played in 'RADA-cockney' style by Margery Fleeson. She wears an apron in tiny airless rooms and says things like, 'Have a nice quiet listen to the wireless.' The best dialogue, though, goes to Russell Waters as Dad, Ken's father-in-law. He has exquisite lines like, 'Do you remember that bloke – er, I've forgotten his name – whose boy's got a hare lip and his girl got that French prize?' *The People at No. 19* is a well-made, if depressing, film that resembles a particularly gripping episode of *EastEnders*.

As the 1940s got into their stride, the scientific approach to sex and sexuality was beginning to make serious inroads into the philosophical attitude of the ancients, the dogmatism of the Church and the finger wagging of various do-gooders. So, in 1947, just two years after the end of the war, the time was ripe for Alfred Kinsey (1894–1956), an American professor of animal biology, to found the Institute for Sex Research at Indiana University, which is what he did.

Kinsey's parents were strict and old-fashioned in their morals and he rebelled against their attitudes. In 1948, he published *Sexual Behavior in the Human Male*, the biggest sex survey ever undertaken. It was based on responses to a detailed, coded questionnaire that covered every conceivable sexual attitude and activity. Kinsey's eye-opening findings really upset the apple cart, prevailing assumptions and nervous old librarians. But it sold like bottled water in the desert.

In 1953 Kinsey and his team followed up with *Sexual Behavior in the Human Female*, which also sold very well. There's more about Kinsey in chapters VI and VII.

Kinsey's research did much to encourage unemotional discussion of human sexuality and the Kinsey Institute for Research in Sex, Gender, and Reproduction is still going strong today.

'Huntley and Palmers'

On 4 September 1957, four years after the first publication of *Sexual Behavior in the Human Female*, the Report of the Departmental Committee on Homosexual Offences and Prostitution was published in Britain. Better known as the Wolfenden report, it was named after the committee's chairman, John, later Baron, Wolfenden (1906–85), and its publication followed the high-profile conviction for homosexual offences of a number of well-known British men, including Lord Montagu of Beaulieu – the motor car man.

The Wolfenden committee consisted of twelve men and three women, including Mrs Mary G. Cohen, vice-president of the City of Glasgow Girl Guides, who, coming from the world of woggles and dyb dyb dyb, presumably knew nothing about homosexuality, and Dr Desmond Curran, MB, FCP, DPM, who, being psychiatric consultant to the Royal Navy, probably knew rather a lot about the rum, bum and concertina department.

To show how modern and forward-thinking the committee was, Wolfenden, who had been a headmaster, and who later became director of the British Museum, suggested that 'Huntley & Palmers' be used as code to spare the blushes of the ladies in the room. 'Huntleys' would stand for homosexuals, and 'Palmers' for prostitutes. Huntley & Palmers (who presumably knew nothing of this strange abduction of their name) were famous biscuit manufacturers based on the Thames in Reading, the town in which Oscar Wilde had famously been jailed for homosexuality, and the same town where Wolfenden held the university vice-chancellorship, thus being well aware of Reading's custard cream credentials.

The committee heard evidence from police, psychiatrists, religious leaders and gay men whose lives had been affected by the law, and recommended in their report that 'homosexual [Huntley] behaviour between consenting adults in private should no longer be a criminal offence'. They found that 'homosexuality [Huntleyism] cannot legitimately be regarded as a disease, because in many cases it is the only symptom and is compatible with full mental health in other respects', adding, 'It is not, in our view, the function of the law to intervene in the private life of citizens, or to seek to enforce any particular pattern of behaviour.' This enlightened view did not, however, extend to tarts – custard or otherwise – whom the Wolfenden committee associated with 'community instability'. Given the green light, the police subsequently cracked down on ladies of the night in Reading's Palmer Park, and elsewhere.

The report's recommendations led to the Sexual Offences Act 1967, which replaced the law on sodomy contained in the Offences against the Person Act 1861 and the 1885 Labouchere Amendment (see chapter III). As a fascinating sidelight, it was later revealed that Wolfenden's son Jeremy – newspaperman, British spy and fan of the bottle – was himself an enthusiastic Huntley.

At the time of the Wolfenden report's publication, William Masters (1915–2001), a gynaecologist, had begun to research sex at the Department of Obstetrics and Gynecology at Washington University in St Louis. With his research assistant Virginia Johnson (b. 1925) he began a huge lab-based study of human sexuality, using a 'copulating machine' containing recording equipment (of which more in chapter VII). The two married in due course and together published groundbreaking research on human sexuality. They influenced sex research around the world and launched the Masters and Johnson Institute, which is still at it today. Their books, *Human Sexual Response* (1966) and *Human Sexual Inadequacy* (1970) were both red-hot bestsellers and are still available, despite being drily written to deter men in dirty raincoats. Masters and Johnson divorced in 1992 and Masters remarried the following year. He is no longer with us but, at the time of writing, Virginia Johnson is still going. You can read more about them in chapters VI and VII.

Growing Up

By 1971, the year Masters married Johnson, a groundbreaking film for schools was produced in the UK in association with the Institute for Sex Education Research Ltd. In traditional style, *Growing Up*, part of the *New Approach to Sex Education* series, featured soothing classical guitar music, animated line illustrations of the human reproductory organs, gently undulating abstract shapes and, less traditionally, graphic full-frontal masturbation.

The film had been written, directed and narrated by Dr Martin Cole, a lecturer in genetics and sexual reproduction at Aston University in Birmingham, whose aim had been, he said, 'to try and deal with the subject of human sexuality in a straightforward manner', and, 'to dispel some of the shame and guilt'. Whether *Growing Up* dispelled the shame and guilt is hard to know but the film's straightforwardness is undeniable.

In well-lit scenes, set in domestic bedrooms, Dr Cole and his team made use of extended shots of undisguised sexual intercourse and languid masturbation – both male and female. The non-simulated female masturbation scene caused especial fury, and, quivering with outrage, an affronted Birmingham City Council banned the film as obscene. Not to be outdone, Birmingham Education Committee fired the masturbation 'demonstrator', a pleasant-looking young teacher, but later reinstated her.

The most vitriolic reaction came, though, from the general public, in piles of correspondence addressed to the long-suffering Dr Cole. Furious 'housewives', 'mothers' and 'Christians' – most if not all of whom had probably never even seen the film – vented their spleen. Cole was called a 'dirty PIG' and a 'perverted bastard', in sometimes nicely spelled and grammatically correct letters. One vociferous member of the impromptu 'Critics' Circle' earnestly hoped for Cole's castration, while another recommended that he be 'birched out of society' as 'a sexual maniac *of the worst kind*'. Quite where this description left murderous child-rapists was not explained. Here are a couple of scrumptious examples from these fan letters:

> Dear Pervert, [. . .] if I had my way you will be either shot so as to end the evil that you are spreading, or you would be committed to a mental institution [. . .]

> Dear Dr. Cole, [. . .] I suggest that in your next film you show yourself being buggered by a long-haired hippy. That will make them sit up. You could also do a masturbation piece, why not? Also cock-sucking. You are, I am told, an expert at it.

The sarcasm was Wildean. It was a tough life being a genetics lecturer in Birmingham during the early seventies.

As the decade wore on, long hair, hippies, purple flairs and the Sexual Revolution continued to flourish despite the prudes. But there was a thorn in the Permissive Society's side. It was called Mary Whitehouse.

Mary Whitehouse

Mrs Whitehouse was a British Christian social activist known for her prominent opposition to everything, and her pursed lips. Almost single-handed she fought a PR-savvy campaign against swearing, sex on telly and free love – which was the only sort many youngsters could afford. Circling above the Permissive Society like a vulture, in vicious-looking spectacles, she launched the Nationwide Petition for Public Decency in January 1972. As expected, people carried on swearing in pubs, looking at pornography, laughing at dirty jokes and going to bed with each other's wives just as they always had.

But Mrs Whitehouse was a fly in the K-Y Jelly. So pervasive was her irritating presence that she received an unofficial, and, one would think, thoroughly unwanted accolade in 1975, when David Sullivan, London University Economics graduate and millionaire pornographer, named his dirty men's magazine *Whitehouse* in her honour.

But, unknown to the free-lovers, the storm clouds were gathering. After little more than fifteen years of hippies, the Pill, the Beatles and untrammelled sexual licence, the Sexual Revolution came to a grinding halt in the early eighties with the emergence of HIV/AIDS.

HIV/AIDS

Acquired Immune Deficiency Syndrome was first officially recognized in the US in 1981 and its dangers quickly appreciated. By the mid-eighties the 'safe sex' message was being heavily promoted and was widely understood. A series of impressive British public information TV spots, narrated by the craggy John Hurt, showed the AIDS acronym being chiselled into a gravestone. The chilling tagline warned the public not to die of ignorance.

For once, a sex education film could be shown to be having an immediate direct effect. People were thinking twice before leaping into bed with strangers, and more young women were staying in to wash their hair.

VI

STUFFED AND MOUNTED

A PENETRATING LOOK AT SEXUAL INTERCOURSE

*

'Life in Lubbock, Texas, taught me two things. One is that
God loves you and you're going to burn in hell. The other is
that sex is the most awful, filthy thing on earth and you
should save it for someone you love.'

BUTCH HANCOCK

Sexual intercourse, also politely known as mating (in animals), copulation or coitus by scientists, and informally as 'sleeping together', in court as 'intimacy taking place', or down the pub as 'screwing', 'shagging', 'rogering', 'fucking', 'banging', 'humping' and more (see chapter VIII) is the sexual act in which a male animal, including Man, inserts his penis into the female's vagina. But not only that (see below). Unlike most animal intercourse, human sexual intercourse is not linked to periods of fertility (oestrus) and can happen at any time during the reproductive cycle, including pregnancy.

One hundred million acts of sexual intercourse occur *every day* around the globe. I did not get these figures by staring through people's bedroom curtains with a clipboard, I got them by browsing through the World Health Organization's fascinating statistical charts. Anyway, the purpose of this curious pastime is a mixture of business and pleasure: sexual reproduction and plain fun.

The mechanics

If there was a maker's handbook for intercourse, the instructions would read something like this. Following a period of foreplay, the erect penis is inserted into the vagina. This is known as intromission. The partners then move their hips to and fro, causing the penis to travel backwards and forwards inside the vagina. The friction caused by this movement excites the sensitive nerves in the male and female sexual organs until (usually) orgasm and ejaculation in the male and often – in humans anyway – orgasm in the female. Men tend to be quicker off the mark in this respect, so a certain amount of care is required from the male partner not to finish the business too quickly so that the female partner can also get her money's worth.

The average man is said to reach his sexual peak between the ages of seventeen and eighteen. For some reason, women's sexual peak is seldom referred to in statistics, either as a result of sexist indifference or residual embarrassment from the old days. There is an urban myth that women don't reach their peak until they are thirty-two, though I haven't found this born out in my own personal research. About seventy-five per cent of men and women alike are said, in these same statistics, to have had sex by their late teenage years. In the case of my old school chum Bob Biggins, this would be '*early* teenage years', daily, behind the bike sheds and with anything that moved.

And it's now been proved: lots of sex is good for your health. In 1997 a *British Medical Journal* study of men aged between forty-five and fifty-nine found that those who had less sex than normal, or no sex at all, were twice as likely to be dead ten years later than those who had two or more orgasms a week. In a follow-up study they found that having three or more orgasms a week was linked with a fifty per cent reduced risk of heart attack or stroke. A win–win situation all round.

One of the most frequent sex-havers of the modern age was

Georges Simenon (1903–89), a prolific Belgian writer, and the creator of Inspector Maigret. At the age of about seventy-four, Simenon boasted to a bemused journalist that he had had sex with 10,000 women, mainly prostitutes. If you assume, for the sake of argument, that this was fifty-five years of sexual activity, that would be 181 ladies a year or 3.4 different ladies a week, every week, non-stop. His second wife later put the figure at a more believable 1,200. That's still a lot and, in any case, how did she know? Georges Simenon died at the grand old age of eighty-six after decades of heavy pipe smoking. So maybe all that intercourse did protect his health.

On a shorter timescale, porn star Chester Anuszak (alias Jon Dough, 1962–2006) is recorded as having had sex with 101 women over two days, doing fifty-five on one day and forty-six two weeks later. Surely a case of 'never mind the quality, feel the width'.

On the female side of the sex-maniac fence, Julia the Elder (39 BCE–14 CE), daughter of Roman Emperor Augustus, is said to have had sexual intercourse with 80,000 men, though not all on the same evening. That's about 2,000 men a year from the age of fifteen, or thirty-eight a week, or almost five-and-a-half a day. She reportedly took passing gentlemen up an alleyway for a quick knee-trembler when she was feeling especially frisky, which must have been nearly always. Goodness knows how many orgasms the poor woman had.

La petite mort

An orgasm is the sudden release of sexual tension in pleasurable rhythmic muscular contractions, particularly in the pelvic region, often accompanied by grunts, groans, moans, shrieks, you name it. The French have a descriptive term for the orgasm, which is *la petite mort*, meaning 'the little death'. The first known use of the word 'orgasm' itself, though, was around 1763. It comes from the

Greek *orgasmos,* from *organ,* to grow ripe, be lustful.

It's worth remembering that the sneeze is a kind of orgasm, and the only one you are allowed to have in public. It is also the only other physiological response that you cannot stop voluntarily once it has started. As a function of intercourse, the inside of the nose reacts by swelling, along with the genitals and breasts. But, never fear, sex is a natural antihistamine and will unblock a stuffed nose before you can say 'pass the Kleenex'. Now you know what to do next summer at Wimbledon, when the grass pollen starts playing merry hell with your hooter in the royal box.

The male orgasm

In 1966, American sex researchers Masters and Johnson described different phases of the orgasm – a complex affair, involving the vascular, nervous and endocrine systems. During the first stage, the man feels the ejaculation coming and two to three seconds later it happens. Masters and Johnson noted that the man 'cannot constrain, delay, or in any way control' this.

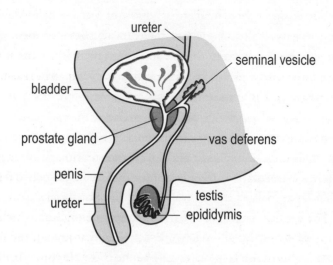

In the second stage, the ejaculation, the man feels contractions beginning in the anal sphincter and travelling to the head of the penis. The sperm are forced from the testicles up the vas deferens and through the seminal vesicles into the prostate gland to produce semen. The fluid from the prostate gland is responsible for semen's characteristic perfume. Contractions become harder and faster as the orgasm approaches, until finally they project the semen through the urethral meatus (opening) into the vagina.

Along with a lot of water, semen contains spermatozoa, or 'sperm', which are the male gametes (sex cells). It also contains more than thirty other ingredients, including fructose (used in ketchup), sorbitol (used in toothpaste), ascorbic acid (used in fruit juices), citric acid (used in ice cream), lactic acid (used in fruit gums) and vitamin B12 (used in cornflakes). There's also some zinc and calcium, both of which are good for your teeth. Semen is full of protein too but isn't fattening, each serving containing only about twenty calories. It does contain cholesterol, but unless you are eating quite a lot of the stuff, this shouldn't worry you too much.

Over his lifetime, the man on the Clapham omnibus will ejaculate gallons of semen. Just hope you are not sitting next to him. It's typically about one level tablespoon of semen per ejaculation, if you want to look at it the way Delia Smith would, though getting it to land on that spoon is going to be a hell of a job. If you are of a more scientific frame of mind, it's about ten cubic centimetres, which is said to account for the name of the rock band 10cc, though this is disputed by band members. Masters and Johnson reported sensations of greater pleasure the greater the volume of ejaculate. By 'volume' here they obviously didn't mean the noise it makes.

The speed of travel of ejaculated semen (spurt speed) is open to some debate but I have heard that it can approach the speed limit in most built-up areas. The furthest anyone has been recorded projecting an ejaculation is a little more than eighteen feet (5.5 metres), though one to two feet is a pretty good go for most chaps. Lucky he didn't have somebody's eye out with that one.

An average of 2 to 5 million sperm are let out into the world with each ejaculation and the entire population of the earth could reportedly be replaced using only the sperm (not semen) you could cram into a headache capsule. In studies, men who were shown pornography depicting two men and one woman were found to produce more sperm than those who looked only at women. The theory is that witnessing male competition causes men to increase their sperm production.

Anyway, once out there, sperm can swim at the remarkable speed of seven inches an hour. So it would take them little more than a year to get from Piccadilly Circus to Leicester Square, so long as they didn't stop at all the pubs along the way.

After the orgasm there is for the man, though not for the woman, what Masters and Johnson called a 'refractory period' (see chapter VII) during which he is unable to experience orgasm, or ejaculate again. For Masters and Johnson the male orgasm and ejaculation were actually the same thing. In young blades the refractory period may be a trifling amount of time but it gets longer the older you get and in very old men it can be several hundred years between orgasms – or seem like it, anyway.

The female orgasm

The orgasm in women is the same, but different. As a woman nears orgasm, the vagina lengthens and dilates, becoming congested with blood. The nipples become erect and, as more blood flows to the skin, some women show a 'sex flush' across the body. As with the man, the woman can feel the imminent orgasm. Then a series of pleasurable contractions overtake the uterus, vagina, anus and pelvic muscles.

During a female orgasm there is decreased blood flow in the orbitofrontal cortex, the part of the brain that governs behavioural control. Those women who describe being 'out of control' during orgasm are right.

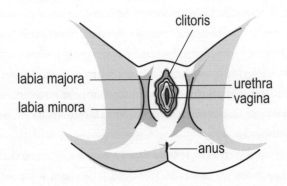

Unlike men, women can experience multiple orgasms over a short time. Alfred Kinsey's sex research team (see chapter VII) discovered a super-orgasmic woman who could have between fifteen and twenty orgasms in twenty minutes, while doctors at California's Center for Marital and Sexual Studies recorded 134 in one hour in one particularly enthusiastic subject. On the other hand, in one study of female orgasm, forty-eight per cent of subjects said they had faked it at least once in their life, 'because', as one put it, 'it just makes things easier'.

Hormones and other substances
There's an ancient joke that goes, 'How do you make a hormone?' To which the answer is, 'Don't pay her.' It may not be going to win the Perrier Award for hilarity but it's appropriate here because a whole variety of interesting chemicals suffuse the bloodstream during and after sexual intercourse. These are a few of them.

PHEROMONES

They say the more sex you have the more you want and the less sex you have the more you want. This seems self-evident. They also say that the more sex you have, the more you will be offered, because of your pheromones. A pheromone is a chemical that triggers a social response in members of the same species, and more sex pheromones are released by a sexually active body than when you are just watching the snooker. Many insects release sex pheromones; moths can sniff out a mate from as far away as six miles (10 kilometres). Some body-spray manufacturers whose products contain human sexual pheromones claim that their sprays act as an aphrodisiac. But none has been shown to attract mates from six miles away, and the evidence that they work at all is very thin on the ground.

ENDORPHINS

Endorphins, such as dopamine, are not hormones but morphine-like neurotransmitters that create a high analogous to that produced by opiates. They are produced during painful or stressful activities and strenuous exercise, creating a pleasurable, calming euphoria. The 'runner's high' is an endorphin effect, as is the relaxed glow after a very spicy curry. Endorphins are also released during belly laughs and orgasm. Indeed, exercise and laughter are now used in the treatment of depression and pain. Surely it's time to put orgasms on the National Health. We could all go on a march, shouting, 'What do we want? Orgasms! When do we want them? Now!'

TESTOSTERONE

Widely regarded as the 'male aggression' hormone, testosterone is also important for the sex drive in women. A shortage of testosterone can result in a reduced libido in both sexes. Testosterone produces feelings of confidence, desire and virility.

OESTROGEN

During sexual intercourse, women produce the hormone oestrogen, one benefit of which is as a beauty treatment. Oestrogen is responsible for shiny hair and smooth skin.

ADRENALINE

Another 'get-up-and-go' hormone is adrenaline (epinephrine). It's the 'fight-or-flight' chemical produced when a man with a knife jumps out at you from behind a tree. During intercourse, the amount of adrenaline in your body goes up, causing exhilaration, a racing heart and increased blood supply to your muscles.

SEROTONIN

Serotonin is mostly used to control intestinal movements but it is also released during orgasm, producing sensations of happy contentment.

OXYTOCIN

Oxytocin is known as the 'cuddle hormone', and the *Journal of Neuroscience* recently reported that if you squirt some up a man's nose it will make him 'empathetic', to the extent that, when shown pictures of a girl hugging a cat, he will become as 'tuned in' to the girl's feelings as a woman would be. Oxytocin is what causes all that cuddling after sexual intercourse. It also stimulates the prostate gland and intensifies orgasms.

PROLACTIN

Prolactin is the 'switch-off' hormone that reduces sexual arousal following orgasm. It is the chemical that makes a man start thinking of sorting through his stamp collection or decarbonizing his motorbike while he lies there after sex.

National differences

Different nationalities vary significantly in the amount of sexual intercourse, and the number of sex partners, they say they have over their life. The Swedes tend to have many sex partners, which may be why they smile so much. I went out with a Swede once but she resembled the vegetable more than the people. US women have fewer than five sex partners. The Chinese generally have the fewest. Perhaps a bit more humping and pumping in the mystic Orient could use up some calories. Intercourse is said to burn off about 100 calories per go, which is worth about two Jaffa Cakes or one small banana. And if you've got a small banana, congratulations on all the sex you're getting.

Smokers have about twice as many sex partners as non-smokers while *General Medicine* magazine recently reported that those who drink coffee not only have more sexual intercourse than those who don't, they also enjoy it more. I must say it gives me a throbbing headache (the *coffee*). The nation with the highest index of sexual satisfaction is reportedly Ukraine. The lowest must be India. Twenty-six per cent of Indians – who have intercourse seventy-six times a year – said that their sex lives were 'monotonous'. Condom makers Durex discovered in a survey that fifty-three per cent of Norwegians also wanted more than the ninety-eight whoopee-making sessions a year they were getting. Maybe it's just costing them too much. I went to Norway not so long ago and the prices were high (try £18 for two pints of beer), so the Norwegians have devised a nifty trick. The idea is to drink as much as possible at home before going out for your ruinously expensive evening's entertainment at the pole dancing club and then run back to someone's house afterwards for a drink-sodden orgy. They have two words for this, '*Vorspiel*' and '*Nachspiel*', meaning 'foreplay' (rather unfortunately), and 'afterplay'.

Prizewinners

Clellan S. Ford and Frank Beach noted in their book *Patterns of Sexual Behavior* (1951) that at the prizewinning end of the sex-having spectrum were the Aranda of Australia, who had sexual intercourse up to five times a night, sleeping between each performance. This makes them the world leaders by anyone's standards. The Greeks reportedly have sex about 138 times a year, or 117 times a year, depending on which survey you look at. But with their economy in the state it's in, perhaps they just have more time on their hands. The Americans come in third, at 124 times, and bringing up the rear are the Japanese, who report a rather lacklustre yearly intercourse index of just forty-five, or less than twice a fortnight. But I'll bet there are cultural differences hidden in these reports. I mean, we all know how boastful the Mediterraneans can be.

Timings

In a North American survey, researchers Eric Corty and Jenay Guardiani asked experienced doctors, nurses, psychologists, social workers and marriage therapists about how long their patients thought an ideal session of sexual intercourse should last, from intromission to ejaculation. The surprising answer was between three and thirteen minutes, with an average of seven minutes. Alfred Kinsey's team found one lady whose first orgasm occurred within two to five seconds after entry, which must really have tested the mettle of her partner.

Corty and Guardiani also reported that thirty minutes was too long, which you can understand, unless you are one of a pair of pigs, whose sexual intercourse lasts for about half an hour – that's a whole episode of *Songs of Praise* with Aled Jones. A pig's penis is shaped like a corkscrew, which might account for the delay. Intriguingly, Alfred Kinsey reported in 1948 that something like seventeen per cent of men from rural areas had had at least one sexual encounter with an animal, preferring pigs to sheep, by all accounts.

Corty and Guardiani found that one or two minutes was too short and I'd agree here. I mean it's hardly enough time to unlace your brogues and hang up your suit. I spoke to psychosexual therapist Dr Liz West at her delightful cottage up a narrow lane in the Sussex village where she lives. She told me that the youngest client she has ever seen was a seventeen-year-old boy who had saved up to consult a sex therapist because he was so worried. 'I can't keep going all night like my friends say they do,' he complained. 'I can only manage half an hour.' Dr West gently explained that when it comes to stories of their sexual prowess and stamina, men are not upon oath. And anyway, half an hour isn't bad.

But even the briefest of penetrative acts may constitute inter-course under the penal (not *penile*) code of England and the USA. The legal definition of 'carnal knowledge' has been unchanged since the Offences against the Person Act 1828 and in both English and American law the statutory definition is *sexual penetration*, however slight. Sticking blindly to this definition, the New Hampshire Supreme Court ruled in 2003 that lesbian sex could not be sexual intercourse. A wife in a divorce case who had had a same-sex relationship was therefore found not guilty of adultery on this technicality, no matter that she may have been in endless naked embraces with her partner, having orgasm after orgasm.

Holding fire

The male act of deliberately refraining from orgasm, termed *coitus reservatus*, takes quite a bit of concentration, but it was practised by the Oneida Community, a religious commune founded in 1848 by utopian socialist John Humphrey Noyes in Oneida, New York. The community called *coitus reservatus* 'male continence' and insisted that the man should put his penis inside the woman's vagina for periods extending to well over an hour, before withdrawing, without ejaculation. During this heroic task the woman would have several orgasms.

Coitus reservatus has been practised around the globe throughout history. Chinese businessmen even found time to run their office while at the sexual coalface. They would sign legal documents and discuss urgent matters with callers, while making occasional movements so that the erection was not lost. Anyway, all this hanging around gave the male members of the Oneida Community time to think and they developed several successful industries, eventually becoming a gigantic silverware company, Oneida Limited, which is still going today.

Most chaps under the age of forty can get an erection in a twinkling – less than ten seconds – though it's a harder slog the older you get. In *Sexual Behaviour in the Human Male* (1948), sex pioneer Alfred Kinsey noted some men who could manage it in three seconds. Men frequently have erections during the day, even while occupied in other tasks and the situation is more pronounced at night. The number of erections while sleeping averages nine for most fellows. (Nocturnal erections are probably good if you suffer from 'Ithyphallophobia', the morbid fear of seeing, having or thinking about an erect penis.) Many men also wake up with what is called 'crepuscular penile tumescence', otherwise known as the 'morning glory', 'dawn boner' or 'EMBV' ('early morning blue-veiner'), the chief advantage of which is to stop you rolling out of bed.

Sect maniacs
Religious groups have traditionally regarded sexual intercourse as an essential part of marriage, and consummation of the marriage is often prescribed (though usually, not much encouragement is required). Interestingly, the first American couple to be shown in

84

bed together on primetime television were Fred and Wilma Flintstone.

Catholics are encouraged to produce offspring till the cows come home while the United Society of Believers in Christ's Second Appearing, the religious sect known as the Shakers, are allowed to shake only in church, not in bed. The Shakers made superb and beautiful furniture but no babies, believing that sexual intercourse is the root of all sin and that everyone must therefore be chaste, including married couples. Their T-shirt probably read, 'Chaste – but never caught!' The obvious problem of how to procreate and keep the sect going was overcome by adopting and converting the children of others. But, as you might have guessed, by 2009 the community had shrivelled to just three members.

The Catholic Church not only encourages its members to go forth and multiply, for centuries it got involved in the micro-management of sexual intercourse, prescribing the man-on-top position as the only proper one. The 'missionary position', as it is called, has attracted to itself a delightful urban myth that it was so named because Christian missionaries taught it to foreign 'savages' who were doing it in a lot of very disagreeable ways, possibly even involving bananas.

Pioneering sex researcher Alfred Kinsey may have accidentally started this rumour in *Sexual Behavior in the Human Male*, when he misinterpreted details of *The Sexual Life of Savages in North-Western Melanesia* (1929) by Bronisław Malinowski. He reports him saying that 'caricatures of the English–American position are performed around [. . .] campfires, to the great amusement of the natives who refer to the position as the "missionary position".' It has recently been decided that Kinsey got in a bit of a muddle in his research and coined the term himself. Before Kinsey got to grips with it, the missionary position was known in the English-speaking West as the 'matrimonial', the 'English–American' and the 'Mama-Papa'. For some unknown reason some Arabic-speaking peoples call it the 'manner of serpents'.

In his bestseller *The Joy of Sex* (1972), Alex Comfort popularized the term and by 1976 it had made its way into the *Oxford English Dictionary*. Continental Europe has now enthusiastically adopted the word too. *Postura del misionero* is Spanish, and *position du missionaire* is French.

Insex

Insect sex or 'insex' is a curious business and is fraught with danger for the male bug, who may well be eaten by his mate before, during or after copulation. The female praying mantis thinks nothing of eating her boyfriend after intercourse and sexual cannibalism is common with many spider and scorpion families too. We probably all know women like this. It's a tricky business for the male who, before mating, must spin a small web and ejaculate on to it before storing the sperm on his 'feelers' and transferring them to the female.

Generally the female of the species is bigger than the male and has no trouble eating her husband. It is much less common for the male to eat the female. If the female is starving, a passing male will be more useful as food than as a mate. Females may even eat small or otherwise undesirable males in an unsentimental form of mate rejection or extreme 'Dear John' letter.

Some male spiders take a *kamikaze* approach to this problem, with the male just sacrificing himself to the female after mating. The evolutionary advantage of this self-immolation is that the male, having mated with the female, will increase the chance of his genes surviving as baby spiders by providing food to the female, even though it spells death.

Other spiders have evolved a nifty escape mechanism to avoid both suicide and becoming lunch. These brave chaps 'emasculate' themselves during sex by breaking off the entire sex organ while it is still inside the female. This allows them to keep injecting sperm while they make a run for it – though possibly somewhat slower than normal.

If this seems a bit weird, it is nothing compared to the things that human beings get up to, as we shall discover . . .

VII
SEXUALITY UNDER THE MICROSCOPE
FROM MONKEY GLANDS TO THE 'COPULATING MACHINE'

*

*'Women might be able to fake orgasms, but men
can fake whole relationships.'*

SHARON STONE

Over the four hundred years or so that science has been with us it
has got absolutely nowhere at understanding anything about love.
But it has made a pretty good fist of getting to grips with sex. The
mechanics and behaviour of animals, including us humans, are
much better understood today than they were just fifty years ago
although some of the research does look a bit weird in retrospect.
But weird is good, so here is a snapshot of some of the most
interesting and unusual sexual science of the modern age.

Monkey business

In 1923 Sir Arthur Conan Doyle wrote a Sherlock Holmes story
entitled *The Adventure of the Creeping Man.* It tells of an ageing
Victorian professor who fancies the pants off a young woman and
gets hold of some strange elixir extracted from monkeys in order
to rejuvenate his flagging sexual potency. Unfortunately, the
monkey juice turns him into a sex-crazed ape-man during the
night, and he climbs the ivy-clad walls of the lady's residence and
gibbers in at the windows, terrifying the household silly.

The details of this tale bear such a strong resemblance to the
work of Serge Abrahamovitch Voronoff (c. 1866–1951), a wealthy
Russian-born French surgeon who is best remembered today for

his 'monkey gland' experiments, that it seems clear that Conan Doyle used them as the basis for his terrific story. His interest in the subject may not have been unconnected with his own waning sexual prowess. Conan Doyle had always been a ladies' man and in his mid-sixties, when he wrote the story, he might well have been lamenting the loss of his former vigour and been looking round for a remedy, finding it in Voronoff.

As a young man, Serge Voronoff had studied the effects of castration on eunuchs, like you do, and this had led him to become interested in exploring the surgical transfer of tissue from one species to another (xenotransplantation), in an effort to discover whether the effects of castration could be reversed.

Experiments in the field had already been done by Charles-Édouard Brown-Séquard, a member of the Royal Society, who was a fan of injecting people with a juice made from the testicles of guinea pigs and dogs, the so-called Brown-Séquard elixir. Brown-Séquard had reported tests on himself that resulted in what he called 'rejuvenated sexual prowess' after he had eaten 'extracts of monkey testis'.

Enlarging on Brown-Séquard's work, Voronoff's purpose was not just to perk up the sex life of subjects, but also to extend their life. Between 1917 and 1926, Voronoff did more than five hundred experimental transplantations on sheep and goats, grafting testicles from younger to older animals. He observed that the operations caused the older animals to regain the vigour of youth, though it doesn't seem to have occurred to him that they might just have been dancing about in discomfort. In any case, he came to the conclusion that monkey glands – a delightful euphemism – could be used to treat the senile.

Voronoff began by transplanting the testicles of executed criminals into willing millionaires whose sexual get-up-and-go had got up and gone. The problem was that criminal testicles were in short supply so he began using monkey testicles instead, following in the footsteps of another expert in the field, Skevos Zervos, a Greek who had started as a naked sponge diver when he was young, and who went on to become a transplant surgeon. He had already done ape-to-man testicle transplantation in 1910.

Voronoff did his own first monkeygland transplantation in June 1920, grafting Salami-thin slices of chimpanzee and baboon testicle into the scrotum of a brave patient. The toe-curling operation seemed to go well and just three years later the International Congress of Surgeons in London pronounced Voronoff's rejuvenation work a success.

Once news was out, Voronoff's monkey-gland treatment took off, becoming the latest thing, like phrenology or the Atkins diet. In his book, *Rejuvenation by Grafting* (1925), he describes the boost to the libido, improved stamina, longer life and the reduced need for glasses that monkey testicles could provide. A new cocktail of gin, grenadine, orange juice and absinthe was even named the Monkey Gland in his honour.

But was this rejuvenation a real effect, or was it, like phrenology, a seductive idea that had no actual scientific merit? In 1927, the University of Chicago's Professor of Physiologic Chemistry, Fred C. Koch, managed to get hold of a lot of bulls' testicles from the Chicago abattoirs. This would have made some great 'Koch and Bull' headlines. With his student, Lemuel McGee, he extracted 20 milligrams of a mystery substance from the testicles and gave it to castrated pigs, rats and cocks. The elixir reportedly 'remasculinized' these animals, though it never extended their life. In 1935, the Dutch named the newly discovered hormone testosterone.

By the early 1930s, thousands of ageing men around the world had already received monkey-gland treatment. The remedy was by this time a global business, and recipients included everyone up to Mustafa Kemal Atatürk, the balding and somewhat past-it president of Turkey. Then, one day in 1937, a chemist called

Menzies Sharp approached Frank Buckley, the manager of Wolverhampton Wanderers, with a 'secret remedy' that would, he said, give his players 'confidence'. The remedy was the Voronoff testicle transplant and he was given the OK to go ahead. Sharp administered the 'monkey-nut' treatment to several of the team, some of whom reported improved sexual oomph. But whether they scored more often I do not know.

The thing was that, although patients did often feel rejuvenated, this would turn out in the end to look like nothing more than the placebo effect. They got no younger, nor did their mechanical sexual prowess improve. But if they *thought* it had, maybe that was success of a sort.

Nonetheless, Voronoff, who was already rich, was getting richer and was living the high life on the entire first floor of a Parisian hotel with a vast staff and two mistresses. But the shine was beginning to come off the monkey-gland penny. By the 1940s scientists, who had been pointing out the obvious fact that foreign animal tissue would be rejected by the human body, were beginning to be listened to. It was becoming clear that monkey-testicle transplants really had none of the beneficial effects that Voronoff had claimed, beyond what would be expected from the placebo effect, and he stopped doing the transplants.

When the eighty-five-year-old Voronoff died, in 1951, he was generally regarded as nothing more than a sort of witch doctor, and was the subject of ridicule and opprobrium. Years after his death, however, it was discovered that the testicles are an 'immunologically privileged site' for the transplantation of 'foreign' tissue, owing to the presence of special cells that form a barrier to the immune system, reducing the chances of rejection. These cells have recently been used to reduce rejection in transplant patients. So maybe the monkey-gland treatment wasn't bollocks after all.

The magic box

Many authors have used weird science as a subject for their writings. *The Ordeal of Gilbert Pinfold* is a 1957 novel partly based on the experiences of its author Evelyn Waugh during a period of mental illness, and was written at the prompting of a psychiatrist at St Bartholomew's Hospital, who thought it would be good therapy. The tale concerns a novelist who is briefly going round the bend, and who hears voices that he imagines to be caused by a mysterious box belonging to his neighbour, who has been using it to experiment on Pinfold's wife. The machine in the story bears comparison with, and seems to have been based on, a real device, the so-called 'orgone accumulator', invented by an Austrian-American psychoanalyst called Wilhelm Reich (1897–1957) who believed that the libido was a 'universal life force'.

Reich had been a member of Sigmund Freud's Vienna circle, but emigrated to the USA in the thirties, where his radical sexual theories ruffled feathers. He attempted to measure the male orgasm, concluding that in 'better' orgasms more 'energy' was released. He called this phenomenon 'orgastic potency'.

Reich developed something he called 'body psychotherapy' – touching his patients in order to relieve tension. Or so he said. He asked men to take all their clothes off, and women to strip down to their undies. He would then press hard on their 'body armour' to awaken repressed memories of childhood events. He said that visible waves of spontaneous pleasure called 'bio-electricity' would move through his patients' bodies as he did this. Reich even decided to call this new treatment 'orgasmotherapy' but came to his senses just in time.

The authorities were not taking kindly to any of this but what really got their backs up was Reich's most famous discovery, something he called 'orgone' (a word he invented, basing it on *orgasm*). He believed that atmospheric orgone was 'trapping' sexual energy and that each orgasm topped up the world's supply.

Orgone, he believed, was everywhere and was responsible for gravity and the formation of galaxies. Orgone energy controlled the weather, he said. In fact, he made several 'cloudbuster' machines to produce rain, a process he called 'cosmic orgone engineering'. On one occasion he pointed his cloudbuster into the Maine sky during a drought and soft refreshing rain duly fell, saving the threatened blueberry crop.

In 1940, Reich built some homemade boxes he called 'orgone accumulators' inside which a patient would sit while 'orgone energy' was concentrated from the atmosphere, boosting their orgastic potency like crazy. At this point, many members of the caring professions, not to mention weather forecasters, started making circular finger movements beside their heads. Nonetheless, Reich's theories greatly appealed to many people, including enthusiastic orgonomist writers Norman Mailer, William Burroughs and Jack Kerouac.

In his novel *On the Road*, Jack Kerouac's character Sal Paradise (a thinly disguised version of himself) says that after using the orgone accumulator, 'I always rush up and take off ninety miles an hour for the nearest whorehouse', though it should be remembered that Truman Capote said of Kerouac's work, 'That's not writing, it's typing.' Norman Mailer actually built several orgone accumulators in his barn, one lined with carpet. William Burroughs also built one and in a 1970s article wrote that he had 'achieved spontaneous orgasm, no hands', claiming that it gave him 'an aphrodisiac effect similar to good strong weed'. This was a machine simply *made* for the Beat Generation.

Possibly feeling that a bit of gravitas was required for his 'orgone heat' theories, Reich asked Albert Einstein – famous scientist and ladykiller – to be involved in his research. Einstein agreed but found no evidence that the orgone accumulator he was given was any more use than a tea crate and wrote a polite letter to Reich, suggesting more rigour and scepticism in his work. Reich then sent

Einstein a twenty-five-page reply, going on about how 'air germs' had messed up Einstein's experiment.

Hearing of Reich's work, *Harper's* magazine described him as the leader of a West Coast cult of sex and anarchy and, in 1947, feeling that he was being unfairly treated, he wrote, 'I would like to plead for my right to investigate natural phenomena without having guns pointed at me.'

But in 1954 the US Food and Drug Administration got an injunction to stop Reich distributing his orgone accumulators. When he broke the injunction he was jailed for two years. Reich died in jail little more than a year later, believing that the world was under attack from UFOs. He was buried at his home, laboratory and research centre in Rangeley, Maine, which he had named Orgonon.

Kinky Kinsey

In 1947, just two years after the end of the war, and just as Wilhelm Reich was pleading for the right to be wrong, Alfred Kinsey (1894–1956), a bowtie-wearing American professor of entomology and zoology, founded the Institute for Sex Research at Indiana University.

The following year, Kinsey published *Sexual Behavior in the Human Male*, the biggest sex survey ever, and the most controversial. Kinsey and his colleagues reported, for example, that premarital sex was commonplace, and that half of married men admitted to having had sex outside wedlock – a town near Boston, as one wit put it. So far, not so astonishing. But according to Kinsey, and contrary to popular belief, ninety per cent of the men he spoke to also told him that they masturbated, seventy per cent said they had oral sex (then classified as 'sodomy') with their wives, and more than a third acknowledged that they had had at least one homosexual relationship, including the 'happily married' Kinsey himself. It looked like Ancient Greece all over again.

Despite being very thick, and twice as expensive as other books of its size, *Sexual Behavior in the Human Male* became an instant bestseller and, naturally enough, sent the media bananas. Nothing so comprehensive or so shocking to established opinion had ever been printed before. Six- and seven-page spreads appeared in respectable magazines such as *Time*, setting out the startling findings. This fantastic free publicity boosted sales while causing much delicious huffing and puffing among 'ordinary' people, who didn't like the earth-rending conclusions that flowed from some of those numbers, if they even dared to think about them.

As if this weren't enough, five years later (1953), and one whole year before bread stopped being rationed in Britain, Kinsey published *Sexual Behavior in the Human Female*, based on personal interviews with nearly six thousand women. This book, which revealed how often women got up to various types of thing, was a truly heroic research project, especially when you consider what listening to six thousand women talking about their sex lives might do to a chap.

Of course, *Sexual Behavior in the Human Female* sold even better than *Sexual Behavior in the Human Male* and the publishers did a little champagne dance around the office. The author even made the cover of *Time* in his bowtie, with his hair nicely combed, surrounded by some tastefully illustrated birds and bees. Included amongst the flora and fauna are several pink roses, some of them in full flower, others just budding. This is what is known as a visual metaphor, though the risk of getting pricked was not mentioned.

Like its male predecessor, *Sexual Behavior in the Human Female* made a point of calling a spade a spade, to the distaste of many. How many English vicars dining off rationed bread and dripping wanted to be told by some foreign academic fancy-pants in a bowtie that women not only *could* have orgasms but *were* having them, and *on purpose*, because they *enjoyed* it?

Unorthodox practices

The controversy over Kinsey's conclusions lasted well into the rather un-relaxed 1950s, but not just because of public distaste. The professor's work also attracted a certain amount of academic criticism. For instance, the so-called 'Kinsey Scale', which gave a score for sexual orientation from 1 to 6, with *completely heterosexual* at one end and *completely homosexual* at the other end, has been criticized for being far too simplistic a picture. Moreover, some of the professor's unorthodox research practices led a few academics to question the reliability of his findings.

One of the most criticized aspects of Kinsey's research is his attitude to paedophiles. He established relationships with a number of imprisoned child molesters and maintained a correspondence with a German named Fritz von Balluseck whose unlovely CV included not only paedophilia and suspected murder but also his sometime job as a senior Nazi party official. One especially repulsive and prolific child abuser was a US government employee by the name of Rex King who was not in prison, or even known to the police, but at large in the community. King's first sexual experience had been intercourse with his grandmother, followed up by sex with other members of his family, and, for a bit of variety, romantic encounters with animals. King kept meticulous records – with timings – of his criminal and cruel-sounding abuse of some eight hundred boys and girls, storing these diaries not in his library, but, for not unsurprising reasons, in the sands of the Arizona desert, where he dug them up so Kinsey could have a butchers. To protect the identity of this creep, Kinsey gave him the pseudonym 'Mr Green'.

Chapter 5 of *Sexual Behavior in the Human Male* reproduced parts of these diaries in 'scientific' tables. Kinsey was uncritical (or non-judgemental, depending on your attitude) of Mr Green's meticulous descriptions and time-keepings of the distressed babies and children he was standing over with an erection and a stopwatch. In November 1944, he wrote to Green (King), 'I rejoice at everything you send' and his conclusions, based partly on the bald, self-serving and, for all anyone knows, underplayed accounts of this violence, was that children were sexual beings who could enjoy such 'interactions' with adults, and get erotic pleasure from them. It seems not to have occurred to him that the right thing to do might be to tell the police all about Mr Green because they might have wanted to invite him to help them with their enquiries. An unattractive colleague of Kinsey's, Dr Clarence Tripp (1919–2003), once spoke to Yorkshire Television about this, suggesting that children were only upset by being interfered with by Mr Green because they had small genitals and he had very large ones so it was just a 'fit' problem, akin – so I'm guessing – to trying to get a quart into a pint pot. He went on to say that it was absurd to regard a bit of 'tickling' as harmful to children. I didn't like this man's false teeth, powder-blue suit, or strange tie knot, and neither would I have wanted to bump into him in the toilet at Saturday Morning Pictures.

Kinsey had been the child of strict, not to say repressive parents and he rebelled by cultivating a hatred of middle-class morality, regarding it as entirely harmful. But his unrestrained interest in sex was not entirely academic. Kinsey was, for one thing, a masochist and enjoyed, if that is the word, stimulating himself by inserting objects into his urethra. This eye-watering diversion was not the only evidence of his rebellion against his repressive parents because Kinsey, who presented himself as upright and happily married, was sexually attracted to men. His academic interest in homosexuality overlapped with his personal interest to the extent that at least one uncomfortable male colleague found himself having to decline an invitation from the neatly coiffed and nattily dressed prof to join him in a bit of man-on-man 'research' in the basement area.

Home movies

Continuing his keenness to involve his assistants, Kinsey arranged for consenting colleagues and some outside volunteers to be filmed while they indulged in sexual acts with each other up in his attic at home, rather than in the university's laboratory. A solicitous Mrs Kinsey provided a steady supply of clean towels and the occasional tray of milk and biscuits.

Many have wondered whether the professor was getting more out of his little movie-making hobby than he let on. Heterosexual copulation, masturbation and masochism were all recorded in these attic sessions, next to the hot-water tank and the stored Christmas decorations, presumably. I wonder if he got his films out to show guests, like my Uncle Bob used to do when you went round for dinner.

The incessant study of every conceivable part of the sexual spectrum had a curious effect on Kinsey and his colleagues: it inured them to sexual arousal by visual stimulation no matter how extreme, so that they needed something more physical to get them going. This crossed the border into nuttiness when, one day, Kinsey deliberately circumcised himself with a pocketknife. Now, that's not normal.

Nevertheless, it ought to be said that despite the criticisms and the weirdness, Kinsey's research did much to demolish the shadowy fortress of sexual repression and middle-class hypocrisy, and allowed newspapers and housewives to talk about sex openly and without quite so much embarrassment. No longer could the political and intellectual elite prescribe acceptable sexual behaviour or orientation without question, and ordinary consenting grown-ups could now decide for themselves what they wanted to do together in their bedrooms.

The professor's two books, together known as *The Kinsey Reports*, are both in print today and have proved profoundly and enduringly influential. In spite of its acknowledged shortcomings, his work laid the foundations of the subject which is today known as Sexology. Alfred Kinsey's institute is still going too, though under its new name, the Kinsey Institute for Research in Sex, Gender, and Reproduction. I was going to say that this is hard to get your mouth around, but I thought better of it.

Ten thousand orgasms

In 1957, William (Bill) Masters (1915–2001) was a gynaecologist in the Department of Obstetrics and Gynecology at Washington University in St Louis, where he had begun to research sex. I guess he'd noticed Professor Kinsey's name in the papers. Like Kinsey, he was a bowtie wearer, though he favoured black skinny ones rather than big colourful ones. Also like Kinsey, he had a healthy sexual appetite.

In 1957 Masters decided he needed a research assistant and hired an attractive young lady who brought to the project no academic qualifications but a gift for administration, a good deal of street-smart oomph and a terrific pair of legs. This was Virginia Johnson (b. 1925) who was to help Masters undertake a comprehensive study of human sexuality (yes, *another* one). The pair were to become the new front-page people in the developing field of sex research.

In contrast to the Kinsey team's personal interview technique, Masters and Johnson conducted most of their research in the lab. From 1957 until the 1990s they recorded the anatomy and physiology of the sexual response of some 700 volunteers, male and female, by filming them as they masturbated and copulated under laboratory conditions, dressed in their signature white lab coats (Masters and Johnson wore the lab coats, not the volunteers).

Over the years, the team made direct observation, so they said, of about 10,000 orgasms and were able to show that men have a post-climactic 'refractory' period during which they cannot ejaculate again, without going cross-eyed. The absence of such a phenomenon in women, they revealed, makes them capable of multiple orgasms. You'd have thought that both these facts might have been more easily revealed if they had just asked the young lab assistant about his weekend away with the missus.

But their research was nothing if not businesslike. Men and women were arbitrarily paired with each other to create 'assigned couples' who could be filmed through a one-way mirror, also confusingly known as a two-way mirror. To preserve the anonymity of subjects – at least that is what they claimed – they offered them hoods to wear. On one occasion a naked young lady subject took off her hood and was recognized as one of the researcher's own previous conquests. They were maturely polite about it all.

In the early sixties, Masters was aware that people were still a bit jumpy and that a public outcry might erupt if his project became widely known. So he kept it under wraps. In 1964 he moved the team off the university campus, setting up with Johnson his own privately funded non-profit research institution in St Louis. Named the Reproductive Biology Research Foundation, it was renamed the Masters and Johnson Institute in 1978.

But social change was rapid, if uneven, at this time, on both sides of the Atlantic. In 1961 British Minister of Health Enoch Powell announced that the oral contraceptive pill could be prescribed on the NHS at a subsidized price of two shillings a month, unwittingly inaugurating the Sexual Revolution in Britain. Before this time, contraception had been touch and go, with the advice to young rakes, 'Sow your wild oats on Saturday night, then on Sunday pray for crop failure.'

Despite the Sexual Revolution, by the time of the Apollo Mission in 1966 humans still found themselves in the strange position of knowing more about landing a man on the moon than they did about what was going on when a woman was having an orgasm. However, Masters and Johnson were beginning to make giant steps in this area, offering some welcome new information on the subject. Amongst other things, they revealed that orgasms were physiologically identical whether stimulation was clitoral or vaginal. This idea, based on careful scientific observation, overturned Freud's notion that there were two sorts of female orgasm: 'vaginal' – the 'proper', 'mature' sort – and the 'neurotic', 'immature', 'clitoral' kind. This idea, that one of the claimed sorts of orgasm was superior to the other, was based on whimsy and should have gone the way of some of Sigmund's other mistakes – into the bin. It continues to be clung to by some people, even today.

The 'copulating machine'

One of the most closely guarded secrets of Masters and Johnson's research was a nifty little gizmo that has been referred to as a 'copulating machine'. It has also been called, more bluntly, a 'screwing machine', and worse. Nicknamed 'Ulysses', this clever device consisted of a clear plastic phallus containing a camera, and a motor that would make it 'go in and out'. Using Ulysses, Masters and Johnson found themselves in a unique worm's-eye position and were able to record the rhythmic contractions of the female orgasm, which they were the first to describe. The team recorded one woman having a forty-three-second orgasm, with about twenty-five contractions. These contractions were measured in men too, coming (if you'll forgive the word) at 0.8-second intervals in both sexes and then gradually dying away.

Masters and Johnson's research papers were rejected for publication by several journals so the pair wrote up the work as a book, entitled *Human Sexual Response*, which was published by Little, Brown in 1966. To avoid sensationalism, the authors made sure that the publication's language was unemotional and 'unsexy' but Little, Brown, sensing an interested market, printed 15,000 copies, just in case. *Human Sexual Response* was an overnight smash hit and sold out within a day. According to Masters, the team were obliged to employ three secretaries just to answer the huge sackloads of post that poured in, of which 'eighty per cent' was hostile. Their next book, *Human Sexual Inadequacy* (1970), from which neither suffered, was also a bestseller and both titles remain in print, having become highly influential and having been translated into more than thirty languages.

Over time, the relationship between the bald gynaecologist and his striking research assistant had become close and, possibly as part of his research, Masters suggested to Johnson that they should themselves have sexual relations. They did, and in 1971 Masters divorced his wife to marry Johnson.

Working with couples who were having sexual problems, Masters and Johnson invented a therapy which they called 'sensate focusing', a routine of sexual exercises aimed at developing interpersonal awareness of the needs of one's partner rather than desperately trying to provoke orgasms.

In the first stage, the couple are allowed to touch each other's bodies, excluding breasts and genitals. No sexual intercourse is permitted at first. Instead, there is a focus on the whole body, exploring what have been called the 'non-penis' aspects of sex. All the senses are used, especially touch, taste and sound. Subsequent stages bring the breasts into the picture, followed by the gradual inclusion of the genitalia and finish finally with intercourse. Sensate focusing was, and still is, also used as a treatment for erectile dysfunction. The technique is hilariously lampooned in Kingsley Amis's novel, *Jake's Thing*, in which the anti-hero, for whom the treatment is not really working, points out to his wife that 'sensate' is not the right word and has only been used because the proper words, 'sensual' and 'sensuous', have already been 'used up'.

From 1968 to 1977, the Masters and Johnson Institute ran one of the team's dodgier-sounding projects. This was the plan to turn homosexuals into heterosexuals. A seventy-one-per-cent success rate was claimed for this so-called 'conversion therapy', over a six-year treatment period. But, in April 2009, *Scientific American* carried a report which said that colleagues of Masters, including Johnson, had had reservations about the programme and questioned the veracity of his claims.

The Dutch newspaper *NRC Handelsblad* recently reported a more robust form of conversion therapy from 1956, when Henk Hethuis, a pupil at a Catholic boarding school, was castrated on the instructions of Catholic priests after telling police he was being abused by a Dutch monk. The boy was told that castration would 'cure' him of his homosexuality, though you have to ask yourself if this wasn't really just a punishment for snitching. Ten other boys were also treated in the same way, the newspaper said.

Somewhat surprisingly, non-surgical 'conversion therapy' continues. In 2012, former Archbishop of Canterbury Lord Carey was among several signatories to a letter supporting sixty-year-old psychotherapist Lesley Pilkington, a Christian counsellor who was appealing against a British Association for Counselling and Psychotherapy ruling that she was guilty of professional misconduct in conducting a therapy session with a gay man who said he wanted her to 'make him straight'. The gay man was actually an undercover reporter who objected to this 'reparative therapy', which he said aimed to 'pray away the gay'. Mrs Pilkington claimed that the BACP hearing discriminated against her Christian faith and was unfair.

Whatever the case, it does sound highly unlikely that more than two thirds of 'Dorothy's friends' could be permanently converted into lawn-mowing suburban heterosexual husbands, by Masters and Johnson's conversion therapy or whatever other means.

Anyway, after two decades the gilt was coming off the gingerbread at home, and Masters and Johnson divorced in 1992, ending the pair's fruitful and influential research and business partnerships. Masters remarried the following year.

Like Kinsey and Reich before them, the team and their work did not meet with universal praise. Amongst their critics is the feminist sexologist Shere Hite (the famous spoonerism), who criticized the pair for allowing cultural attitudes to get into their research. This may well be true. Masters, who died in 2001, did once put his opinion of the fairer sex this way: 'Women are marvellous,' he said, 'the whole skin surface is an orgasmic platform', which could, I suppose, be regarded as a cultural attitude. Some said that Shere Hite had turned her feminist sexology into a fetish, but that would be a very mild sort of fetish, as we shall learn.

VIII
Wash Your Mouth Out!

A CONCISE GLOSSARY OF FILTHY LANGUAGE

*

*'Sex is a three-letter word which needs some old-fashioned
four-letter words to convey its full meaning.'*

ANON.

I used to know a fellow who did ornithological talks for elderly
people. When he was on the marshes he used to delight in
shouting out 'Tits like coconuts!' and making the old ladies jump.
The brain processes swearing in its more primitive regions, along
with emotion and instinct. This is why you swear without thinking
when you stub your toe or hit your head on the vicar's cupboard
door. The section of the brain where swear words, including sexual
swear words, live is the hypothalamus. It is part of the limbic
system, one of the most primitive bits of the human brain. As well
as swearing, the hypothalamus is home to emotions and impulses,
and it plays a major role in regulating the 'four Fs': Feeding,
Fighting, Fleeing and Reproduction.

Sexual swearwords have a strong emotional component and
many nicely spoken young ladies who would never dream of
saying 'Oh, Mercy!' when they drop their Yorkshire puddings on
the kitchen floor, will, at the height of sexual excitement, shriek
like sex-crazed sluts, emitting staccato bursts of these most explicit
sexual terms. 'Talking dirty' seems to be intertwined with lust, and
it can have a powerfully stimulating effect on a sexual partner. In
tests, these blunt words have been found to be more memorable
than non-sexual, non-emotional words, and they provoke a

physical effect on the sayer as well as the hearer.

The words in the following lists of sexual slang are often more jocular than the very bluntest words, and though these are not exhaustive glossaries they do contain some of the most poetic and delightful terms, mainly of British and US origin.

Sexual intercourse
Slang terms for sexual congress are many and various. 'Sexual congress' isn't so much slang as polite – not to say coy – evasion. 'Sexual intercourse' is the 'scientific' word and like 'sexual congress' it is a euphemism, that is to say, a nice word for a nasty one. Some of these words appear below, and though some are short and plain-spoken they tend to be humorous and celebratory too.

Ball	Copulate
Bang	Couple
Beat	Dance
Bed	Dash up the Channel
Blaze	Diddle
Bit of the other, a	Dig out
Blow the groundsels	Dip one's wick
Boff	Do
Bone	Do a bit of ladies' tailoring
Bonk	Do it
Bore	Do the dishes
Bounce	Do the mattress jig
Bounce refrigerators	Dog's match (sex in the bushes)
Bump uglies	Dunk one's biscuit
Bunk-up	Empty one's trash
Bust one's nuts	Exercise the ferret
Carnal knowledge	Fire
Coitus	Fluff
Congress	Fool around

Fornicate

Frig

Fuck

Funny business

Get guts

Get it on

Get laid

Get lucky

Get one's banana peeled

Get one's end away

Get one's greens

Get one's jollies

Get one's oats

Get one's tip wet

Give her a beef injection

Give her the bone

Give her the business

Give the lizard a run

Go all the way

Go at it

Go to the ballet

Grease the weasel

Grind

Hanky panky

Have a go

Have some curly greens

Hide the salami

Hit

Hit skins

Horizontal bop

Horizontal mambo

Horizontal refreshment

Hose

How's yer father

Hump

Indoor sledging

Interior decorating

Intimacy

It

Jiggery-pokery

Knee-trembler (standing)

Knock boots

Know (biblical)

Lay

Lay some pipe

Leg-over

Make babies

Make the beast with two backs
     (from Shakespeare's *Othello*)

Make whoopee

Mate

Monkey business

Nail

Nobbing

Nookie

Old in-out, the

Play around

Play mumble-peg

Plough

Poke

Pot the white

Pound the duck

Pull the bacon

Pump

Ram

Ride

Ride the flagpole	Sink the sausage
Roger	Slap and tickle
Roll in the hay	Slay
Root	Sleep together
Scour the pipes	Sleep with
Screw	Stable the nag
Serve	Smack
Service	Smash
Sexual relations	Squeeze the lemon
Sexual union	Storm the cotton gin
Shaft	Stretch leather
Shake a skin-coat	Swack
Shake the sheets	Take a bean out of
Shag	Trim
Shenanigans	Wham-bam-thank-you-ma'am
Shine it	Wax ass

The penis

There are more than 100 known Latin terms for the penis, including *vomer* (plough), *vena* (vein) and *penis* itself, which means 'tail'. 'Penises' and 'penes' are both correct plural formations. Curiously, the term for the head of the organ is 'glans', the Latin word for 'acorn'.

Many of the terms for the male pudendum are 'harder' – if you'll pardon the expression – than those for the female anatomy. Weapons and tools crop up a bit, along with active vocabulary.

Ankle spanker	Baby rifle
Arse opener	Bald-headed yogurt slinger
Baby arm	Bean-tosser
Baby maker	Beef stick

Beef thermometer

Beer can

Big foot Joe

Bishop

Blue-veined custard chucker

Bone

Brat-getter

Bum-tickler

Bush-beater

Captain Standish

Cherry popper

Chew toy

Choad

Chopper

Chromosome snake

Cock

Comrade Wobbly

Cornholer

Crab ladder

Crack-haunter

Cream horn

Custard wand

Dick

Dibber

Diddlestick

Dillywhacker

Ding-a-ling

Dingbat

Doinker

Domepiece

Dong

Donger

Fanny ferret

Fanny rat

Fanny spanner

Fiddlestick

Flagpole

Fuck stick

Garden hose

Giggling pin

Girl-catcher

Glory pole

Gooter

Gristle stick

Gut wrench

Hammer

Hampton (Cockney rhyming
    slang: Hampton Wick = dick)

Happy lamp

Happy pole

Honey pump

Jimber (erection)

Jimmy

John Thomas

Johnson

Kennel raker

Kick stand

Kidney wiper (large)

Knob

Lance

Liver disturber (large)

Love muscle

Love pump

Meat

Meatloaf

Member

Middle leg

Milkman

Mr Happy

Mud snake

Noodle

Nudger

Old chap

One-eyed burping gecko

One-eyed trouser snake

Organ

Package

Pecker

Percy

Person

Peter

Piece

Pile driver

Pillicock

Pink bus

Pink oboe

Plonker

Pocket rocket

Pole

Pork sword

Porridge gun

Portuguese round stick

Prick

Pud

Ramrod

Rod

Roger

Schlong

Schmeckel

Schmuck

Shaft

Shooting stick

Skin flute

Smile rifle

Splat gun

Spritz pipe

Stroker

Sugarstick

Summer sausage

Tallywhacker

Thing

Third leg

Tadger

Todger

Tonsil tickler (large)

Tool

Trouser trout

Tube steak

Turkey neck

Twanger

Vein sausage

Veiny bang stick

Wand

Weapon

Whang

Widow-consoler

Willy

Whore-pipe

Yogurt rifle

The breasts

The English word breast comes from the Old English *breost*, akin to Old High German *brust*, and Old Irish *brú* (belly), though I have read that it has its roots in the Proto-Indo-European *bhreus*, meaning to swell or sprout.

The slang terms for the female breasts are many and various. In fact, they could fill a fat book. They are a delightfully humorous and respectful celebration of the female form, with many references to fruits and vegetables – are you getting your five a day? Some initial letters, such as B, seem to have more than their fair share.

Anyway, here's the list, which is a taster rather than the full menu, though it does contain some of my favourites. Commit a few to memory and titillate your bosom friends with them the next time you sit down to tea.

Angel cakes	Bosoms
Apples	Boulders
Bags	Bouncers
Balcony	Bubbas
Balloons	Buds
Baps	Bullets
Bazongas	Bumpers
Bazookas	Busters
Beacons	Caboodles
Betties	Charlies
Bibble chunks	Charms
Bikini stuffers	Cheerleaders
Bonkers	Chihuahuas
Boobies	Coconuts
Boobs	Corkers
Bops	Credentials

Cupcakes

Curves

Dingers

Dirigibles

Domes

Doodads

Doozies

Dugs

Dumplings

Ear muffs

Exocets

Flappers

Floats

Fog lights

Fried eggs

Fun bags

Gagas

Garbos

Gazongas

Gobstoppers

Grapefruits

Grillwork

Gum

Handsets

Headlamps

Hindenburgs

Honeydews

Honkers

Hoohas

Hooters

Howitzers

Hubcaps

Jemimas

Jugs

Kabukis

Kazongas

Kazoos

Knockers

Kumquats

Loaves

Lulus

Lung warts

Macaroons

Mambos

Mammas

Mangos

Mausers

Meatballs

Melons

Milk cans

Montezumas

Moo-moos

Muffins

Mulligans

Nancies

Nards

Noogies

Nose cones

Nuds

Nuggies

Oompas

Ottomans

Pair

Pastries

Peaks

Pillows

Pips

Plums

Points

Pokers

Pompoms

Pumpkins

Rib Balloons

Rivets

Roundies

Sandbags

Satellites

Scoops

Shakers

Shirt puppies

Skin sacks

Smoothies

Snuggle pups

Spark plugs

Specials

Sponge cakes

Spuds

Stacks

Sweater puffs

Taters

Tits

Titties

Tomatoes

Tooters

Torpedoes

Tweeters

Willets

Wind-jammers

Wobblers

Woofers

Yams

Yayas

Zeppelins

Zingers

IX
The Spice of Life
The sexual spectrum, from vanilla to kinky

*

*'If variety is the spice of life, marriage is
the big can of leftover Spam'*
JOHNNY CARSON

First, you've got your so-called 'vanilla sex', the sort, presumably,
that a man and a woman have face to face in a bedroom with the
lights out; and then you've got everything else, all the other
flavours, which I suppose must all be, by definition, sexually
deviant. But, as we know, variety is the spice of life and the sexual
spectrum is so enormous, and sexual taste and appetite so various,
that there can be few human beings who have only ever tasted
vanilla. Are we all perverts?

This chapter is a celebratory overview of the sexual spectrum:
straight, gay, bisexual, transvestite, transsexual and everything else.
It features fetishes galore, from bondage and domination to
exhibitionism, macrophilia and everything else you've ever heard
of (plus a lot you haven't). I've also talked to experts in the field,
young and old, professional, amateur and academic to get their
view through the sexual kaleidoscope.

Masturbation
As Truman Capote said, 'The good thing about masturbation is
that you don't have to get dressed up for it', and it's certainly a
good place to start examining the sexual spectrum. The term
'masturbation' was first recorded in 1603 and is of uncertain

etymological parentage. It refers to the erotic stimulation of one's own genitals by manual or other bodily contact – exclusive of sexual intercourse – by 'instrumental manipulation', or by a combination of these methods. Common accessories of the craft are sexual fantasy or porn, and the result is usually orgasm.

In one description I read of male masturbation, the instructions were to place the fingers and thumb on the penis, before shuttling them back and forth as if playing the flute. Just be aware that it's not music that will come out of the end of your instrument.

After numerous surveys, masturbation is now known to be very common in humans of all ages and both sexes. It has appeared in art since prehistoric times but the practice came under a cloud of disapproval from the end of the eighteenth century until well into the twentieth century. Victorian girls were forbidden from riding horses and bicycles for fear of becoming aroused on cobbled roads and the inhabitants of boarding schools were lectured on the dangers of 'self-abuse'. For a long time it was claimed that masturbation made boys blind, deaf or mad but banning boys from masturbating was about as sensible as making convent girls eat bananas with a knife and fork for reasons of decorum. Nobody took much notice, except for feeling a bit guilty. According to Havelock Ellis in the 1920s, enthusiastic seamstresses used to give themselves orgasms by sitting on the edge of their chairs while pedalling their treadle-operated sewing machines. Whether productivity went up, who can say?

Times have changed, and today masturbation is known for its great medical benefits. It is now considered a normal sexual practice and in a 1997 study, frequent ejaculators were found to be less likely to die from coronary heart disease, with lower blood pressure being recorded in those who had recently masturbated than in those who hadn't. In 2003 Australian researchers also suggested that men could reduce their risk of developing prostate cancer through regular masturbation. Sexual intercourse did not have the same protective effect because of the risk of STIs. Men who ejaculated more than five times a week were found to be a third less likely to get prostate cancer. A 2009 British study found particular benefits for the over fifties but concluded that regular ejaculation in younger men actually *contributed* to prostate cancer. This is typical of science: first it's one thing, then it's another. You don't know whether you're coming or going.

In 2009 another Australian study found that daily ejaculation is important to sperm health, with wankers having more mobile sperm than non-wankers. The same year, in an effort to reduce the rate of teenage pregnancy and sexually transmitted infections, the UK and other European governments officially encouraged teenagers to masturbate at least once a day. Presumably the idea was that after seven wanks a week the teenagers would be too exhausted for intercourse. In any case, the UK's jolly slogan, 'an orgasm a day keeps the doctor away', was music to the ears of British youth.

The word 'wanker' is a well-known British term of disapproval that has even spread to the United States. But I heard its use embroidered recently when an angry political comedian remarked that the prime minister looked like 'a recently wanked penis', a description I found remarkably congenial.

Perhaps the most esoteric finding of all appeared in the 2008 study done at Tabriz Medical University in Iran. It was that ejaculation reduces swelling in inflamed nasal blood vessels, making breathing much easier. So next time you find yourself all blocked up in a stuffy committee meeting, you will know what to do.

Oral sex
Oral sex is the sexual stimulation of a partner's genitals by use of the mouth, especially the tongue. Cunnilingus is the name for oral sex performed on a woman and fellatio is the term for oral sex on a man. The two words were coined fairly recently, their first

recorded use coming within six years of each other: 'fellatio' in 1893, and 'cunnilingus' in 1897. *Cunnilingus,* comes from Latin, from *cunnus,* meaning 'vulva' and *lingere,* 'to lick'. 'Fellatio' is also from Latin, from *fellare,* literally, 'to suck'.

In Ancient Rome, fellatio was taboo, but in modern Western culture, it is widely practised. According to the UK National Survey of Sexual Attitudes and Lifestyles (2000), seventy-eight per cent of men and seventy-seven per cent of women reported having oral sex the previous year.

Two common and delightful slang terms for cunnilingus and fellatio are, respectively, 'muff diving' and 'blow job'. Presumably, the blowing is the culmination of the act rather than the lead-up, which is a 'suck job' if it is anything. The etymology is obscure, though it has been attributed to a street term for fellatio, 'blow-off', which is said to be a prostitutes' vernacular first recorded in 1933. Another idea is that 'blow job' derives from a supposed Victorian slang term, 'below-job', during the execution of which you would, I suppose, have to 'go down'. Anyway, no evidence is provided for any of these and my dictionary remains silent on the controversy. Interestingly, an act of group sex in which a woman fellates several men in a row is known on the street as a 'gangsuck' or 'blowbang'.

Women are from Venus, men can't find their keys

Psychotherapist and sex expert Richard Evans-Lacey runs Psychic Plumbing, a service providing professional therapy to 'force blockages back through the pipes', as he puts it. On his website, Richard sports a huge pointed moustache but he is wearing a truly magnificent beard when I meet him at his place overlooking a delightful church square in London. 'Variety delights me in my work,' he tells me as I drop my hat on to a pile of his own head-wear, including a policeman's helmet and some military hats. He sits down beside a rack of his homemade kilts and tucks into a bowl of cereal as we talk about the sexual psychotherapy he does with his clients.

I wonder if he can enlighten me on the difficult question of whether men and women are after different things between the sheets. The essential difference between male and female sexuality, he says, is essentially one of dominance and submission, or as he prefers it, 'surrender'. In the sexual act the man is 'completely aware, and is witnessing the woman's surrender. His aggression and dominance allow her to submit. She has a willingness to give up control for pure abandon, because she is safe.' Women's popular fantasy subjects – the cowboy, the fireman, the dark, mysterious, powerful stranger – might bear him out here, but I don't know.

Women are certainly more inclined to talk about sex to their friends. Few men are going to gossip about the geography of their girlfriend's anatomy to their mates in a giggly circle down the pub. But a woman's friends will be well briefed not only about what floats her man's boat in the bedroom but how well he performs, and all his horrid little quirks and foibles. So be warned, chaps.

Male homosexuality

They say that if you offend the gay mafia they don't shoot you, they send round a couple of heavies to criticize your curtains. Now, before you report me to the thought-police for that joke I should tell you that it came from one of my gay friends.

Homosexuality in animals is well documented, with male bats having the highest rate of homosexuality of any mammal, but the precise percentage of homosexuality in humans is still open to debate. Alfred Kinsey reported that thirty per cent of post-adolescent US men and thirteen per cent of women had had an orgasm through physical contact with another person of the same sex but his results have been disputed owing to their probable experimental bias. In a 2001/2002 Australian telephone survey, more than 19,000 males between the ages of sixteen and fifty-nine were interviewed. The survey reported that 1.6 per cent described themselves as gay while 0.9 per cent said they were bisexual. However, 8.6 per cent of men said that, although they did not classify themselves as homosexual they were attracted to members of the same sex, or had had some same-sex experience.

The prevalence of homosexual sex in single-sex boarding schools, prisons and the military is well known but it is not clear how many of these beggars-can't-be-choosers homosexuals revert to straight sex on their release.

GAYS IN THE BIBLE

Despite the prevalence of homosexuality in the clergy, the Bible never has anything nice to say about gay men. In the Old Testament, the ancient book of Leviticus is especially full of don'ts on this topic. In verse 22 of chapter 18, for example, it says, 'Thou shalt not lie with mankind, as with womankind: it is abomination', which couldn't be clearer. In Genesis 19, two angels in disguise visit the city of Sodom, where a local man named Lot offers to do them bed and breakfast, with, one imagines, somewhere to put their wings overnight. The men of Sodom tell Lot to hand over his guests so they can have sex with them but Lot says no, offering instead his two virgin daughters. The men of Sodom aren't having it, though, and insist. In the end, the angels have to blind them for being so cheeky, and the town is consumed by fire.

This religious intolerance is still going, although not in quite such an extreme form. In 2011, a British Christian married (heterosexual) couple who had refused a single room to a gay couple for religious reasons were ordered to compensate them. But, though we have come some way down Tolerance Road and nobody had their eyes put out in that case, gay tolerance is still patchy. Also in 2011, India's health minister Ghulam Nabi Azad told a conference on HIV/AIDS that gay sex was 'unnatural' and that homosexuality was 'a disease which has come from other countries'. AIDS campaigner Anjali Gopalan said the health minister was 'living on another planet' but Mr Azad later said he had been 'quoted out of context'.

Anti-homosexual remarks have also been recorded in parliament. Right-wing Scottish MP Sir Nicholas Fairbairn (1933–95), who described his role as Solicitor-General for Scotland as forming 'a second pair of hands and often a first brain for the Lord Advocate', was well known for going about with a fully working silver revolver attached to the belt of his extremely loud and allegedly homemade tartan costumes. He was also said to be the only remaining MP to use the House of Commons snuff box.

Despite being a onetime Honorary Vice President of a lesbian and gay rights organization, Fairbairn made a surprising intervention during a 1994 parliamentary debate on the age of consent:

Mr Blair: Let us be clear about the issue before us tonight. It is not at what age we wish young people to have sex. It is whether the criminal law should discriminate between heterosexual and homosexual sex . . . The argument – and the only argument – advanced to justify that discrimination and its attendant tragedy is that it is necessary for the protection of young people. Without it, it is said, young men unsure of their sexuality may be preyed upon by older homosexuals and induced to become homosexual when they otherwise would not. I will attempt to deal with that argument tonight.

Sir Nicholas Fairbairn (Perth and Kinross): I hope that the Committee will not be misled by the fact that heterosexual activity is normal and homosexual activity, putting your penis into another man's arsehole, is a perverse—

The First Deputy Chairman: Order. We can well do without talk like that.

Decades of heavy drinking finally took their toll and Sir Nicholas died the following year, aged 61.

The American military went further than this, even going as far as to investigate the possibility of a 'non-lethal gay bomb'. This was not designed to single out gays but, rather, to turn the enemy militia gay. The plan was to squirt female sex pheromones over enemy forces to make them sexually attracted to each other and cause 'homosexual behaviour' to break out. This project followed two other rather bonkers plans, firstly, to hide beehives in combat zones and then spray the enemy with bee pheromones, and, secondly, to give the enemy bad breath with a fiendish-sounding chemical weapon: the so-called 'halitosis bomb'.

GAY VARIETY

Disapproval has never done anything to stop homosexual activity. In past times it just drove it underground. Guy Haines, a retired actor from Brighton, described to me how the illegality of gay sex in the sixties only made it more exciting. He recalled once going back with a man to the London flat he was taking care of for a friend who was away. 'It was a very agreeable apartment,' he told me, 'and we had sex on the couch in the sitting room. Interestingly, the place belonged to Noël Coward.' Haines also told me another story that somehow involved an artificial leg but I was laughing so much as I jotted down notes that I cannot read them well enough to tell you the details.

In recent times, the Internet has made it easier for gay men to contact each other, just as it has for everybody else. Tony Wendice, who works for a multinational consumer goods company near St Paul's Cathedral, agreed to meet me to discuss his sex life. We found a nearby All Bar One and sat down under a sign for the toilets.

Tony told me he realized he was gay at a very young age. 'When I was five years old I was on holiday at Butlins in Minehead with a friend,' he said. 'My friend's dad came into our bedroom to say goodnight and he was stark bollock naked. I remember I liked what I saw, and I liked it afterwards. I knew that something wasn't quite right. I tuned in very early – I knew I was gay.'

Tony grew up in a working-class environment, where men were expected to be men. He was teased a bit at secondary school. 'My personality was shining through,' he says, 'but I really wanted to fit in so I tried three girlfriends. I managed the mechanics fine but it wasn't really doing it for me.'

Tony told his mother he was gay when he was nineteen. She accepted it immediately and offered to help the mother of an Oxbridge-educated friend who had recently come out as gay. 'Charles's mother was a twin-set-and-pearls lady,' explains Tony, 'and she was taken aback when Mum suddenly mentioned what she called "bum sex". The "up-the-bum" stuff was so alien to this counties lady.'

Tony has had a partner, Leonard, for twenty years but they separated when he had a 'mid-life crisis'. Tony says he went on to Gaydar, which styles itself 'The premier gay dating site. Home to millions of men', and started going to gay clubs. 'It would be drinks from 11 o'clock then clubbing,' he says. 'It was all about looking thin, being beautiful, getting eye contact. I was going to the gym five times a week. I had lots and lots of fun, weekend after weekend.'

I wonder about the dangers of HIV and AIDS. Tony thinks the government did an excellent job with the television information films. 'I always wore a condom,' he says. 'It's all about safe sex. It was a lot of fun but towards the end it had got depressing and empty. It became so pointless and unfulfilling. Anyway, Leonard and I got back together in 2008 and now I watch *Emmerdale* five days a week.'

Lesbianism

One day the actor Kenneth Williams was walking down the Edgware Road with his mother. 'Oh, look!' she said. 'There's another of those lesbian restaurants.' 'It's not "lesbian", Mother,' said Williams. 'It's "*Lebanese*".' 'Yes,' she replied. 'It's *disgusting*.' The causes of lesbianism, if 'causes' is the proper word, are still poorly understood. But research is under way.

Dr Andrea Burri of King's College, London, is a sex researcher who believes that genetics, hormones and upbringing together have an effect on female sexual orientation but has had trouble drumming up funds to investigate this fascinating subject further. At one point she offered to run naked across Westminster Bridge to raise money for a study into possible links between genetics and female homosexuality. 'I don't always get the funding, so it is a struggle,' she said. 'It has been frustrating, because you are often not taken seriously doing this kind of work.' I wonder how far her proposed naked sprint over the bridge improved her academic gravitas.

All this reminded me of that story about the young actor who goes to a theatrical agent and asks him if he will represent him. 'Sure,' says the agent, 'but you've got to change your name – it's ridiculous! I simply can't sell an actor called "Penis Van Lesbian".' The actor angrily refused, saying that Penis Van Lesbian is the name he was born with and he is sticking with it.

Years later the agent receives a letter from the same actor, who, bursting with gratitude, explains that, in the end, after many rejections, he had taken the agent's advice and changed his name.

'As you may have noticed,' he said, 'I've since had considerable success, all thanks to your brilliant suggestion. Yours sincerely, Dick Van Dyke.'

'Plastic' women

A growing body of research shows that women seem to be more 'plastic' or 'fluid' in their sexuality than men. In 2001/2, in a huge Australian telephone survey, 0.8 per cent of women described themselves as lesbian and 1.4 per cent as bisexual (more than men). Interestingly, though, a whopping 15.1 per cent of women said that, though basically straight, they were attracted to women or had had at least one same-sex encounter. More women than men in happy stable heterosexual relationships agree that they have fantasized about same-sex encounters, or describe themselves as bisexual or, in that ghastly term, 'bi-curious'. Men tend to be more rigid in their sexual partner preference and typically classify themselves strictly as straight or gay, and only much more infrequently as bisexual. Psychosexual therapist Dr Liz West suggests that 'women are more open to admitting relationships of this kind and they find it easier than men to be intimate with each other. A lot of those sex encounters with women may be more about intimacy.'

To test the idea of 'plasticity', Marta Meana, a professor of psychology at the University of Nevada at Las Vegas, asked a group of heterosexual men and women to look at pictures of straight sex while wearing eye-tracking goggles. She found that the men stared at the women more than they did at the men (no surprises there), whereas the women looked at both sexes equally.

Lisa Diamond, author of *Sexual Fluidity: Understanding Women's Love and Desire*, showed men and women a video involving men, women and apes having various types of sex – both gay and straight – though not all at the same time. The men told her their reactions, which she wrote down. At the same time, she also measured their physical reactions to the video with a plethysmograph, an instrument that records changes in blood volume in an organ (in this case the penis). The plethysmograph used to be a simple little doohickey, like a rubber band that slipped over the penis and expanded upon erection. Today these things are higher tech. The female equivalent is the vaginal photoplethysmograph, a clear acrylic rod-shaped gizmo with a kind of torch on the end, which is inserted into the vagina, where it measures the circulating blood, recording the physical signals of arousal.

What Diamond found was that as well as reacting to a much broader range of stimulus than men, the women focused on the men's *faces* and on the women's *bodies*. She suggests that women, whose sexuality is more 'fluid', might be enjoying the women's curves while searching for signs of sexual desire in the men's expressions.

Objects of desire
Marta Meana says that being desired sexually is profoundly important for women. She maintains that the object of female desire is to *be the object* of desire. This must be why women love receiving compliments and getting presents, spend hours doing their hair and makeup and take five years dressing for a date, while men run a comb through their hair, if they have any, while sitting on the car bonnet. It is probably also why flowers and chocolates always work.

Men who give presents increase their chances of getting sex in return, and humans are not alone in this behaviour. In a recent paper, *Payment for Sex in a Macaque Mating Market*, it was reported that male macaques used food to 'pay' for sex with females in a straightforward exchange. Chocolate is a good gift (for humans) because it contains phenylethylamine, the chemical responsible for the high that comes from sexual attraction. It must be said though that chocolate remains the least popular flavour of edible underwear, at least according to the managers of sex shops.

Bisexuality

Virginia Woolf's family seemed to cover the entire sexual spectrum. Her novel *Mrs Dalloway* (1925) was about a bisexual man and woman in a sexually unsatisfactory marriage. Then, in 1928, getting the bit between her teeth, Woolf wrote *Orlando: A Biography*, the tale of a man who changes into a woman. In fact it is really a lesbian story based on the life of Woolf's girlfriend Vita Sackville-West, who, like Woolf, was married. The wily author made Orlando a man to prevent the book being banned because of its homosexual subject matter.

Bisexuality is not the same condition as hermaphrodism (intersex), or transgenderism. It is merely the sexual attraction to both sexes. Sometimes this is an evenly spread attraction but very often there is a preference for one sex over the other. The American composer Leonard Bernstein (1918–90) described himself as 'half-man, half-woman', but Arthur Laurents, who worked with him on *West Side Story*, said he was merely 'a gay man who got married. He wasn't conflicted about it at all. He was just gay.'

Nonetheless, both male and female bisexuality have been recognized for centuries. Augustus Caesar was famously said to be 'every man's wife and every woman's husband', though the Ancient Greeks and Romans were less troubled by labels and had no word for bisexuality. Edward Gibbon said that, of the first fifteen emperors, Claudius was the only one whose erotic tastes were entirely 'correct'. Hadrian was another bisexual emperor, and had a close romantic relationship with a young Greek fellow called Antinous.

Animals also indulge in bisexual behaviour, including the bonobo, killer whale and bottlenose dolphin, as do some gulls, penguins and worms.

Cross-dressing

Most mornings I walk past the sometime retirement flat of Lady de Frece, better known as Vesta Tilley (1864–1952), the most famous male impersonator of her day. Vesta Tilley said she felt that she could express herself better dressed as a boy, though she was happily married. People go in for cross-dressing (transvestism) for various reasons. Performer and heterosexual transvestite Eddie Izzard, who amusingly describes himself as a 'male lesbian', says that he fancies women but just wears what he likes. Cross-dressing, for him, is not a sexual fetish, and he described J. Edgar Hoover and Hermann Göring, who were both said to like wearing women's clothes, as 'weirdo transvestites'. But whether it is weird to put on women's clothes for sexual gratification is a matter of opinion. Hoover and Göring were certainly weird, but for other reasons.

Many male transvestites say they get a psychological rather than a sexual boost from wearing women's clothes, though, for some, the thrill of stepping into a pair of stockings is unambiguously sexual. Ed Wood (1924–78) was a heterosexual transvestite Hollywood B-movie director who, while serving in the Second World War, was prone to wear women's undergarments beneath his uniform, though not for sexual purposes. Wood directed and starred in a film drama entitled *Glen or Glenda* (1953), which concerned a cross-dressing man with a fetish for angora sweaters. He admitted that the film was the story of his own psyche.

Stunned churchgoers amongst the audiences for *Glen or Glenda* sprinted home to check their bibles and, after a stiff lemonade and a lie down, they flipped them open to Deuteronomy 22:5, where they found this: 'The woman shall not wear that which pertaineth unto a man, neither shall a man put on a woman's garment: for all that do so are abomination unto the LORD thy God.'

Women who dress as men are fewer and further between but the notorious case of 'man-woman murderer' Harry Crawford is an interesting one. When dressed as a man, Harry Crawford looked like a man, as can be seen in mug shots from the twenties. But Harry was really Eugenia Falleni, an Italian woman who lived in Australia and looked like a woman when she dressed as a woman – albeit a raddled-looking one.

Falleni had spent most of her life since 1899 dressing and acting as a man and in 1913 she married a widow named Annie Birkett, who must have had bad eyesight. Three years later, shortly after announcing to a relation that she had discovered something amazing about Harry, Birkett disappeared. Her wounded body was later discovered, but Falleni was not arrested until 1920. Amid the male clothing in her suitcase the police discovered a cloth-wrapped dildo made of wood and rubber. In court rum duck Falleni appeared in male and female attire on different days.

Transvestism should not be confused with drag, a term used to describe female clothing worn by a male performer. Drag queens are generally homosexual men who portray in their act a grotesque version of femininity but dress in men's clothes when they go to the shops.

These days, fewer eyelids are batted at all this and a Friday-night crowd on the Underground can resemble the cast of *Cabaret* to the extent that you can't tell the sex of half of them – or whether some are even human.

But, as prejudice has died down, the language of sexual politics has become increasingly aggressive, inventing its own angry and abrupt, not to say mystifying jargon. Today, a heavily bearded man wearing a dress while shopping at Waitrose will no longer be described as having gone off his rocker but instead be lauded as an example of 'genderfuck'. It's a shame that the gobbledegook-suffused articles about this interesting subject are too often fuddled or badly written, or both.

Transgenderism

Gender dysphoria is a condition in which a person feels that their 'gender identity' is different from their anatomical sex, as though they are trapped in a body of the wrong sex. The condition is also sometimes known as transgenderism or transsexualism, though 'transgender' is sometimes used to describe people who want to live as a member of the opposite sex without having sex reassignment surgery. I read somewhere that transgender people may be heterosexual, homosexual, bisexual, pansexual, polysexual (the famous parrot) or asexual, so it's a complicated business, and a fast-moving one. In 2004 the English Gender Recognition Act allowed transsexuals and people with gender dysphoria to marry in their preferred gender and get a new birth certificate and passport. In 2010, France became the first country in the world to remove transgender identity from the list of mental diseases.

But transgenderism isn't a new phenomenon. In 1865 Sophia Bishop, a charwoman who was looking after the recently dead body of respected British army surgeon James Barry (c. 1789–1865), discovered that the fellow's anatomy was female, and may well have had an attack of the vapours, which was fashionable at the time. Though the army sealed the records, Barry is believed to have been Margaret Ann Bulkley and been anatomically female at birth. Nonetheless, James Barry (two male names, notice) lived his entire adult life as a man – with rather a prickly personality. By the end of his career he had become Inspector General in charge of military hospitals but got cross if anyone referred to his features or voice, rather camply fighting duels over the matter. Barry also once got into a fight, presumably about bedpans or something, with the strong-willed Florence Nightingale.

Another transgender person whose anatomical sex was only realized by many after his death was Billy Tipton (1914–89), an American jazz pianist who was born female but who began living as a man at the age of twenty-six. Although not officially married,

Tipton lived with his 'wife' and adopted three boys. All this was before the days of gender reassignment surgery.

Jeanette Schmid (1924–2005) was a professional transsexual whistler. Born Rudolf Schmid in what is now the Czech Republic, Schmid liked dressing up as a girl from an early age and, despite not being the ideal blond Aryan male, joined the Nazi armed forces in 1941, before changing tack and becoming a female impersonator. Schmid was a big hit with the then Shah of Iran, who invited him to Tehran, but his female impersonation act was so outrageous that he was obliged to drop it at the last minute and, instead, whistled a bit of Offenbach.

Combining his talents, Schmid then toured his transvestite-whistler routine around the globe, performing alongside such minor support acts as Frank Sinatra and Marlene Dietrich. In 1964, Rudolf had sex reassignment surgery and changed his name to Jeanette. After recovery, with the stage name Baroness Lips von Lipstrill, Jeanette Schmid continued her successful world tours (the whistling tranny competition must have been negligible). She died in Vienna at a ripe old age in 2005.

Barry, Tipton and Schmid seem to have been clear about their perceived sexual identities. Not so Gloria Hemingway (1931–2001), one of Earnest's children, who was born Gregory, a boy. After years of gender dysphoria, Gregory had partial gender reassignment surgery, but then had it reversed. He reportedly seemed like 'one of the guys' in his local pub, but at other times dressed as a woman. He, or she, never seemed completely at home in either sex.

A common medical term for this condition is bigenderism. A bigender is not someone with a 'big end' but a person who shifts between the masculine and feminine genders and the term should not be confused with intersex, which is the congenital presence of physical features of both sexes.

Sex work

The term 'sex worker' was coined in 1978 by activist Carol Leigh. Sex work covers a broad field from street walking to phone sex, peep shows, pornography, webcam artistry, go-go dancing, lap dancing and striptease, just for starters. And it's big business. Strip clubs generate more money in the US than theatre, classical music, opera and jazz combined.

In chapter 41 of his book *London: The Biography*, Peter Ackroyd discusses the history of sex and sex work in the city. Apparently, the Romans held jolly priapic celebrations in what is now Leadenhall Street, and dotted herms (statues with erect penises) about town, their pudenda shining in the sun. The Law has always rubbed up uncomfortably against the sex trade and by the fourteenth century, brothels were being regularly prosecuted. So numerous were the city's whorehouses that the lawyers really had their work cut out. By the eighteenth century even Casanova had managed to catch gonorrhoea in London – in the Canon tavern. 'Mollie houses' and 'sodomitical clubs' catered for gays and 'buggerantoes', including the aptly named Mother Clap's in Holborn.

Ackroyd lists some of the delightful historic nicknames for prostitutes: 'doxies', 'molls', 'punks', 'jilts', 'drabs', 'smuts', 'wagtails', 'mackerels', 'blowzabellas', 'buttered buns', 'cats' and 'trulls', which is reminiscent of the 'trolls' of today. But my favourite tart nicknames are the delightful 'trugmoldies' and the prizewinning 'punchable nuns'.

Sex has always sold, and the historical commercialization of the product is exemplified by the early temple brothels, which handed over all their income to priests. The first recorded brothel of this sort operated around 2300 BCE in Mesopotamia, while the world's biggest brothel, the 450-room Nymphia, was built in San Francisco in 1899 to accommodate members of the flourishing trade in tarts. It had windows in every door with coin-operated shades so people could watch. It's only surprising that the oldest profession is not listed in the FTSE 500.

In 1990 a peer-led charity called POW was launched in Nottingham to support working prostitutes in a poor area of the city, a group which they say is 'very chaotic, vulnerable and hard to reach'. POW has 1,500 clients on its books and provides information on occupational hazards such as drug use and sexually transmitted infections. It also helps those who want to get out of the business.

Although there are still many prostitutes at work on the streets, the Internet and mobile phones have made home-working and sex-freelancing easier.

Kitty Stryker describes herself as a 'seductress and self-taught sex goddess'. She is, she says, 'a politically and socially conscious, well-educated sex worker/performer with experience and/or knowledge of many aspects of sexuality, from threesomes and bondage to the history of fetish and fashion and the psychology of kink!' Kitty, who is in her twenties, has been a sex worker for eight years and now works in San Francisco, where I tracked her down for a chat.

As a student, Kitty studied psychology and anthropology but always knew what she wanted to do. 'Some people want to be astronauts,' she says. 'I wanted to be a sex worker.' She started her career at a local 'domination house' but was shocked by the attitude. 'They didn't like BDSM (bondage and domination fetish, see chapter X) and had no respect for the client. They had no idea about safety either and I knew it would end in tears.' So she set up on her own, doing role-play phone sex, and got some good reviews. 'My parents were really cool about it,' she says. 'They're open-minded, and they told me to make sure my prices were high enough. They were concerned about violence but I find that the deeper you go down the sex hole, the safer it is. When I was a fetish model these guys would try to grab me and I had to let them know – hey, you don't touch me.'

Kitty has also worked in London, where she says she began her PhD on the subject of prostitution as therapy, especially in the area of disability. 'Most of my clients in the UK had disabilities,' she tells me. 'It's hands-on instruction.'

She explains that the Internet has been a hugely useful tool for her and other sex workers, with whom she does outreach work. Twenty-five years ago it would have been trickier for her to set up. 'It would just have been more difficult for people to find me,' she says, 'and more expensive. Prostitution is often a money issue. If you are a single parent you have to make enough to pay the nanny, and in the US you have to work three jobs. If you do sex work you can be home with the kids; it gives you time, which is a valuable commodity. Why the fuck work at McDonald's? Which is the more degrading?'

Somebody once said that the big difference between sex for money and sex for free is that sex for money usually costs less. Kitty tells me that she charges about £400/$800 a session and not being a big spender she works three or four times a month, which leaves her with plenty of time left over. It's stable work and she can plan financially. I wonder if she enjoys her work. 'Sometimes you think, wow! Do I get paid to do this? Sometimes it's just a bit "huh". It totally depends on the client. It's like any other job.'

This reminded me of a story about the author Douglas Adams, who, in his early days, was a bodyguard for some foreign potentate or other. One evening as he sat on a hard chair outside the man's hotel room a prostitute emerged, nodding glumly to Adams before remarking, 'At least you can read while you're on the job.'

'Open' relationships

I wanted to find out about 'open' sexual relationships so I arranged to meet Max Doray, who writes a sex blog that includes stories and musings on her various interesting sexual experiences. It is unusually well written, frank and not remotely obscene.

She asked to meet me at Tate Britain, where we spoke in hushed voices on squeaking sofas under the watchful eye of a nude man – a statue, I mean – just round the corner from the gallery shop. Max is an attractive, talkative, witty and intelligent lady, and she is also much tattooed, with everything from flowers to a handlebar moustache.

She believes monogamy is not the only way to live your life and describes herself as 'monogam*ish*'. This is to say that she has a stable relationship with her boyfriend but both of them have other sexual encounters too. 'People need to loosen up really,' she says.

I read on her blog an account of a party she went to with her boyfriend that contained some jolly useful advice for beginners in the field. This is what she says: 'You need to get to the person you fancy early in the evening, boys anyway, because most men have a limited number of encounters in them before they are done for the day.'

I'd also learned that Max was a Tantric sexual practitioner, working with clients. But she tells me that she doesn't do Tantric sexual practice any more, explaining that she felt 'violated by the hands-on stuff'. 'I decided it was not for me,' she says. 'I found it repulsive. All the love is sucked out of you. I've moved on to being an 'ecstasy aunt'.

She explains that she now gives out sexual advice, but, instead of agony, it's ecstasy. She tells me about a man who was on the swinging scene who wanted to go 'mono' (monogamous). However, the woman he was in a relationship with still found herself tempted by other men. Ecstasy aunt Max suggested that this fellow's girlfriend should ring him when she was round at some guy's place after a couple of drinks and was considering a 'shag', and get him to talk her down – like an Alcoholics Anonymous sponsor. Was it a success? 'Yes,' says Max. 'It stops her doing it. It works. But even if it fails one day, at least it won't come as a surprise to him.'

As the conversation draws to a close our attention is distracted by a well-dressed middle-aged lady in one of those green quilted jackets who has suddenly appeared and is looking at some photographs on the wall beside us. She has good hair and a middle-class accent but is talking loudly to nobody in particular about 'pissoirs' and other incomprehensible stuff. It may be Tourette's or it may be that she is just bonkers; we can't decide. The situation, which was already unusual, is now surreal.

Spreading it around

Wife-swapping parties were much talked about in the seventies, mainly by middle-aged men who were getting a bit tired of the old furniture. A typical scenario involved half a dozen suburban couples going round to one of their suburban houses, eating a few suburban sausages on sticks and all the chaps then dropping their car keys into a fruit bowl. The ladies each picked a key and zoomed off with the chap whose car it belonged to for a night of unbridled sex. A lovely wife-swapping tale concerned the unlucky man who went off the whole idea after getting his own wife back. How much of this actually went on and how much was wannabe gossip is hard to say.

In any case, the term 'wife swapping' was soon overtaken by 'swinging', a related activity in which partners switched each other at parties or in swingers' clubs. The rise of the Internet made the whole thing enormously easier and today there are numerous websites putting like-minded people in touch with one another.

A popular activity in the world of swingerdom is threesomes, sometimes called troilism, a common example of which is a husband secretly – or not – watching his wife having sex with another man. The word *triolisme* exists in French and the English 'troilism' is sometimes also spelled 'triolism'. If *triolisme* has something to do with the French word *trois*, meaning three, then 'triolism' and *triolisme* are classic spelling mistakes. The other possibility is that the word comes from Shakespeare's play *Troilus and Cressida* (c. 1602), in which the Greek character Ulysses obliges Trojan prince Troilus to hide, and watch his (Troilus's) lover, Cressida, in the tent of another man, a fellow called Diomedes. Just in case you cared.

Another word whose origins are hard to track down is 'dogging'. This is the practice of having sex in a public place, often a car park or lay-by, or watching others in the act. The practice is said to have emerged in the UK during the latter half of the twentieth century. The use of the word allegedly arose in the seventies to describe men who 'dogged' couples by spying on them as they indulged in a bit of outdoor- or car-sex. In this sense the practice is a kind of voyeurism.

After seeing a clip of some dogging going on, I wish I hadn't. The male participants, of what was headed a 'gang-bang', looked like pie fans. They had grungy jeans, dirty fingernails and beer bellies, while the frankly elderly lady was on the stout side, had lank hair and looked short of a tooth or two.

More group sex
I once worked with a chap called Michael Logan whose best friend was an assistant to a very senior Tory politician. This friend used to organize high-class sex parties at nice Kensington venues to which Michael used to go. He said he was a bit nervous at the first one and just sat there on a sofa in his cords and brogues watching developments. At later dos he told me he became more involved. He said that although everyone knew why they were there, proceedings started rather slowly, with mildly flirtatious chat. But then at about 1 a.m. things quickly turned into a proper orgy. Apparently, there were often more women than men, which could be explained by ladies' more social natures.

I needed to speak to the experts so I contacted Julie and Tobias of Kinky Salon, London, a non-profit sex-party setup. The Kinky

Salon website says they are open to all, 'vanilla or kinky, people of gender, queer, gay, straight, heteroflexible, bi or try-sexual, all of the above or none of the above', which I suppose covers all the bases.

I meet Julie and Tobias in the Hilton hotel in Paddington because Julie is just off to Eroticon, a conference for sex bloggers and erotic writers, in Bristol. They tell me that Kinky Salon, London, which is celebrating its second anniversary, was inspired by Kinky Salon in the USA. 'We were dissatisfied with what was out there,' says Tobias. 'We are non-commercial, open, more friendly and less frightening than other places – safer than a nightclub in Milton Keynes.'

'We are quite fluffy,' adds Julie.

Kinky Salon rents a venue in London every couple of months for their next private party. There are no tickets on the door and about 200 guests come along each time, including, I'm told, 'quite a few sex nerds and geeks'. It is compulsory to dress up and the mood is light-hearted. 'Everyone looks completely daft,' says Julie. There is a different theme each time, with music, stand-up, singing and burlesque. The Kinky Salon private playroom has fifteen beds. This is no small cocktail do and requires a crew of half a dozen people to set it up all day, from 10 a.m. to 9 p.m. After the party a truck arrives to take everything away again. 'We have fifteen large shipping-containers'-worth of decorations, beds and BDSM equipment to store,' explains Tobias.

The evening starts with an ice-breaking game, and twenty-five performers are available to provide a cabaret from 10.30 until 12.00, with prizes awarded for the best costumes. At 12 o'clock 'the wave breaks', Tobias tells me, and the action starts. I learn that the power across the sex scene is 'with the women', though I never doubted it. Julie says that they have control over multiple-partner sex.

'Some people have never had sex while they've been coming,'

adds Tobias, and one gay man who helped with organizing said he didn't want to participate because there was 'too much flange'. Gay men are a hard-to-reach sector, apparently.

For those who might suggest this all resembles the decadence of the Roman Empire before its collapse, Tobias has a different suggestion. 'It's like a cricket club,' he says. 'It's evolving and continues to live.'

'I want to do something that makes the world a better place,' says Julie. 'I want to give something back.'

X
FETISH ME SIDEWAYS!
UNUSUAL DESIRES, FROM RUBBER TO ROBOTS
*

*'There is no more unhappy being under the sun than a
fetishist who pines for a boot and has to content
himself with an entire woman.'*

KARL KRAUS

Scientists call fetishism 'paraphilia', from the Greek *para*, meaning
abnormal, and *philos*, loving. This word was popularized by US
sexologist John Money (1921–2006), who used it as a non-
judgemental term to describe unusual sexual interests and
behaviour. To make himself clear he explained that it was 'a
sexuoerotic embellishment of, or alternative to the official,
ideological norm', which just goes to show that, like many
sexologists, his jargon was needlessly impenetrable and pompous.

There are so many fetishes that you feel spoilt for choice. They
go from tickling to trampling; in fact, homosexuality was still
classed as a 'paraphilia' in the USA until 1973. There's even one
dedicated to amputees. I suppose it would be a dull world if we
were all the same.

One of the UK's most successful fetish clubs is Torture
Garden (TG), described as the world's largest fetish/body art
club, for open-minded individuals. It caters to fashionable
clubbers, 'alternative arty weirdos' and burlesque cabaret fans 'of
every sexual orientation and gender'. Thousands of people, aged
from eighteen to sixty-plus, attend their events at various London
venues.

During the 1990s, 'fetish' leaked into the mainstream, becoming fashionable, and, along with others, Torture Garden has developed its own latex fashion label. However, many who turn up make their own costumes. These are extremely imaginative but I wonder quite how you get to the club without being molested. I'm not getting on the Tube dressed in an outfit of huge white balloon breasts, stripy tights, diving mask and latex body suit. Not for all the tea in China.

Fetishism covers all the bases really, so I've done a lucky dip and here is a quick look at a few of the most interesting paraphilias that came up out of the fetish bran tub.

Podophilia

Just as the snapdragons in my grandma's garden were known to her as *antirrhinums* so fetishes seem to attract Latin or Greek names, maybe to make them seem more 'proper'. When it comes to sexual interest in non-sexual parts of the body, podophilia is undoubtedly the commonest fetish. In fact, 'podophilia' is merely a fancy name for foot worship. Foot fetishism is not new either; Sigmund Freud wrote about it long before websites had sprung up to cater for its adherents.

Shoe fetishism, a related paraphilia, does not have a Latin name. It is known as 'retifism', after Nicolas-Edme Rétif (1734–1806), a communist pornographic writer who had a sexual appetite for shoes. Footwear scores very high on the fetish scale. In 2006 AOL accidentally released some analysis of fetish-related search queries, the so-called 'AOL Fetish Data'. Sixty-four per cent of these queries involved footwear.

BDSM

BDSM is a fetish with several sub-types. The unpronounceable abbreviation comes from several fetish terms: B&D (Bondage and Discipline), D&S (Dominance and Submission) and M&S

(Marks and Spencer). No, sorry, I meant S&M (Sadism and Masochism).

The BDSM 'scene' is one in which groups of BDSM fans meet at parties, often dressed in masks, leather or whatever takes their fancy. Theatricality and sexual role-playing are high on the agenda. Creativity is often noticeable and a tattooed BDSM fan is likely to have high-quality needlework on their curves, rather than 'LOVE' and 'HATE' self-administered with a penknife on the knuckles.

BDSM encounters are bound by rules and rituals, with a requirement for proper forms of address, correct behaviour, and a prescribed dress code. In some respects it sounds like the Church of England, or the military.

Power relationships are important in a BDSM relationship, where the submissive partner lends control to the dominant partner, who will frequently restrain, punish or humiliate him or her. In many ways, this resembles a routine marriage. Active partners are known as 'doms' (dominants) or 'tops', and passive partners are known as 'subs' (submissives) or, more unfortunately, 'bottoms'. For every female masochist there are some twenty male masochists.

One of the better-known masochists of recent times was English theatre critic Kenneth Tynan (1927–80). Tynan used to dish it out in his theatre criticism, once referring to Orson Welles's Othello as 'Citizen Coon'. His first wife, Dundy, wrote that Tynan also liked to take it, mentioning one especially heroic orgy in which four canes got broken. In his diary he refers to 'Nicole', a lively disher-out who after dinner one night injected 'a large glass of vodka into my anus via an enema tube. Within 10 minutes the agony is indescribable . . . NB three days later I am still seeping blood.'

The aphrodisiac qualities of pain have long been understood, but to avoid the risk of physical harm, bondage and sadism require the explicit consent of partners, involving what has become known, apparently, as 'SSC', 'safe, sane and consensual' behaviour, or, more piquantly, 'risk-aware consensual kink' (RACK).

Bottoms (submissive partners) who have had enough humiliation and whipping are able to stop the business at any time by use of an agreed 'safeword'. 'Stop', 'no' and 'ouch' don't count since these may be mistaken for role-play words. Better are terms unlikely to be used during BDSM, such as 'Yorkshire pudding!', '*Newsnight!*' or 'Hilary Benn!'

One BDSM sub-group is so-called 'second-skin' fetishism, in which fetishists dress in exotic materials, such as rubber/latex, leather, fur or even, I'm told, nylon – whether drip-dry or not I don't know. Latex fetishists, or 'rubberists' as they like to be known, probably squeak a lot, especially when moving down a vinyl banquette at Pizza Hut. PVC fetishists benefit by wearing equally shiny 'wet-look' outfits, made from polyvinyl chloride (PVC), which won't squeak too much sliding down a fireman's pole.

A dominatrix in a figure-hugging 'spray-on' black PVC catsuit is a cliché of this fetish, but raincoats and Wellington boots are not uncommon either. This is a good job too, with some of the weather we've been having. Rubber trousers, gas masks, latex medical gloves and splash suits are also favourites, though those gas masks must get very steamed up.

Trampling

Trampling is a BDSM sub-fetish, related in an odd way to foot and shoe fetishism, in which the subject is trampled underfoot. Generally the way it works is that a man is trampled upon by a woman, so in this respect it resembles everyday life (that was a joke; don't send me letters). Trampling can be done barefoot or in shoes of any kind, including stilettos.

Spanking

As we've seen, not all fetishes have Latin or Greek names. Some have made-up *Latin- or Greek-sounding* ones, and 'spankophilia' is one of these. Spanking, the 'English vice', continues the dominant/submissive theme, and might be classed as a sub-genre of BDSM. It is an ancient fetish, with the *Kama Sutra* detailing the correct way to spank a woman – in case the mechanics were beyond you. The practice was especially popular with the Victorians and is enthusiastically gone in for today. Canes, bespoke paddles and bare hands are among the contemporary implements of choice.

Until fairly recently this fetish was disguised as legitimate punishment for children by creepy birch-swishing masters in some boys' boarding schools, and weird hairbrush-wielding games mistresses in some girls' schools.

Formicophilia

Formicophilia is the fetish for having small insects crawl on your genitals. What more do you need to know?

Voyeurism and exhibitionism

For the less energetic fetishist, voyeurism and exhibitionism are good bets. The desire to expose the rude parts of one's body to strangers is fairly commonplace. Who among us hasn't seen a flasher hurtling across the pitch at some football match or other, their equipment swinging in the breeze, often being chased by a policeman, helmet at the ready? However, voyeurism and exhibitionism both inhabit a legal no-man's-land so you need to go careful. There's a fine line between a cheerful exhibitionistic boob flash and having your collar felt for indecent exposure. For their part, voyeurs can find themselves arrested as Peeping Toms at the drop of a hat, not to say skirt.

In 2012 a chap who took a nude tea-time stroll through a

popular Yorkshire beauty spot, bollock-naked except for a backpack, boots and a cap, was arrested by a jogging off-duty policeman who saw a woman dog-walker with a 'disgusted frown' on her face. The man denied any wrongdoing, saying nudity was not an offence. 'The surprise of seeing a naturist whilst you're out walking,' he remarked, 'I don't think would be much different to seeing a steam train on the East Coast Main Line.' The judge commented drily, 'I note with some interest that he would not walk with his clothes off in the city centre of Leeds', and fined him £315.

The practice of spying on people who are naked, undressing or having sex is, if anything, more common than exhibitionism. I daresay quite a lot of voyeurism goes on at the beach during the summer, when middle-aged dads, melting cornet trickling down their fingers, find their eye roving the dunes in search of a naked breast or two. With the development of smart phones, nifty voyeurs can now even take surreptitious snaps of their targets, for 'research purposes' back at base.

A specialist sub-genre of this practice has developed which is especially popular in Japan, for some reason. Called 'upskirting', it is the art of furtively taking pictures up a woman's skirt, on the train, in the library or on the escalator, though lighting the subject must be fiendishly difficult. In Australia, 'upskirting' in public places without the subject's consent has been made specifically illegal, though obtaining consent is going to be a thankless task.

Presumably upskirting is related to stocking and underwear fetishism, in which the observer gets a thrill seeing, handling or wearing underwear of various kinds from panties to suspender belts. Usually it's men admiring or wearing female attire. Seldom do you see websites depicting women lolling around in men's pants.

Macrophilia

Macrophilia is an infatuation with giants. Most macrophiles are men. While some macrophiles fantasize about women only slightly taller than themselves, others are obsessed with enormous giantesses, as tall as a tower block. The poster for the 1958 film *Attack of the 50 Foot Woman* shows a gorgeous babe, in short skirt and ill-fitting bra, straddling a motorway flyover and picking up cars. This is a macrophile's delight.

Pegging

Whether pegging is strictly a fetish, I'm not sure, but these days it can be hard to tell the usual from the unusual. After all, dildos have been around since classical times, but a recent boost in the sale of so-called strap-on dildos has led to the naming of the sexual practice of 'pegging'. This hobby is mentioned in William Burroughs' novel *The Naked Lunch*, but the word is a new one. It was invented in a contest run by Dan Savage (born 1964), an American gay author of a sex advice column called *Savage Love*, who bemoaned the lack of a word for the act, which, in case you are wondering, involves a woman penetrating a man while she is wearing a strap-on. There are now many DVDs available on the topic, including sixteen editions of *Babes Balling Boys* and more than twenty-five editions of *Boss Bitches*.

Cameltoe

'Cameltoe' is possibly the most delightfully evocative jargon fetish term. It refers to the supposed resemblance of a lady's crotch or 'pudendal cleft', when constricted by a pair of figure-hugging shorts or panties, to a camel's twin-toed forefoot. The male equivalent is known, for who knows what reason, as a 'moose knuckle'. It may be an entertaining diversion but it's hardly worth having a whole fetish for, surely.

While on the subject, I should mention the pubic wig, or 'merkin', which has been a conversation starter since the fifteenth century, when it was worn by ladies of negotiable morals, who had shaved their pubic hair off to deter lice. Victorian prostitutes are also said to have made use of merkins to hide evidence of the pox. Merkins have been deployed by members of the so-called 'Muffia', in London, who go on something called the Muff March to protest against 'designer vagina' surgery, waving striking banners proclaiming things such as, 'Keep your mitts off our muffs!' and 'You've put my chuff in a huff!'

Sploshing

Sploshing is another lovely name. Also known as wet and messy fetishism (WAM or wamplay), it involves wet or messy substances such as mud, cream, baked beans, beer, custard, gloop or gunge being liberally applied to subjects, who may also sometimes be required to sit on cakes. Related in some strange way to female mud-wrestling, once a common spectator sport in rough northern pubs, it even has its own magazine, *Splosh!*. On the *Splosh!* website

I read this: 'You are about to enter the wacky, wet and messy world of SPLOSH!, where women behave very badly indeed. Food fights, pie battles, mudlarking and deliberately wet or wrecked clothing are the norm.' One unlucky fan, a teacher from West Yorkshire, was hauled over the legal coals when his searches for sploshing-related material were found on a school computer.

Agalmatophilia

Among the more esoteric fetishes is agalmatophilia, from the Greek *agalma* (statue), and is the sexual attraction to a statue, mannequin, doll, robot or similar object. Robot fetishism is also known as 'technosexuality'. The nice thing about robot girlfriends and boyfriends, presumably, is that you don't get any backchat. It reminds me of that fellow I read about who was sentenced to eighteen months in an American prison for repeatedly smashing shop windows to get at the female mannequins. On one occasion police found him up an alley behind a women's clothes shop in the company of three lingerie-clad dummies. His behaviour 'strikes fear into the community', said the judge. Amusement, more like.

Smoking

I knew a chap once who used to go on, in rather a lurid manner, about women smoking, and I guess he would have made a good secretary of the smoking-fetish club. Sexual arousal at the sight of a person smoking cigarettes or cigars (not pipes, I note) is chiefly a male fetish, and women – often unclothed – are frequently the subject of smoking-related porn. Several websites are currently devoted to it. Let's just hope they are careful with that hot ash.

XI
CAUGHT WITH THEIR PANTS DOWN
FOUR FRONT-PAGE SEX SCANDALS

*

'To have news value is to have a tin can tied to one's tail.'

T. E. LAWRENCE

Scandals always involve people who ought to know better. You don't get a scandal when the milkman goes to bed with a woman who is not his wife. No, you have to be prominent or religious, or hold yourself up as an example.

Owing to the unique combination of stiff upper lip, not pushing in, taking it like a man and pretending not to have sex, the British have long found themselves leading the world in being caught with their pants down. Sex scandals in Britain took off in the fifties and sixties, when the post-war bowler hat and tightly rolled umbrella were being unceremoniously elbowed aside by long hair, rock and roll and extreme grooviness. The press was becoming less deferential to the toffs in government who had sex only by post, and instead of fawning adulation the aristocratic ruling class now found loud raspberries ringing in their ears.

Whereas French leaders tended to assume that any government minister without a mistress was a homosexual (and maybe still do), the remarkably ungroovy English Prime Minister Harold Macmillan was stuck in the Edwardian tradition of passing the port to the left, warming the pot and taking a fellow at his word. If a chap denied being a homosexual, he must be telling the truth and if he said he hadn't been to bed with a prostitute, you believed him.

During his premiership, Macmillan had more sex than he could shake a stick at – *sex scandals*, I mean. The most humiliating of these entered his own bedroom, when his wife, Lady Dorothy Cavendish, began an affair with the bow-tied bisexual Bob Boothby (see below), a colleague of Macmillan's. On top of his personal woes, Macmillan also had to deal with John Vassall, a gay staffer at the British embassy in Moscow who had been snapped by the KGB doing unspeakable drunken things with some men at a party and blackmailed into spying for the Soviet Union. There was sex in Macmillan's Cabinet, too, in the form of the Profumo scandal, and the Headless Man case, which involved the Duchess of Argyll (see below). They had never had it so good.

Of course, sex didn't just spoil things for British prime ministers; it has spoiled things for American presidents too. John Fitzgerald Kennedy is notorious for his voracious appetite in this department. In 2012, Mimi Alford, who was a nineteen-year-old Whitehouse intern in 1962, revealed her affair with the president, which, at the time, Kennedy had managed to keep out of the papers and away from the public, along with all his other philandering. Less lucky was one of his successors . . .

The girl who bit off more than she could chew
On 17 January 1998, the name on everybody's lips was Monica Lewinsky. On Monica's lips was the name, and not only that, of President Bill Clinton. News had surfaced on the *Drudge Report* website of an alleged sexual relationship between Lewinsky, a twenty-five-year-old White House intern, and Bill Clinton, the married President of the United States.

Drudge reported that *Newsweek* editors were in possession of a story by reporter Michael Isikoff, which they were treating as a very hot potato. On 21 January, the *Washington Post* announced that the story concerned a possible relationship between the President and a White House intern, sending journalists into a frenzy, and presidential aides into a damage-limitation exercise. Five days later, President Clinton, with his wife beside him, addressed a televised news conference with what seemed to be a straightforward denial: 'I did not have sexual relations with that woman, Miss Lewinsky,' he said, with a strange look in his eyes. And that was that. Except, of course, that it wasn't, because Bill Clinton had form.

Before becoming president in 1993, Clinton had been governor of the state of Arkansas and a number of allegations of sexual inappropriateness had raised their ugly heads. Leaving aside Monica Lewinsky for a moment, Clinton admitted sexual encounters with only one woman – apart from his wife, obviously. This lady was Gennifer Flowers, whose name had emerged during his 1992 presidential election campaign. Clinton denied at first that there had been any relationship with Flowers but his position was somewhat undermined by recordings of him talking amiably to her on the phone, which she played at a news conference.

Now, all these years later, a former Arkansas employee, Paula Jones, had filed a sexual harassment lawsuit against Clinton, and this blast from the past had made its way to the US Supreme Court. Rather inconveniently, Monica Lewinsky's name had popped up during the proceedings, though she denied any sexual relationship with the president. Clinton likewise denied having sexual relations with her. But things were about to unravel like a string vest, and once again tape recordings would do some damage to a president's credibility. These tapes, along with an unlaundered navy blue dress, were going to refresh Clinton's memory rather publicly.

MONICA

But who was this Lewinsky woman, and where had her story come from?

Born in San Francisco to affluent Jewish parents, who divorced unpleasantly when she was a young teenager, Monica had taken a degree in psychology before using her family connections to take up an internship in the office of the White House chief of staff, in July 1995. In April the following year she was moved to the Pentagon because of fears that she was spending too much time with the president.

On Easter Sunday, Lewinsky told the president that she was being transferred and he promised to get her back to the White House after the 1996 election. They then had a 'sexual encounter', during which he apparently spoke on the telephone to political consultant Dick Morris, a sort of double-dick conversation, and multi-tasking of the most presidential kind.

At the Pentagon, Lewinsky became friends with a lady with a large face called Linda Tripp (*she* was called Linda Tripp, not her face). She was some two decades older than Lewinsky, but, as ladies do, Lewinsky spilled the Clinton sex beans to Tripp, at one point showing her a blue dress that was stained with 'a substance'. When Lewinsky said she was going to have it cleaned, Tripp advised her not to and said that she should put it in a safe-deposit box because it could be evidence one day. Lewinsky said she remembered wearing the dress on 28 February, when she had had her picture taken with the president. He had then told her he had something for her and his secretary Betty Currie went with her into the study next to the Oval Office before retiring into a nearby pantry. She hung about there for about fifteen minutes while Lewinsky and the president had another 'sexual encounter', which led to the soiling of the garment.

Afterwards, rather touchingly, Clinton gave Monica a hatpin and a copy of Walt Whitman's poetry collection, *Leaves of Grass*, which, when first published in 1855, a critic had called 'a mass of stupid filth'. Whitman was then fired from his government job. Here were shadows of things to come.

Tripp encouraged Lewinsky to document details of her relationship with the president and spoke to her friend Lucianne Goldberg, a literary agent and Clinton critic, who advised Tripp to secretly record her own phone conversations with Lewinsky. In October an anonymous woman made three phone calls to the Institute that was funding the Paula Jones case, alerting them to a probable affair between the president and an intern.

In January 1998, FBI agents wired Tripp with a hidden microphone and recorded a conversation with Lewinsky at the Pentagon City Ritz-Carlton Hotel. With all this cloak-and-dagger stuff it was starting to look like *Tinker Tailor Soldier Spy*. Did Tripp see her own book in the offing?

'THERE IS NOT A SEXUAL RELATIONSHIP'

The same month, Clinton was deposed in the Jones case and was asked, 'Have you ever had sexual relations with Monica Lewinsky, as that term is defined in Deposition Exhibit One?' Clinton answered, 'I have never had sexual relations with Monica Lewinsky.' He later denied perjury, rather unpersuasively, I think, on the grounds that the agreed definition of 'sexual relations' meant that, because fellatio was performed *on* him, not *by* him, he had therefore not had 'sexual relations'. When challenged about his assertion that 'there is not a sexual relationship, an improper sexual relationship or any other kind of improper relationship', he remarked that as he had been using the present tense in his answer, and as, at the time he was being questioned, there *was* no relationship, this was a true statement. 'It depends on what the meaning of the word *is* is,' he said. He seemed to many to be splitting hairs.

The big newspapers, along with ABC News, now reported the investigation and Lewinsky only survived the media blitz, she said, by knitting. She spent weeks hiding at her mum's home in the famous Watergate complex and the Lewinsky affair itself inevitably became known as 'Monicagate'. In interviews, the president, who was under even more intense scrutiny, continued to deny a 'sexual relationship' with the intern.

Linda Tripp now learned that Lewinski had signed an affidavit in the Jones case, denying a sexual relationship with Clinton. On literary agent Lucianne Goldberg's advice, she smartly delivered the Monica tapes to Special Prosecutor Kenneth Starr who was investigating Clinton separately over his Whitewater investments. Goldberg also arranged for Tripp to speak to *Newsweek* reporter Michael Isikoff, who had been rooting around Clinton's sex life. Tripp helpfully pointed out to Starr that Lewinsky's denial in the Jones lawsuit was false, and said that Lewinsky had encouraged her to help in the cover-up. Tripp also told Starr about the navy-blue dress. Starr, who may have begun salivating at this new evidence, now broadened the scope of his enquiry to include the possibility of perjury by Clinton and Lewinsky.

DNA TESTING

In July, Lewinsky was given 'Monicagate' immunity in exchange for testifying about her relationship with Clinton. She now remembered nine encounters in the Oval Office between November 1995 and March 1997 involving sexual contact, including fellatio, but not sexual intercourse. She supplied Starr with DNA evidence in the shape of the blue dress and its stain, completely undermining Clinton's denial of 'sexual relations' with her. On 3 August, Clinton was asked for a blood sample for DNA testing. Starr concluded that he had committed perjury.

At one point Lewinsky had been asked, 'Did you and the president ever engage in sexual relations using cigars?' and had replied, 'Yes. Just once. Just once.' Her testimony, along with the DNA results, finally forced Clinton to come clean (if you will pardon the phrase). On 17 August he admitted 'inappropriate intimate contact' with Lewinsky but refused to go into detail. That evening he went on television and acknowledged a relationship which was 'not appropriate'.

Linda Tripp maintained that she had acted out of 'patriotic duty', but Lewinsky felt differently. In her final words to the jury, she said plainly, 'I hate Linda Tripp,' and you kind of knew where she was coming from.

Starr's 445-page 'Monicagate' report was published on the Internet, listing ten sexual encounters between the president and Monica Lewinsky and eleven grounds for impeachment. Clinton ruled out resignation but by December it looked as if the president would indeed be impeached. However, in February 1999, after the end of a twenty-one-day trial, senators voted to acquit President Clinton of perjury and obstruction of justice, much to the surprise of some.

Though Clinton remained in office, Judge Webber Wright, who had judged the Paula Jones case, held him in civil contempt of court and he was fined $90,000 for giving false testimony, though he denied, and always has, having a sexual affair with Paula Jones. Nonetheless he agreed to pay Jones and her lawyers $850,000 in an out-of-court settlement.

TELLING TALES

After the end of the Jones and Lewinsky (or 'Zippergate') scandals, Monica Lewinsky hit the news big time. On 3 March, she was interviewed by the stupendously famous Barbara Walters in a programme watched by 70 million US viewers, which ABC said was a record, plus many more around the world. She comes across in the interview as a rather sweet, possibly naive young lady, at one point telling Walters that she had asked the president if he was interested in her just for the sex. She reports that Clinton had become emotional before giving her the well-worn adulterer's assertion that he didn't want her to believe this of him. You'd have thought that a lady with a degree in psychology might have understood a bit more about the way ambitious, successful men are prone to behave. Anyway, Lewinsky's immediate publicity earnings totalled well over a million dollars.

Over time the scandal faded and Clinton earned the name Teflon Bill from his apparent ability to survive anything. Lewinsky was finding the continuing media scrutiny intolerable and in 2005 she moved to London, where she graduated from the London School of Economics with a master's degree in social psychology. She has since kept a low profile. Her friend Linda Tripp started an open-all-year Christmas shop, in Middleburg, Virginia, thus confirming her impeccable poor taste. A dignified Hillary Clinton stood by her husband throughout the scandal. But you can just imagine the ferocious tongue-lashings over the dinner table.

The minister and the showgirl

John 'Jack' Profumo, CBE (1915–2006) was a baron (an Italian one) and a British soldier and politician. He was mentioned in dispatches during the Second World War and was elected to the House of Commons as a Conservative MP while still a soldier.

Profumo was always independent of mind and quite early in his parliamentary career voted against his government, leading a whip to write him a letter calling him an 'utterly contemptible little shit'. In 1954 he married the actress Valerie Hobson, who had appeared as Baroness Frankenstein alongside Boris Karloff (real name, Bill Pratt) in the delicious film melodrama *Bride of Frankenstein* (1935).

In July 1960, Profumo was appointed secretary of state for war and the following summer he and his wife were invited to a pool party at Cliveden, the country estate of Viscount Astor, at which he used to entertain influential guests and show off. This party was being run by a fellow called Stephen Ward, who had been a carpet salesman in Houndsditch and was now a society osteopath. (I'm not making this up.) Ward had squeezed the deltoids of anyone who mattered, including Winston Churchill, Ava Gardner, Mahatma Gandhi, Douglas Fairbanks Jnr, Duncan Sandys (pronounced Sands) – both of whom crop up again below – Lord Astor and Anthony Blunt, the spy and homosexual surveyor of the Queen's pictures.

Ward also kept a stable of 'girls' whom he would introduce to his swanky friends. At the Cliveden party he introduced Profumo to an attractive young showgirl named Christine Keeler. Struck by her charms as she was climbing naked out of the pool, Profumo began an affair with her. This always struck me as unlikely because the fellow was a rather unprepossessing bald-headed skinny little man who, though always well dressed, was old enough to be her grandfather. I suppose it was the money and power that did it.

SUSPECTED RUSSIAN SPY

But Profumo's fling with Keeler had hardly got going before the head of MI5, Sir Roger Hollis (another of Ward's patients), advised the cabinet secretary to have a word in Profumo's ear. Profumo had picked the wrong girl. Unknown to him, she was also having it off with a young naval attaché at the Soviet Embassy, Yevgeny Ivanov, who was a suspected Russian spy. MI5 man Peter Wright interviewed Keeler and was unnerved when she volunteered the term 'nuclear payload', a phrase not in general use by topless dancers at the time, even in relation to their own assets. Wright decided that the Soviet attaché had been trying to use Keeler to extract secrets from Profumo. Whatever the case, Profumo wrote Keeler a note ending the affair.

Christine Keeler had been brought up in two converted railway carriages in Buckinghamshire before becoming a topless showgirl at Murray's Cabaret Club in Soho. Here she met Stephen Ward and the pair set up together at Ward's mews property in what Keeler remembered as a platonic 'brother and sister' relationship. Keeler had met another showgirl at the club called Mandy Rice-

Davies and she introduced her to the slum landlord Peter Rachman (yet another of Ward's clients). Rice-Davies became his mistress and replaced Keeler in Ward's flat.

In December 1962 Keeler was visiting Rice-Davies at the mews when one of Keeler's less urbane 'boyfriends', Johnny Edgecombe, fired several shots at the door after she refused to come out. He was arrested, and when Keeler failed to appear at his trial at the Old Bailey, in March 1963, the Profumo story, which had been sloshing around the rumour mill for a while, hit the front pages.

For weeks journalists and politicians had been aware of the growing gossip. The innuendo was not, as one wit suggested, an Italian suppository, but a deadly torpedo heading towards the terrified government, who feared being caught up in the most damaging political scandal of the twentieth century. It would have made a good film, with toffs, tarts, sex, spies and drug-running gunmen. And in fact it did. *Scandal* (1989) was a successful fictionalized version of the story.

'MODELS'

Chris Moncrieff, the much-respected parliamentary journalist, remembered in the *Guardian* that reference to the Cabinet minister's alleged relationship with a 'model' – a press euphemism for 'call girl' – was niftily smuggled into a dull standing committee on the subject of sewage machinery by Labour MP George Wigg. He demanded to see an example of the new sewage equipment, saying, 'The trouble with this House is that we can never get the truth of anything unless we have the *models* available. Where is this *model?*'

Profumo, a man tipped as prime-minister material, was suddenly about as attractive to colleagues as a fishwife's hankie. Hauled in by the whips for a grilling in the small hours, he blandly assured them that he hadn't had sex with the svelte model. And in the tradition of taking a fellow at his word, they believed him.

Prime Minister Harold Macmillan, who was especially naive in such matters, was greatly relieved by this dodgy late-night promise. Profumo then made a personal statement to the House in which he acknowledged 'acquaintanceship' with Keeler but said there was 'no impropriety whatsoever' in the relationship, and threatened with libel writs anyone who said there was.

But the newspapers kept publishing stories about Keeler and the pressure became too much. In June 1963, Profumo confessed the affair to his wife and then admitted to the prime minister that not only had he been having it away with a lady who was not his wife but that he had lied to the House about it – an unforgivable sin. He resigned.

In a damage limitation exercise on 21 June 1963, Harold Macmillan asked the Master of the Rolls, Lord Denning, to lead an enquiry into the affair. His report, which was published in September 1963, was a bestseller, shifting 105,000 copies. It blamed Profumo for his relationship with Keeler, and especially for lying in the House of Commons.

The affair had holed the Tories below the water line and Harold Macmillan resigned shortly thereafter on the grounds of ill health. He was replaced by another toff, Sir Alec Douglas-Home (pronounced Hume) who lost the general election a year later to Labour's pipe-sucking man-of-the-people, Harold Wilson.

AFTERMATH

Shortly after his resignation, Profumo began working as a volunteer, cleaning toilets at Toynbee Hall, a charity with one foot in the establishment and the other amongst the poor of the East End. In what looks rather like a penance he continued to work there for the rest of his life, helped by his wife, who had stuck by him, as she continued to do until her death in 1998. Profumo eventually became the charity's chief fundraiser and his contacts and political skills brought in large sums of money. Jack Profumo was awarded a CBE for his work in 1975 and died in 2006, at the age of ninety-one, never again having spoken about the Keeler interlude.

Of the others, Stephen Ward was prosecuted for living off immoral earnings – though some pointed out that his 'girls' appeared to be living off him. He committed suicide during the trial.

Keeler got nine months for perjury in an unrelated matter and continues to keep her head down. Despite being dismissed as a mere 'tart', she always denied being a call girl, on the grounds that she had no phone.

Mandy Rice-Davies, who always had a felicitous phrase upon her lips, shot to fame, mainly because of her quick wit and her gift for the apt quote. When it was pointed out to her in court that Lord Astor not only denied having been to bed with her but asserted that he had never even met her, she replied, 'Well, he would, wouldn't he!' This *bon mot* has made it into numerous books of quotations.

Rice-Davies made the most of her notoriety, giving interviews in which she talked fascinatingly about salacious subjects such as a dinner party where a very well-known man wearing nothing but his birthday suit and a mask waited on tables as a nude slave, while guests abused him. He appeared, it was said, to be enjoying it. Journalists tried guessing the chap's identity, which remains a delightful mystery to this day. Duncan Sandys (see below), was one name that cropped up, but this was strenuously denied.

Perhaps the last word should be left to Mandy Rice-Davies, the girl who had not so much kissed the Blarney Stone as sucked it off. She hilariously described her life after the high-profile scandal as 'one slow descent into respectability'.

The Dirty Duchess
Margaret, Duchess of Argyll (1912–93), was born Ethel

Whigham, a rather unromantic name, you might think. Still, she was the eye-catching daughter of a Scottish millionaire and was privately educated in New York City, where she grew up, and also in London and Paris. So she had everything else going for her, really. She was debutante of the year in 1930 and had numerous youthful romances with playboys, millionaires and publishing tycoons, and her gay coming-out party was attended by many of the beautiful people of the time. *Note for younger readers:* 'coming out' has nowadays attracted an entirely different connotation, as has 'gay' (see glossary).

In 1933, after avoiding marriage to the 7th Earl of Warwick by just a whisker – the invitations had already been sent out – wealthy 'Margaret' Whigham got spliced to American gentleman-golfer Charles Sweeny, at Brompton Oratory, holding up the Knightsbridge traffic for three hours in her fancy dress.

The slim young socialite was described as a great beauty and was frequently photographed. But in these snaps she seldom smiles, and her deep-set eyes always look troubled. Though Whigham was much written about, flattered and admired, the piquant Alastair Forbes once remarked of her that she had been given 'fine ear-rings but nothing to put between them', and it is unlikely that it was the lady's brains which had attracted either the earl or Sweeny. No, her motto was, apparently, 'Go to bed early and often,' and she was gaining quite a reputation as an enthusiastic sex fan.

GOING DOWN

But her hobby seemed to turn to compulsion in 1943 when she suddenly plunged forty feet into an open lift shaft on her way to have her feet looked at by her Bond Street chiropodist. The fall nearly killed her. 'It was later found that all my fingernails were torn off,' she said. 'I apparently fell on to my knees and cracked the back of my head against the wall.' This was not the last time that the striking-looking Margaret was to be discovered on her knees.

Apparently, the bang on her head caused her to lose all sense of taste (as her choice in husbands was to indicate) and smell. Moreover, it appeared to her friends to exacerbate her lively sexual appetite to the extent that she became a nymphomaniac. The bang on the head leading, as it were, to bangs anywhere else she could find.

Margaret and Charles Sweeny were divorced in 1947, and in 1951 she married Ian Douglas Campbell (1903–73), 11th Duke of Argyll and Hereditary Master of the Royal Household in Scotland. He had had two previous wives himself.

The duchess was now mistress of a historic castle. But things came unstuck and her marriage to the duke hit the rocks, ending in divorce in 1963 when he stumbled upon her salacious diaries, in which she had listed the technical specifications of the genitalia of a number of her gentlemen friends.

After four years of legal faffing, the case finally came to court in 1962. The cuckolded duke named eighty-eight men he believed had been diddling his missus, apparently including two government ministers and three royals. But the most shocking item amongst the duke's evidence bundle was a series of 'instant' Polaroid photographs showing a chap apparently having a bit of a wank in the refined surroundings of the duchess's delightful Mayfair house, at 48 Upper Grosvenor Street. Each snap had its own scribbled caption: 'before', 'thinking of you', 'during – oh', and 'finished'. The Polaroid camera was a rare thing in 1957, when the pictures had been taken, and the advantage of it in this instance was that the duchess didn't have to take her naughty negatives down to Boots to be developed, where they would have been seen by all those people.

ART DECO BATHROOM

Amongst the photos of the chap – or conceivably chaps – was one of the duchess naked, except for her ever-present three-strand pearl necklace. In this artistic study she had been photographed sucking off a nude man in her Art Deco bathroom. Whether this fellow also gave her a pearl necklace was not recorded in the picture. Fortunately for him but not for the judge, his head had been cut off, in the sense that it couldn't be seen in the photo.

The court case lasted eleven days, and in May 1963 the presiding judge Lord Wheatley issued his verdict. The duchess was found to have committed adultery with three men identified by the duke, and with a fourth, unidentified man. Bringing all his wisdom and experience to bear on the mystery, Judge Wheatley granted the divorce, describing the duchess as 'a highly sexed woman who has ceased to be satisfied with normal sexual activities and has started to indulge in disgusting sexual activities to gratify a debased sexual appetite . . . A completely promiscuous woman whose sexual appetite could only be satisfied by a number of men, whose promiscuity had extended to perversion and whose attitude to the sanctity of marriage was what moderns would call enlightened, but which in plain language was wholly immoral.' Judging by the pictures, and leaving aside the judge's ideas of what were normal sexual activities, this was something of an obvious conclusion.

The press, fired up over the continuing Profumo affair, started to wonder about the identity of the shadowy figure in the picture, nicknamed 'the headless man', who was rumoured to be a well-known Cabinet minister. The government, who were getting tired of ministers' libidos making it into the papers, called upon the bowler-hatted Lord Denning, who was already looking into Profumo, to hunt down the headless man without delay.

HANDWRITING ANALYSIS

In true bloodhound style, Denning decided to compare the handwritten captions on the photographs with the handwriting of five of the headless-man suspects, including the handsome actor Douglas Fairbanks, Jr and Duncan Sandys, who had for some years been the son-in-law of Winston Churchill, and who was defence minister in January 1957, when the pictures were taken. Sandys offered to resign from the Cabinet over the allegations but Harold Macmillan refused him.

In later years Lord Denning's astute fairness would be exemplified by pronouncements such as, 'It is better that some innocent men remain in jail than that the integrity of the English judicial system be impugned', but he was not a handwriting expert. He needed handwriting samples so, Sherlock Holmes-style, he invited his five likely lads to the Treasury to help him out. When they arrived, they each signed the visitors' register. At which point Denning probably shouted out, 'Gotcha!'

The signatures were analysed by his 'expert' graphologist, and the conclusion reached that the headless man was Douglas Fairbanks, Jr. How this was done from five wobbly signatures and a few scribbled captions beats me, and possibly it beat Denning too, who didn't include it in his report. Fairbanks denied the allegation until his death and, for once, the duchess kept her mouth shut. With great good luck – and the duchess needed a bit of that – John Profumo resigned barely a fortnight later to huge fanfare, and the searchlight turned away.

Human relationships had never been the duchess's forte and she was only lucky that her boozy maid Edith, who called her mistress 'a Mayfair whore' and 'a silly old bitch' in front of guests, was not providing a character reference. In the end, her most enduring personal relationships turned out to be with a series of poodles. Quite apart from her disastrous 'love' affairs, Margaret had never been any good at managing her financial affairs, and her fortune began to dwindle. To raise cash she tried putting on tours of her lovely house (I expect the bathroom was extra), but her extravagance and unlucky investments finally obliged her to sell it, and in 1978 she moved into a suite at the fancy Grosvenor House Hotel.

DOGGED BY TROUBLE

Neil Kirby, longtime staffer at the Grosvenor House, remembers that on one occasion the hotel's general manager went up to persuade the duchess to pay an outstanding £27,000 bill. As he sipped his drink on her tasteful sofa, one of her poodles, which had eaten something that didn't agree with it, defecated extravagantly on the rug. She went to fetch cleaning equipment but the dog, covered in pints of the unspeakable liquid, jumped playfully all over the manager, who fled screaming from the room. The duchess was finally evicted in 1990 and spent the rest of her days in an un-fancy Pimlico nursing home, where she died in 1993.

The Duchess of Argyll once summed up the important things in her life: 'Always a poodle; only a poodle. That, and three strands of pearls. Together they are absolutely the essential things in life.' It seems rather a feeble selection.

The beguiling bow-tied bisexual bounder: blackguard Baron Bob Boothby, of Buchan

Robert (Bob) Boothby (1900–86) was educated at Eton and Oxford, becoming an MP in 1924, and top-hatted parliamentary private secretary to Chancellor of the Exchequer Winston Churchill in 1926. He remained an MP until 1958, when he became Baron Boothby, of Buchan and Rattray Head in the County of Aberdeen.

Boothby was naturally charming and had a flair for self-publicity. He was a great admirer of herrings, and, from the look

of him, all other kinds of food, being often photographed with a glass of something congenial in his hand. A dapper man with a penchant for ostentatious bow ties, he was always turned out in beautiful suits, which, in later life, needed to be generously cut around his phenomenal tum.

An early example of the prominent, media-savvy Tory, the grinning Boothby frequently appeared on *Any Questions* and was once the subject of *This Is Your Life*. He was also briefly chairman of the Royal Philharmonic Orchestra. How urbane, avuncular and polished he seemed.

But there was more to the bubbly baron than met the eye – *which is saying something*. At Eton, Boothby gained an early reputation for his active homosexuality, going on, as an Oxford undergraduate, to attract the nickname 'the Palladium' for his twice nightly performances.

After trying men for size, Boothby decided to have a go at

women too. He was, he said, twenty-five when he switched from promiscuous homosexuality to enthusiastic bisexuality.

FURTHER SHENANIGANS

Lord Boothby's politics were, like his private life, pragmatic, and in 1941 he was obliged to resign after making a speech in the Commons in which he had failed to declare a financial interest. So he joined the RAF, completing his training as a pilot officer with the rank of flight lieutenant. He was knighted in 1953.

Boothby knew that he was committing a criminal offence every time he had sex with a man but was entirely unembarrassed about his nature or his sex life, and from 1954 he campaigned openly for homosexual law reform.

His appetites were ample, and from 1930 he had a long affair with the unlikely-looking Dorothy Macmillan, wife of Harold Macmillan (prime minister, 1957–63). The affair gave the cuckolded Macmillan the willies and he had a nervous breakdown in 1931. Boothby was also twice married, first in 1935 to Dorothy's cousin Diana Cavendish, a union that lasted only two years. In 1967 he tried again, this time with the delightfully pretty Wanda Sanna, a Sardinian lady three decades younger than him. This relationship was said in private to be 'platonic'.

The broadcaster Ludovic Kennedy, who was related to Boothby and knew him well, said he was certain that he had fathered at least three children by the wives of other men. He once told Boothby to his face that he was a 'shit', to which the lord replied, 'Well a bit. Not entirely.' Another curious baron, Woodrow Wyatt of Weeford, claimed that in 1991 the Queen Mother had described Lord Boothby to him as 'a bounder, but not a cad'.

No doubt the lord's ever-present charming smile, and network of friends in very high places kept the heat off him, rather as they had done for Profumo. In fact, the press did indeed know of bisexual Boothby's illegal sexual shenanigans and had some excellent evidence, but found themselves unable to print the stories, sometimes under the direct influence of their proprietors, who went to the same parties as Boothby himself.

Although Boothby did well in keeping his private life out of the papers, the shit hit the fan in the summer of 1964 (the year after the Profumo and Headless Man scandals), while Boothby was on holiday with Colin Coote, the editor of the *Daily Telegraph*. In July the *Sunday Mirror* published a story about an alleged homosexual relationship between a prominent peer (a 'household name') and a leading underworld thug. The *Mirror* had, they said, a photograph they couldn't print, though they did describe it.

THE TWINS

The picture, taken at Boothby's posh flat in Eaton Square, Belgravia, showed Boothby – though they didn't name names – sitting cosily on a sofa with London gangster Ronnie Kray. Ronnie Kray was one of a pair of unattractive East End homosexual gangster twins who supplied Boothby with good-looking young men, and arranged sex parties at a boring-looking block of flats in north London. In fact, there was another man on the sofa, a shiny, blond cat burglar named Leslie Holt, whom Boothby had met at a gambling club, and with whom he was having 'a relationship'.

The *Sunday Mirror*'s talk of the photograph threatened a scandal to surpass the Profumo affair, and the queasy Tories were in absolutely no mood for it. Neither was Boothby, so he phoned his friend, senior Labour MP and journalist Tom Driberg, for help.

Though they were on different sides of the House, Boothby and Driberg were on the same side of the sexual fence. Driberg had been described as 'a voracious homosexual', and 'the most disreputable man in parliament'. However, in 1951, somewhat to his parliamentary colleagues' amazement, Driberg had announced his engagement to Ena Binfield. Whether this was a cosmetic arrangement was hotly debated, and a witty policeman at the House of Commons remarked, 'Poor lady, she won't know which way to turn.'

Driberg maintained that there were no heterosexual men, only obstinate ones, and few chaps were able to escape his unsavoury predations. A note was reportedly pinned in the lift at the offices of *Private Eye*, where Driberg worked, forbidding men from descending alone on the days when Driberg was in the office.

In fact, unknown to Driberg and Boothby, their gay connections had already been documented by two Tory MPs, who reported the pair 'importuning' young men at the dogs. One of Driberg's unlovely boyfriends was a young gangster called Teddy Smith, who was in deep with the Krays, and, like Boothby, Driberg was also a regular on Ronnie Kray's sofa.

POLITICAL FIX

If this were all to come out, the Labour lot would be shown to be as bad as the Tory lot and it was perhaps unsurprising, therefore, when, after talking to Driberg, the Tory Boothby was mysteriously approached by two movers and shakers from the Labour Party.

Gerald Gardiner was an up-and-coming QC, and Arnold Goodman was Harold Wilson's obese and oleaginous solicitor. They offered to represent the Tory baron in any forthcoming libel action. They also advised the unflappable Boothby to write a letter to *The Times* suggesting that the *Sunday Mirror* had been referring to him in its article, and announcing that he was going to sue them silly for libel. Boothby duly signed such a letter, which *The Times* published. In it the louche lord fibbed his head off: 'I am not a homosexual,' he said nonchalantly. 'The whole affair is a tissue of atrocious lies.'

Everybody on the paper wanted to defend the story but the newspaper's chairman Cecil King gave in, personally signing the *Sunday Mirror's* grovelling apology on the front page.

Boothby's cronies had not only engineered a surrender, but netted Boothby £40,000 in an out-of-court settlement. The lying lord later told author John Pearson that somebody he called the 'Little Man' had been behind the cover-up. The 'Little Man' was his unflattering nickname for Harold Wilson, who, he said, had got Goodman to do the deal so as to protect the Labour Party from a worse-than-Profumo-type scandal.

Tom Driberg survived politically, and was made a peer in 1974, dying in the back of a taxi two years later. The smiling Boothby lived on to a ripe old age, refusing to snuff it till 1986, when he was 86. Having always warmed his hands before the fire of life, he told Ludovic Kennedy that after the age of eighty-five, when it was all a lot less fun, that euthanasia should be made 'compulsory'.

XII

A Helping Hand

DILDOS, VIBRATORS AND SUNDRY SEX AIDS
DOWN THE YEARS

*

*'There are a number of mechanical devices which increase
sexual arousal, particularly in women. Chief among
these is the Mercedes-Benz 380SL convertible.'*

P. J. O'ROURKE

England can boast some delightfully rude place names, from
Scratchy Bottom to Brown Willy, Nob End, Piddle, Cocker-
mouth, and Fanny Hands Lane. There are even two Twatts in
Scotland – some say more. But while travellers see only charm in
the straightforward nomenclature of our rude forefathers, civic
prudes have fallen upon Oxford's Gropecunt Lane, for some
reason renaming it 'Magpie Lane' – maybe they wanted to keep
the 'bird' theme going. Three cheers then for Worcestershire's
Minge Lane, which, despite the discomfiture of the intolerant, is
hanging on to its immodesty by a hair.

Perhaps the most amusing case of renaming is that of Muff, a
town nestling at the mouth of the River Foyle in County
Donegal on the border between Northern Ireland and the Irish
Republic. The name has, of course, been a persistent nuisance.
The editor of the Muff Diving Club website had an overwhelming deluge of filthy posts flooding his forum page on
launch day. Understandably, the club quickly decided to change
its name – to the Scuba Association of the Town of Muff, hoping
against hope that this would lick the problem.

But this state of affairs is not exclusive to the British Isles. France famously has an Anus and the United States revels in the delightfully ambiguous Bald Knob, Beaver and Wankers Corner. Australia maintains the masculine motif with Chinaman's Knob, a town conjuring up all the glamour of the mystic Orient: joss sticks, sweet-and-sour pork balls and kimonos swinging open in the breeze. Not everybody is happy about all this though. Siegfried Hauppl, mayor of the village of Fucking in Austria, complained, 'The British keep stealing our Fucking road signs.' He reported that signage had also gone missing from Windpassing, and Wank-on-the-Lake near the Bavarian border.

The dildo
All of which brings me to the town of Dildo, established in the early 1800s and situated attractively on the island of Newfoundland, in Canada. The town's name, first recorded in 1711 and spelt 'Dildoe', comes, say the Dildoians (they aren't called 'Dildoes', by the way – in case you plan on visiting) from a place in Spain or Portugal. Anyway, it's foreign. Dildo is home to the Anglican All Saints' Church, though 'All Saints', Dildo' doesn't sit well on the tongue.

Down the years the notoriety of the town's vulgar appellation has led various cocksure Dildoian do-gooders to attempt to change it. Every one of these attempts has been a dazzling failure on account of un-bothered residents simply thumbing their noses at the stuffed shirts. The people of Dildo, it seems, rather like their name.

The origins of the word 'dildo' to describe the well-known sex toy remain blanketed in mystery. The Spanish, rather charmingly, call the thing a *consolador*, or 'consoler', though the Welsh have no time for such niceties, their *cala goeg* meaning nothing more than 'fake penis'. Which makes one wonder about the significance of the Welsh national vegetable – the leek. The first recorded written example of 'dildo' hails from 1598, at which time the word was applied to any number of diverse tubular or todger-shaped objects, such as the *dildo glass* – what we would today call a 'test tube'. The term has also long been used as an insult for a stupid or ridiculous person, as in, 'You great dildo, Colin! Where's yer manners? Offer His Holiness a fag,' but is of course mainly used today to indicate what the *Oxford English Dictionary* calls 'an object shaped like an erect penis used for sexual stimulation', (not to say, *simulation*).

The word used in its modern sense first appeared in a piece of doggerel entitled, 'Choise of Valentines, or the Merie Ballad of Nash his Dildo' (c. 1593), by playwright and satirist Thomas Nash. There are nearly eighty verses to Mr Nash's Hallmark-type Valentine's ditty, making it quite a mouthful. Here's just a taster. Excuse the spelling; they all wrote like this then.

> My little dilldo shall suply their kinde:
> A knaue, that moues as light as leaues by winde;
> That bendeth not, nor fouldeth anie deale,
> But stands as stiff as he were made of steele;

Seventeen years passed before the word's next recorded occurrence, in Ben Jonson's comedy *The Alchemist* (1610) and also, for good measure, in Shakespeare's *The Winter's Tale*, which was written at about the same time but published later. The term 'dil doul' was also used in a coarse seventeenth-century folk ballad found in the library of Samuel Pepys, a famous lecher whose wife once gave him a ferocious tongue lashing when she stumbled on him upstairs absent-mindedly rogering his maid, a 'girle' named Deb. Anyway, this song was called, 'The Maid's Complaint for Want of a Dil doul' and it's clear from the context that the expression here refers not to an imitation, but to the real thing. This is a bit of verse two:

For I am a Maid and a very good Maid,
And sixteen years of age am I,
And fain would I part with my Maiden-head,
If any good fellow would with me lye:
But none to me ever yet proffer'd such love,
As to lye by my side, and give me a shove
With his dil doul, a dil doul. dil doul, doul
O happy were I, &c.

Seventeenth-century England has left us a notably rich gift of literary references. In 1673 John Wilmot, 2nd Earl of Rochester, rude poet, and a 'profane and lewd' English libertine, published his satirical poem *Signor Dildo*. The political ballad, somewhat embellished by subsequent authors down the pub, was so well known that the term *Signor* became another word for 'dildo'. Modern literary references are ten a penny but the most famous is probably the dildo named Steely Dan III from Yokohama, mentioned in William Burroughs' novel, *The Naked Lunch* (1959). The rock band Steely Dan (not to be confused with the wholesome Steeleye Span) named themselves in its honour.

But before we go any further on this etymological excursion, and just in case the vicar asks you for information, we ought to define our terms in a bit more detail. A dildo, precisely speaking, is a non-vibrating sexual tool, toy or aid generally made these days of silicone, metal or glass, which more or less resembles an erect male member in shape, size and what marketing men call 'look and feel'. Excuse me if I'm teaching my grandmother to suck eggs.

New and different variations are popping up all the time and the ingenuity and variety of contemporary designs are most impressive, which reminds me of the joke about the inquisitive old lady who visits a sex shop and asks the assistant if she can buy the huge dildo with the tartan shaft and scarlet head that she sees on the shelf behind him. 'No, Madam,' he replies, unwrapping his sandwiches, 'that's my Thermos.' You can understand her confusion; the choice is endless. There are inflatable dildos, vibrating dildos – overlapping in dildo taxonomy with vibrators proper (see below) – face-fitted dildos, multicoloured dildos and so-called strap-ons, which are worn in a harness. An intriguing variation on the theme appears in a nineteenth-century Chinese painting of a woman using a dildo attached to her shoe.

A *godemiche* is a dildo with the bonus of fake testicles, and you can even get long, flexible 'double-enders' for use by two people at the same picnic, thus reducing your carbon footprint. Dildos with suction cups at the base are known as 'wall mounts', which I guess is self-explanatory (all stand for the national anthem) though I hear they can also be stuck down and sat upon. Manufacturers are now also doing a nice line in furniture-mounting straps. Is this beginning to sound like a Heal's catalogue?

Those with money to burn can easily get hold of a hand-carved hardwood dildo of great beauty and impressionistic verisimilitude. If you are interested, have a look at hardwooddildos.com where the blurb says it all:

> . . . handcrafted from exotic woods, sanded to perfection, and finished with a food-grade varnish. The elegance of natural wood lends class to these fully functional tools of pleasure . . . a Hardwood Dildo also makes a great gift [!]. Each dildo comes with free shipping and a velvet pouch.

Now, while I'm all for free shipping, I don't really want the boys from Her Majesty's Revenue and Customs opening my packet to see what's inside and then having a bit of a laugh as they wave my footlong up and down the red channel. Surely the time is ripe for these things to be made available at Tesco next to the sandwiches and newspapers.

The world's most ancient dildo is a 28,000-year-old eight-inch stone phallus from the Late Stone Age, which was pulled (if you'll pardon the expression) in fragments from a German cave in 2005 and reassembled – a job for an expert with an eye for detail and a steady hand. Exactly who may claim ownership of such finds varies from country to country, but in 2007 an 'Ancient Egyptian dildo' appeared on eBay, carved, so they said, c. 1550 BCE. The price for this little wooden hummer was a dildotastic $650, which may be a bargain, I don't know. Coming in at five-and-a-half inches in length, it was about life size but was cracked and fissured with age, like the beam of an old pub, and the chances of a splinter in a very inconvenient place looked insanely high to me.

CLASSICAL DILDOS

The Classical world was jammed with dildos. The Ancient Greeks had a word for the instrument: *olisbos* and sometimes illustrated examples of the thing on their vases.

Dildos are also referred to in Aristophanes' comedy *Lysistrata* (411 BCE), in which the foul-mouthed heroine persuades the women of Greece to withhold sexual privileges from their men until they negotiate a peaceful end to the Peloponnesian War. After a while, as you'd expect, the girls are just gagging for it and turn for satisfaction to their 'eight-fingered [!] leather dildos', which might be the first recorded case of women using sex as a bargaining tool, a practice that continues in the human and animal kingdoms to this day.

Bronze Chinese dildos from around 200 BCE to 25 CE were

reportedly used on upper-crust ladies by their maids, and inventive uses for fruit and vegetables (not prickly pear, one presumes) crop up in *Arabian Nights*. Resin-coated camel dung was the preferred matrix of ancient African cultures, while Polynesian women used green bananas – and maybe still do. Two eighteenth-century polished wooden examples from France were recently sold at auction for £3,600. One measured 10 inches (25 centimetres) and the other 11 inches (28 centimetres), which, you might think, would be enough to put a smile one anyone's face, even after the auctioneer's commission.

The dildo's 'Industrial Revolution' began, though, in 1843 with the patenting by Thomas Hancock (inventor of the 'masticator') of the vulcanization process, which made rubber stronger, stretchier and less sticky. These advantageous properties eminently suited dildo manufacturers right up to the 1930s, when they switched to latex, which has a shelf life of five years, compared to just three months for natural rubber. This obvious bonus was augmented by latex's magnificent fire-proof characteristics, which reduced the risk associated with all dildo factories until then that premises would go up in flames the moment workers stopped to light a fag. At the same time, the bedroom became a safer place for smokers.

The first decade of the twentieth century provided the earliest glimpses of dildos in the mass media; even the shaky, prototype blue movies of the time show primitive porn stars making dildo whoopee. The approach in print was more circumspect. In 1918 the popular Sears, Roebuck mail-order catalogue began, euphemistically, to advertise nifty devices for reducing 'anxiety and female tension'. Despite the linguistic camouflage, American ladies got the idea.

Research and development continued between the wars and in 1918 rubber dildos stiffened with a steel spring became available for the relief of post-war blues. These were superseded by PVC-filled schlongs after a metal component in the older type reportedly injured a male fun seeker to the tune of $14 million compensation. Goodness knows exactly what happened. It makes your toes curl just thinking about it. Anyway, common-or-garden PVC dildos are still knocking about, though for higher-end products silicone rubber has been the material of preference since the 1990s, providing a superior look and feel and doing away with the pertinacious smell of new shower curtains, which, for most aficionados, lacked allure.

The modern Greeks, like their ancient ancestors, have taken the dildo to their bosom and on the first Monday of Lent, 'Clean Monday' – or 'Dirty Monday' as some locals call it – the residents of the town of Tyrnavos hold an annual penis festival famous throughout the country. The pagan party includes fine wine, capital nosh, raunchy songs and loads of bloody great phalluses. Festival visitors are often taken unawares by jolly pranksters suddenly stuffing a ceramic dildo between their legs and holding them over a bubbling pot of 'bourani', an aphrodisiac soup made from nettles, before obliging them to kiss a phallus and drink a blindingly strong local spirit called *tsipouro* from its urethral meatus. The rest of Greece marks the holiday by flying kites.

CLONE-A-WILLY

These days you can even personalize your dildo by purchasing a special kit containing all you need to mould the real thing and cast a uniquely eerie replica in silicone. My friends Lisa and Jeff tried this with a 'Clone-A-Willy' kit from the Internet. Lisa told me that they got into trouble straight away, having no blinds in the kitchen, so people could see in. They ended up doing the casting in the hallway, on the telephone table, which wasn't ideal. Jeff told me they could have done with a fluffer, 'because mixing the goo while staying hard long enough to pour it in the mould and then stick your willy in requires faultless timing'.

Lisa was very pleased with the result. 'It looks *exactly* like my boyfriend,' she says. 'I'd show you but it would be like Jeff taking out the real thing and waving it around.' I learn that it is not only a good likeness, but performs well 'under examination conditions'.

Although Lisa could have cloned Jeff's willy till the cows came home in Essex, it would have been *illegal* in several other countries where dildos are outlawed, while a few nations allow their production only so long as they bear no resemblance to human anatomy – a rich source of potentially lucrative employment for a whole new class of willy-resemblance lawyers. You'd have thought the USA would have been one of the enlightened democracies that allowed dildos but in some Great Plains and southern states the making, selling or distribution of sex toys was against the law until very recently. In fact, you should still take care driving across Alabama with a new electric toothbrush in your glove compartment because in 2007, on Valentine's Day somewhat contrarily, a federal court upheld the state's prohibition on the sale of sex toys. The upright William H. Pryor, Jnr, an assistant attorney general in Alabama, was quoted as denying any 'fundamental right for a person to buy a device to produce orgasm', while a Baptist preacher named Dan Ireland stood hard against the dildo, maintaining that, 'there is no moral way to use one of these devices'. I'm supposing Dildo Dan was speaking after a bit of trial and error with a Clone-A-Willy kit or something, otherwise how did he know?

Clone-A-Willy kits certainly provide something for every taste. As well as glow-in-the-dark ones, several come with a 'multispeed vibrating unit' so you can turn your dildo into a vibrator if that's what tickles your fancy (batteries not included, *naturally*).

The vibrator

The vibrator is perhaps the commonest sex aid in use today and is a simple development of the dildo. It has been around for longer than you might imagine; for example, Cleopatra is said to have used a box filled with buzzing bees as an early form of the device, but it was the coming of electricity that really put lead in the vibrator's pencil.

The evidence for the widespread use of the first modern vibrators – some of which, it is said, you could plug into your ceiling light socket – is sparse. In 1880 Dr George Taylor developed a steam-powered vibrator called the 'Manipulator' and Joseph Mortimer Granville (1833–1900), doctor, inventor and author of *While the 'Boy' Waits* (1873), *Nerve-Vibration and Excitation as Agents in the Treatment of Functional Disorder and Organic Disease* (1883) and a number of potboilers, is the man who first patented the electromechanical vibrator, for the relief of muscle aches. It is claimed that 'Granville's hammer', as it was alarmingly called, was almost immediately used for 'the relief of female hysteria' but the not very alluring title of his 1883 book doesn't suggest anything sexual. Indeed, he said he did not use the device on female patients. Whatever the case, it was 1952 before the American Psychiatric Association decided that female hysteria, if it existed at all, was not a disease.

The electric vibrator as sex toy is a pretty modern development. The Hamilton Beach company patented the first electric vibrator available to the public, making it one of the earliest domestic appliances to be electrified, after the toaster and kettle. But there is no evidence that it had been designed for sexual use, and, if it had been, the order in which those bits of equipment were electrified gives you some idea of people's priorities: tea and crumpets first, sex second. It is true that vibrator adverts began to appear in such homely periodicals as *Needlecraft, Woman's Home Companion* and the Sears, Roebuck catalogue, but to the modern eye they look entirely innocuous. The vibrator only really began making waves in 1966, when Jon H. Tavel applied for an American patent for the 'Cordless Electric Vibrator for Use on the Human Body'.

Sex aids have come a long way since Cleopatra's time and Romanian doctor Nicolae Adrian Gheorghiu recently announced a device of his own invention, which, he claimed, could give a woman sixteen orgasms a minute, or two-and-a-half a second. This is not really a conventional vibrator; instead, the doctor puts electrodes on the lady's buttocks and spine, before passing weak electrical pulses through the gizmo. He says it is better than having thirty men, one after the other. Anyway, vibrators are now all over the Internet and several are made to look like lipstick or other innocent items so that ladies can carry them round in their handbags without causing a stir.

Some other sex toys
According to the Adult Industry Trade Association, a record number of sex toys are now being sold, most to young women.

Author, bioethicist and social critic Jacob M. Appel has said, 'Now that we are relatively confident that masturbation does not make little girls go blind, or cause palms to sprout hair, exposure to sex toys shouldn't harm them. On the list of items that I might not want children to be exposed to in stores – guns, matches, poisons, junk food – sex toys are way down the list.' One can't help agreeing with him.

Though dildos and vibrators vastly outnumber other sex aids, the choice is nonetheless vast. Here are a few examples of the more *esoteric* sex toys out there at the moment.

MALE BREAST ENHANCERS

If you are a man who has always wanted to wear a pair of realistic rubber breasts but didn't know where to find them, look no further. Strap-on boobs for men are now available online. They are made of a 'firm' squeezable material and are said to feel 'real', boasting a pair of persuasive pinkish nipples. They attach to your chest just like a normal bra so you shouldn't have much trouble.

THE AUTO SUCK

At a mere £25, the Auto Suck – a fellatio simulator designed to plug into your car cigarette lighter – is just the job. It's perfect for motoring holidays, the car wash, camping and even long traffic

jams. In fact, the power cord is so long that it could easily reach the cigarette lighter in the car next door to yours. The packaging warns, however, 'Do not use while driving.'

KAYLANI'S WICKED FOOT FETISH MASTURBATOR

A pink silicone foot with an artificial vagina in the heel, this odd sex aid is described this way: 'Smaller than the real thing, this velveteen pussy in the sole of a petite foot is ideal to keep in your drawer and take with you on those long business trips. Finished with toes with ruby-red nails, this deliciously kinky toy provides an incredibly lifelike sensation.' Quite what is meant by 'lifelike sensation' and 'smaller than the real thing' is hard to guess, as there can be few men who have actually copulated with a real foot with a vagina in it. On the website where I found this product the blurb was rather spoilt by the blunt, 'This product has been discontinued.'

DILDO GAS MASK

Advertised with the headline, 'OMG! Welcome to the world of extreme vinyl sex toys', the dildo gas mask is a must-have for anyone who's after a super-long vinyl dildo with a gas mask stuck on the end. If you tend to release mustard gas during your lovemaking, or frequently indulge in sex sessions during riots when police are firing tear-gas grenades, then this device will be right up your street. The dildo measures 16.5 inches in length and has a circumference of 4.75 inches.

THE CONDOM

The condom is not a sex *toy*, although various attempts have been made to add flavours and textures to them, but it is a vital *sex aid*, insofar as it allows couples to have sex without worrying about pregnancy or sexually transmitted infections. The condom has always been used to protect against STIs and has only been used for contraception in more recent times.

Like the dildo, the condom has a town bearing its name. Condom-en-Armagnac is a commune in south-western France. It has a lovely church, called Condom Cathedral, which was once the seat of the Bishops of Condom.

Several Latin etymologies have been put forward for the word 'condom', including *cumdum* (scabbard) as well as the surname of an alleged inventor of the product, but its origins are actually completely unknown. The first recorded use of the word came in 1666, when the English Birth Rate Commission referred to the use of 'condons'.

The oldest picture of a condom in use is said to be a painting in a fifteen-thousand-year-old French cave. If this is true, prophylaxis and contraception seem to have taken a step back in sophistication during medieval times, with the recommendation that the man dip his penis in tar or onion juice. How hot that tar would have to be is an interesting question.

The earliest description of condom use appears in Gabriele Falloppio's *De Morbo Gallico*, which was published in Italy two years after his death in 1564. He described linen sheaths soaked in chemicals, which were allowed to dry before being placed over the glans of the penis, tied on with a bit of ribbon. Before the fifteenth century, condoms covered only the tip of the male member.

Condoms have been made from a variety of materials over the years. Before the nineteenth century, fish skin, seedpods, treated linen and animal intestines or bladders were used. In Japan, the devices were made of tortoise shell or animal horn, before Dutch traders introduced condoms of 'fine leather'. Not so long ago reusable bladder condoms dating from the 1640s and believed to be the property of soldiers of King Charles I were discovered in an English privy.

Eighteenth-century intestine-condoms were sold in pubs, open-air markets, barber shops and chemist shops, just as today. They had to be softened with sulphur and lye. But in Europe they were also available at the theatre. In 1740 Thomas Streetser, writing as Roger Pheuquewell Esq., described the condom of his time in his bawdy book, *A New Description of Merryland* (the vagina). Streetser's pen name was not exactly subtle. 'Roger' had been slang for the penis since about 1650 and 'Pheuquewell' is a northern pronunciation of 'fuckwell'. Anyway, Pheuquewell warmed to his subject, describing the condom as being made of 'an extraordinary fine thin Substance, and contrived so as to be all of one piece, and without a Seam, only about the Bottom it is generally bound round with a Scarlet Ribbon for Ornament'.

In 1828, Gray's *Pharmacopoeia* described the making of a Georgian sheepgut condom in a delightful *Blue Peter*-style recipe, from 1824. The home-made process produced four grades: Ordinary, Fine, Superfine and Superfine doubles made from *sheeps' intestina caeca*, which is the pouch connecting the ileum with the ascending colon of the large intestine. I knew you'd want to know.

For the Ordinary, what you do, basically, is soak the gut in water for a few hours, then evaginate it (this just means turn it inside-out; what did you think?), macerate (soften) it once more in a weak alkaline solution, which you must change every twelve hours, and then carefully scrape it to remove the mucous membrane, leaving just the peritoneal and muscular coats. You next expose the thing to the vapour of burning brimstone (this is sulphur – you'd better open the windows) and wash it with soap and water (oh good). Afterwards blow it up, dry it with your sister's hairdryer, cut it to a length of 7 or 8 inches and tie it off at the open end with 'a riband'. Or you could just go down to Boots and get a packet of Durex.

The Superfine sort is much the same but is dressed with the knife, soaked, dried with a clean cloth and scented with essences, before being stretched on a mould and polished with a glass. You can just hear Valerie Singleton saying, 'Here's one I rubbed earlier', can't you?

Before use, this home-made condom had to be soaked in water to make it supple enough, which must have added quite considerably to the inconvenience of the Regency buck.

The first condoms were expensive but in the early nineteenth century they were actively promoted to the poor. Rather surprisingly, advertisements for condoms had first appeared in British newspapers in the 1840s. The first reusable rubber condom became available in 1855, and soon several big rubber companies, including Dunlop, were mass-producing them.

Rubber manufacturers found that full-length condoms in a single size sold best but, unfortunately, early condoms often fell off or broke, and they were frequently full of holes. Casanova had tested his by blowing them up like a balloon. The poor quality did not deter the manufacturers and companies continued to sell rejects cheap until the 1920s. Even by 1935 the quality wasn't much good, and a biochemist who tested 2,000 by filling them with air and then water found that well over half leaked. Nonetheless, business was brisk and huge numbers of used condoms were to be found discarded in parks and streets, offending the Bishop of London on his Sunday strolls.

Before the twenties, condom factories had tended to go bang because of explosive chemicals such as benzene. Latex rubber was invented in 1920 and was much safer to make. In 1932 the London Rubber Company, which had until then been a wholesaler for German-made condoms, became Europe's first latex condom maker, under the brand name Durex. Durex launched the lubricated condom in 1957 followed by the first polyurethane condom in the nineties. Recent research reveals that a modern condom will last for a month in a chap's wallet before friction makes it more likely to fail during use.

At the height of the Cold War, the Soviet Union was running very short of condoms and Soviet leader Nikita Khrushchev decided to ring British Prime Minister Harold Macmillan with an order for some British ones to fill the gap. 'Can you send us about a million?' he asked. 'I'll have them dispatched at once,' replied the unflappable Macmillan, 'in the hope of fostering warmer relations between our countries.' 'Thank you, prime minister', said Khrushchev. 'And, by the way, make sure they're nine inches long and three inches wide because that's the typical size in my country.' Macmillan agreed without demur and rang the London Rubber Company to place the order. In due course the condoms arrived in Moscow and a team of soldiers crowbarred the first crate open. Printed on the packets they read, 'British condoms: MEDIUM'.

XIII
FANCY THAT

THE SCIENCE OF SEXUAL ATTRACTION

*

'Sex appeal is fifty per cent what you've got
and fifty per cent what people think you've got.'

SOPHIA LOREN

I stumbled on a website recently called beautifulpeople.com, which says it provides 'online dating for beautiful people only', and asks users to vote whether prospective members are attractive enough to join. They say they have a membership of about 700,000 lovely people and have rejected well over five million stinkers.

Not so long ago, the site suffered an attack by something called the 'Shrek virus' and inadvertently allowed thousands of people to join who hadn't done the beauty parade test. Beautifulpeople's MD described many of these hopefuls as being 'no oil painting' and the site had to refund them more than £60,000 when they were unceremoniously kicked off.

As well as all the gorgeous ladies and gentlemen, the beautiful-people website also ranks countries with the *least* beautiful people in the world. Near the bottom come Russia, Poland and the UK. Whether those who are accepted on to this unusual website are getting their money's worth or are just gullibly handing over their hard-earned-cash in order to be flattered by strangers is a debatable point.

Height of desire

In any case, attractiveness is a complex business. Take those personal ads that you see in the papers and all over the Internet. A recent study done in a San Francisco café used eyeball tracking to find what men and women look at when reading profiles on dating sites. After analysing the results, they found that men spent much longer looking at the women's pictures, while women spent longer reading the men's text.

In their own personal ads, however, women do tend to stress the physical attributes they require in the man of their dreams. They are always asking to meet *tall* men and even women looking for sperm donors, who you'd think couldn't afford to be choosy, ask for tall chaps. In something like eighty per cent of personal ads, women demand men who are six feet tall or taller. This demand immediately reduces the field of eligible bachelors by something like eighty-six per cent, in the US anyway, where only about fourteen per cent of men are six feet tall or taller, and where they do a lot of this crazy research.

Unfair to midgets though this might sound, the instincts of these women are spot on because tall men tend to be healthier than shorter men. Tall men also tend to have prettier girlfriends, or so I read, and I don't doubt it. As if this were not enough, taller men are also richer and more professionally successful than shorter men. At fifty-eight per cent, the number of CEOs of US listed companies who are taller than six feet is way over the national average of fourteen per cent, and for each extra inch men can add thousands to their salary, with an average gain of £100,000 over an entire career. However, we dwarfs needn't feel bad, because one day that tall, dark stranger those women are so desperate to meet is going to turn out to be the Grim Reaper.

Bodies

As well as height, women find strong, muscular and athletic men

attractive, whether for sexual adventure or longer-term relationships. This is not exactly news to men and they tend to exaggerate the demand, assuming that women want a man with the rippling torso of Arnold Schwarzenegger (in 1967, not now), and can overdo it a bit down the gym.

Women find a V-shaped muscular upper body attractive, with hips narrower than shoulders. They do not lust after podgy love-handles and man boobs but prefer a muscular chest and flat abdomen. Both men and women assume that men with a high shoulder-to-hip ratio are more socially and physically dominant, and broad-shouldered men do indeed report having sex at a younger age than other men. They also report being the object of much female sexual attention. Well, who wouldn't report that about themselves?

While women are after the knight in shining armour, men want gorgeous, pouting Maid Marian, with physical attributes that indicate good childbearing and baby-feeding abilities. Men use a woman's waist-to-hip ratio (the hourglass figure) to judge her reproductive health, along with the well-known breast-assessment index, during the formulation of which they are often caught at it. In a very unfair joke, Australian men are said to have settled on the perfect physical attributes for a girlfriend: she should be four feet tall, toothless and have a flat top to her head so they have somewhere to rest their pint.

Hands

Human hands are an indicator of reproductive health and the level of sex hormones at work in early life. Men like their women's hands to be long-fingered and delicate, rather than great big shovels. Long fingernails exaggerate this feminine quality and many women wear artificial nails to enhance the look. Women find a squarer hand attractive on a man and the shorter a man's index finger is compared to his ring finger, the more aggressively masculine he is likely to be, owing to testosterone exposure in early life.

Face facts

When they are at their most fertile, women are drawn to men with more masculine faces. These square-jawed faces are a result of a high level of testosterone at work during puberty. A more masculine face shows a man to be a virile and healthy chap, able to compete successfully with other men and strong enough to protect his woman. Because high testosterone production can harm the body's immune system and make a man less able to fight parasites and disease, only the healthiest men can afford to risk high testosterone production in adolescence just as only the richest men can afford to squander their resources on a Ferrari. It's rather annoying for most testosterone-fuelled pubertal boys that at the time of their sexual peak, when the pump is primed and they are ready to conquer the world with their unstoppable sexual potency, their acnefied faces look like a pepperoni pizza. What girl wants to kiss a face that looks like the surface of the moon?

Rather counter-intuitively, research has revealed that when they are *not* ovulating, women tend to be most attracted to men whose faces, though masculine, are less exaggeratedly square-jawed, having a hint of femininity about them. The theory of this wavering attraction between very masculine and averagely masculine is that women are seeking out superb male specimens to impregnate them with their super-fit Tarzan genes but want their long-term relationship to be with a less testosterone-full man who can make them laugh, knows how to use a knife and fork properly and who is more likely to play trains with his son than go off on beaver patrol every weekend. Men with less testosterone may not win the arm-wrestling contests but their brains often beat the brawn.

When choosing a mate, men like a smaller chin, higher, thinner eyebrows and an absence of beard and moustache. A more feminine female face indicates more female sex hormones at work at the time of puberty, and therefore a good reproductive system.

Glowing, smooth pink skin on the Caucasian face is attractive to both sexes and it is one of the most powerful markers of good health. Nobody likes a partner's mug to be covered in boils or blackheads – it's a real turn-off. In one Scottish study of light-skinned people, an increase in fruit and vegetable consumption was linked to improvements in skin tone, and an increase in the natural warm colour of the skin. These faces were found to be more attractive in men and women alike. The improvement was attributed to carotenes, the red chemicals in fruits, vegetables and autumn leaves. So eat more of these things – not the leaves, of course.

The cosmetics industry makes a killing from selling products to improve the look of the skin, especially on the female face. There's a skincare product out there for every conceivable skin type and I have even seen one which claims to 'reduce the appearance of wrinkles', or so it says in the television commercials. Put another way this means 'reduce what wrinkles look like', which is clearly nonsense, yet people keep on buying the stuff because unwrinkled, pink, healthy skin is a sign of a good sexual bet and women don't want to be left behind in the beautiful-skin race, or in the going-to-bed-with-hunks race.

As with clear, unspotty skin, the hourglass figure in women and broad shoulders in a man, facial symmetry is important to men and women alike. It is another indicator of good genes and good health. Small changes to facial symmetry can turn a handsome or pretty face into a positively unattractive one.

Sex drive

When we say someone is 'sexy' we are really saying that they are healthy, so it is no surprise that sexy people are referred to as 'fit'. But, while men go almost exclusively for physical attractiveness, women are much choosier in their partners in other respects. This is because they have a lot to lose by picking the wrong mate – nine months' pregnancy and a dad who turns out not to be able to chop down trees, feed his family or protect them from tigers. So in addition to purely physical attributes, women prioritize status, dominance and power. Though they need a man with good genes *and* good dad skills they want deep pockets too, and one of the most obvious tokens of power and status is a man's car.

Researchers have discovered that women find a man with a flashy car more desirable than the *same man* with a Honda Civic. The car lends the man sex appeal. It is not inaccurate, therefore, for a chap to describe his expensive sports car as a 'fanny magnet', though it is rather distasteful. At the same time, these women are not stupid. They understand the status game which these flashy men are playing, and are well aware that they are only interested in one thing, finding them a good bet as a one-night stand but a poor choice as a husband. Despite their intellectual understanding of what is going on, though, beautiful young babes continue to select as husbands raddled old millionaires driving Ferraris. Who knows, maybe they are getting a bit on the side from the rugged gardener in the back of his battered Citroën 2CV.

Bad girls

It has long been thought that men are more promiscuous than women but unless there are a small number of hugely promiscuous women doing all the business, the maths is hard to work out. In fact, anthropologists Elizabeth Oberzaucher and Karl Grammer from the University of Vienna have shown that women actually provoke promiscuity by their behaviour. Moreover, they found that women with a long-term partner behave 'worse' in this respect than other women. Women in a long-term relationship who go out with a male friend tend to show more skin (which men recognize as a mating signal) and dance more sexily than women who are not in a relationship.

And it gets worse: most women have a spike in their libido at their most fertile time and are more likely to commit adultery during ovulation than at any other time. Ovulating women are more flirtatious than non-fertile women and if they are ovulating and also have a steady partner they are the most flirtatious, sexy and provocative of all. Elizabeth Oberzaucher explains that these women will deliberately go out on their *most fertile* days, leaving their long-term partner at home watching the football, and dance about like nobody's business, sending out powerful sexual signals, and maybe, as a result, also 'doing some "double-mating"', as she put it.

Research in the US has revealed just how sexually powerful dance can be. Some women whom researchers spoke to admitted having had sex with a man based on nothing more than seeing his dancing. I'm guessing in these cases that it was probably more 'disco' than 'Mr Pastry', but I don't know. Women are most attracted to men who make large sweeping movements, finding them more erotic. And the same is true when men watch women dancing. Dance is clearly a vertical expression of a horizontal desire.

But, look here, there's more to sexual attraction than dancing, having a flash car or looking like Rock Hudson or Marilyn Monroe, otherwise most of us ugly, spotty, economy-model drivers would be doomed to a solitary partnerless life. There's your personality, of course, then there's the way you smell, and the way you sound, each of which play an important part in your sex appeal, as all train-spotting fishmongers with squeaky voices know to their cost.

Personality

Weedy men who play the guitar in a band need not worry too much, though. Chaps with less testosterone may not win the pushing-in-the-queue contests but they are often more astute, creative and funnier than the boisterous he-men. Characteristics such as ingenuity, musicality and humour are by-products of a mind that can think its way out of trouble, while providing entertainment better than television. If you are a man with a brain capable of devising clever traps for catching antelope, building more efficient tree houses, empathizing better with others and devising a way to start the fire when the tinder is wet, you are in with a good chance – these are all vital skills in communal survival.

For many women, a good personality overrides the physical shortcomings of a prospective mate, and top of the list is a sense of humour. A good sense of humour even has its own personal ad abbreviation, 'GSOH', though the people I meet who claim to have a GSOH often turn out to have a really BSOH or even a FASOH. Married women who say their husbands are 'witty' –

which is different from 'humorous', but let's not split hairs – say they are more satisfied with their marriage than women who say their husbands have a BSOH. Furthermore, humour is one important sexual characteristic that women look for in one-night stands and long-term relationships alike.

While women find men who make them laugh sexually attractive – and this includes Ken Dodd, apparently – men like women *who laugh at them*, whether at their humour, wit, jokes or silly behaviour, such as putting the tea cosy on their head and dancing down the street. Humour is a sign of confidence and intelligence and is a skill with which the skinny man can, and often does, dominate the rippling hunk. Christopher Hitchens once said that a laugh is already a kind of submission and there does seem to be truth in the idea that a man can laugh a woman into bed.

Talking scents

Elizabeth Oberzaucher did a curious 'smell pleasantness test' to discover whether the way a man smells has any influence on his attractiveness to women. After some vigorous exercise, four men – who varied in their physical attractiveness – took off their sweaty T-shirts. These were then smelt by a group of women. The surprising results were that the best-looking and youngest man had by far the worst body odour. Elizabeth Oberzaucher put it in scientific terms: Attractive men 'stink more', she said.

The chemical responsible for this unpleasant odour is called androsterone, a male hormone made from the metabolism of testosterone. The smell of androsterone is heartily disliked by women *except* when they are ovulating, when they find it only slightly less disgusting. The explanation for this strange effect is that it is an evolutionary device by which men repel infertile women, who, from a reproductive point of view are a complete waste of flowers and chocolates. At the same time, a fertile woman will put up with the pong and allow attractive chaps to impregnate her with their genes. This may well explain the incomprehensible success of malodorous body sprays such as Lynx.

And the situation is even more complex. Humans have some interesting genes which fight viruses and bacteria, known as the major histocompatibility complex, or MHC. Women will do better if they mate with men whose MHC genes are *unlike* their own. Mates who have different genes from our own are a much safer bet since reproducing with a close genetic relation is likely to lead to birth defects. Luckily, a woman's sense of smell peaks around ovulation, when she can sniff out men who will be genetically safer as reproductive partners.

To find out more about MHC, Brazilian scientists asked some chaps to wear skin patches for a few days, after which time a group of women smelled the patches and rated them from attractive to unattractive. The researchers found that the odours of men whose MHC was dissimilar to their own were the most desirable to the women, while the smell of men whose genes were like theirs made them shudder with disgust. In her own research, evolutionary psychologist Christine Garver-Apgar found that women whose partners had genes like their own reported wanting sex less often. They also reported more frequent sex fantasies about other men and more sexual infidelity, particularly when they were at their most fertile.

Just as men use a chemical repellent to deter infertile and genetically similar women, women lure mates with sexual odours called 'copulins'. Though they sound horrid, these odours are attractive to men and cause their testosterone levels to rise. Copulin odour varies at different stages of the menstrual cycle. When the woman is at her most fertile, copulins make the man 'less fussy'. They also cause him to secrete androsterone, and round and round it all goes. There's a lot going on in this attraction lark but you'll be OK if you just follow your nose.

Sexy voices

Alternatively, you could follow your ear. The concept of the sexy voice is well understood around the world and many women wish their man sounded like Sean Connery or Jeremy Irons instead of Yoda or David Beckham – no matter how good his legs. Likewise, men would prefer to hear the voice of Marilyn Monroe in their ear in the morning rather than the Wicked Witch of the West.

An attractive voice is linked in men with broad shoulders and a narrow waist and, in women, with an hourglass figure. These attributes are signs of reproductive fitness, so the voice is a useful index of the quality of a potential breeding partner. Men tend to prefer women with high voices, a sign of youth and high levels of oestrogen. According to the journal *Evolution and Human Behavior*, a woman's voice is most attractive to men during ovulation and least attractive during menstruation.

In a study at Northumbria University, a group of men and women were asked to listen to male voices and rate them for confidence, dominance and sexiness. They then marked photographs of the speakers. The men with deeper voices scored better than those with higher voices and they were also found to look more attractive. A deep voice in men goes along with bilateral body symmetry, which, as we know, is a sexy sign in men and women. Women reported that a deep voice made the man sound 'stronger' and 'bigger'. Luckily for squeaky-voiced men, there's always heavy cigarette smoking to improve your chances in the boudoir.

Evolutionary anthropologist David Puts has found that women greatly prefer deeper voices when considering their owners as prospective short-term sexual partners. The attraction to deep voices is strongest during a woman's most fertile phase of her ovulation cycle. From all this research into sexual attraction it looks as though women are lust-crazed vampires during ovulation, whereas at other times they are almost like normal people (*joke* – no letters to the prime minister, please).

Women are like frogs – at least when it comes to finding deep voices alluring. Female bullfrogs are attracted by the male bullfrogs with the most growly croaks. These frogs are also the biggest and healthiest, and it is the same for men.

At puberty, testosterone causes a deepening of the male voice, and the more testosterone there is, the deeper it goes. The trouble for young men is that, just as with spotty faces, their most vigorous period of sexual potential coincides exactly with production of the most embarrassing noises they will ever make. Just as they are yearning to overcome the girl of their dreams with their sexually overwhelming velvet voice, they actually sound more like a motor scooter with a faulty muffler, growling most of the time but with the occasional high squeal that forces girls not into willing sexual surrender but into fits of helpless laughter.

The world of sperm

However, a woman will have to kiss quite a few frogs before finding her prince. According to a study published in the journal *PLoS One*, an analysis of the semen from fifty-four heterosexual men showed that the sperm from those with deeper voices were inferior to those of men with higher voices on seven 'motility' measures. The deeper-voiced men were, it seemed, less likely to make a baby than their less sexy-sounding competition – in short, they were firing blanks.

This effect is true in dominant males throughout the animal kingdom. The more attractive the male, the lower his sperm quality. Like many puzzling results in sexual science the explanation is one of 'trade-off'. Humans have limited resources, so there is a balance to be struck between having rotten sperm but being attractive enough to get a woman to go to bed with you so you can actually transmit your genes, and having prizewinning sperm but being so repellent that you have no chance of getting it out of you and into her.

An intriguing 2012 study has also linked a diet high in saturated fat with lower sperm count. The team, led by Prof. Jill Attaman from Harvard Medical School in Boston, asked men at a US fertility clinic about their diet, and checked their sperm over four years. Those eating a lot of junk food had fewer sperm, as well as, possibly, fatter stomachs. The message is clear, men: cut down on the hot dogs and fried chicken McKing burger nuggets, don't be too handsome, and don't have too deep a voice.

Sperm quality aside, sensitivity to the character of a human voice is pervasive. Few people want to hear the pilot of their jumbo jet come over sounding like Mickey Mouse, and radio listeners are quick to complain if a presenter's voice is too high or low, or lacks warmth and authority. Newsreaders, male and female, are carefully chosen for the quality of their voices, amongst other important things. A few years ago BBC Radio 4 caused a row when Neil Nunes, a new continuity announcer from Jamaica, was unleashed on the listeners. His very low voice was felt by many to be more like a humpback whale mooing in the ocean depths, though a multitude of women thought he sounded delightfully sexy.

Dr Gordon Gallup of State University of New York at Albany says that the voice 'may be a medium for the transmission of important biological information'. The sound of your voice is not only a sign of your attractiveness, it can indicate the age at which you lost your virginity, the number of sex partners you've had, and whether or not you have ever had a bit on the side. Gallup says that attractive voices go with attractive bodies, and it's certainly true that the 'spinster's croak' tells you quite a bit about the way she's going to look once she's taken her nightdress off. Gallup has a word of advice for those considering going on a blind date with someone. 'It would be prudent,' he says, 'to have a telephone conversation with that person first.'

As with body shape, skin condition and smell, the sound of a sexy voice is attractive because it is the sign of healthy genes to pass on to the kids.

The kiss

Also known as 'osculation', kissing has been described as the most intimate sexual behaviour of all. Kissing produces a cornucopia of sensory titillation, exciting five of the cranial nerves, along with which there is often an exchange of saliva. The lips house special touch- and pressure-receptors which fire off highly stimulating messages to the brain. The body processes all the information it is receiving about the prospective sexual partner, quickly rating the attractiveness of the kisser. Dr Helen Fisher of Rutgers University says that during a kiss a person gets a comprehensive physical report on the kissee. 'You can see them, smell them, hear them, feel them and taste them,' she says. '*All five senses.* Within seconds you know if they are likely to make a good mate.' The first kiss is not only fun, it is a vital selection tool, and if the physical signs are wrong it can doom an otherwise promising relationship.

Professor Michael Cunningham of the University of Louisville in Kentucky recently completed a decade-long study of lips in which he concluded that big ones are more sexually attractive than small. He showed subjects pictures of men and women and asked them to rate them for attractiveness. His team found that big eyes, a small nose and voluptuous lips are sexually attractive in men and women alike but that even modest computer alterations to the lips could change the rating of a face from 'a perfect ten' to the equivalent of 'hideous'. Cunningham found that although good lips cannot rescue an ugly face, they *can* make an already attractive face better. 'Generally speaking, big is better than small,' he says. 'But it is possible to go a little too far and then be unattractive.'

Professor Cunningham points out that 'Men are looking for warmth, generosity and sensuality in a woman's lips . . . When someone is genuinely pleased to see you, they flush and become fuller and darker . . . If a woman is holding her lips tightly clenched, it is not a good sign that she wants to get to know you better.' Everybody recognizes the passion-killing spinster's pout: a mouth with the look of an anal sphincter.

The Kentucky team concluded that women are 'simultaneously looking for sensuality and ruggedness. That means a man should look virile – not too sensual and not too feminine.' So there's no need to start with the lipstick then, gentlemen.

Body language
When it comes to recognizing the cornucopia of courtship signals that a lady uses to show a chap that she fancies him, a man is about as clever as a monkey trying to catch his own reflection in a mirror. Women are much better, being experts at flirting and subtle courtship signals. They do this a lot but still men don't get it. Here is some of the body language that men and women use, sometimes unconsciously, to lure a mate.

1. Flirting and seduction can start at a distance. A man will draw in his beer belly, lengthen his stride, adopt an arm-swagger, and lift his head. A woman will swing her hips and may give a backwards glance over her shoulder to a man she is interested in. This signal means 'follow me'. Even men who are a bit slow on the uptake find this one alluring.

2. Another classic female flirting device is the head toss, often accompanied by the hair flick. A woman might also give a man a sideways glance through partly closed eyelids, and as the man catches her eye will look away. The eyelash flutter is now a cartoon cliché.

3. A woman who stands with her thumb in her belt with fingers 'pointing' at her pubic region is being sexually assertive. The male equivalent is to stand in an exaggeratedly masculine and dominant pose, feet wide apart and fingers in belt or pockets,

thumbs pointing towards the 'gentleman's area', just like a cowboy. Thumbs out of pockets is a masculine pose, fingers-out is feminine. If the partners in this strange dance are interested in each other they will start by pointing their bodies directly towards each other.

4. People who are attracted also stand closer together – less than three feet apart.

5. One of the subtlest subconscious signals, and fleetingly brief, is a widening of the eyes and a raising of the eyebrows. It says, 'I fancy you something rotten', but it is easy to miss.

6. Both parties are likely to preen themselves. A man may brush his lapels, straighten his tie and smooth his hair or eyebrow. A woman may twiddle her jewellery, touch her knee or throat and smooth her thigh. Women subconsciously display the inside of their wrists to attract a man. Often this is done while touching the hair.

7. If a woman is seated, she may slowly cross and uncross her legs.

8. A man's head will be held high and the woman may begin to adopt the mouth-open pose: an all-purpose sexual signal.

9. A woman will often flop her heel in and out of her shoe in a frankly erotic gesture.

10. As things warm up a couple will increasingly look into each other's eyes and their pupils will dilate. Big pupils are sexually attractive, so much so that they are created electronically in model photographs in glamour magazines.

11. This may move on to slight knee-touching either with the woman's knee 'accidentally' bumping the man's, or with her frankly squeezing or stroking his leg.

12. If a woman begins stroking or sucking a long object, such as a bottle, cigar tube, bread stick or pepperpot, there is likely to be some serious 'trouser disturbance' for the gentleman.

Attracting a partner

In addition to the subconscious body language, there are several things you can actively do to attract a mate.

1. If you are a lady, bung on a bit of makeup and run a brush through your spun-gold hair. But don't bother with intensive grooming if you are a man – you don't want to look continental. Neat and tidy will do.
2. Ladies should cultivate a bit of charm but men should not try too hard to be nice. Being nice will get you nowhere in the seduction stakes if you are male. Indeed, being a bit of a bounder is likely to increase your flirting power.
3. Although some very dominant men like their blondes to be dumb, most men like the impression that a woman has a working brain. So don't hide it, ladies.
4. Do be confident and assertive if you are a man. Also try to be as tall as possible.
5. Do touch your flirtee. Don't grab hold of his shirt and chest hairs or her bum. Instead, touch lightly on the forearm or on the back of the hand or wrist. Just briefly – there's no need to squeeze hold like you are strangling an eel.
6. Men may pay a woman the occasional compliment but should avoid disasters such as, *I like older ladies*; *You don't sweat much for a fat lass*; *You disguise your heavy midriff cleverly with that poncho*; or, *Do you want to see a trick I learned in prison?*
7. Neither men nor women should try too hard – it makes you look desperate. Instead, maintain a cool, elusive, mysterious intrigue.
8. Scientists have recently discovered that crossing a wobbly bridge or going on a fast toboggan ride with a man causes a woman to become attracted to him. This is worth knowing if you are a chap. I mean, how much does a peek over the top

of a multi-storey car park cost? What it lacks in romance it makes up for in erotically charged shared danger. Just watch her cling on to you.

9. If humour comes naturally and you are a man, be funny. If it doesn't, just stay mysterious.

10. Ask your flirtee about themselves. 'Have you ever tried wife-swapping?' is a good question for an attractive neighbour, though 'Are you a virgin?' and 'Do you like screwing?' diminish your mysterious allure.

Just as you will recognize when the light is green for go, you will know when things are going badly. Signs that you are flogging a dead horse with your flirting include your target pointing him- or herself away from you, constantly looking over your shoulder for someone more interesting, snapping back curt answers to your questions, looking at their watch – and in bad cases, holding it to their ear to check it's working, pursing their lips, holding their arms, drink or bag in front of their body like a shield, raising their eyes to heaven at everything you say, glazing over, tutting loudly at your jokes and questions, and, finally, just walking away. If you *can't* spot that the wheel has come off your technique when they walk away there's not much I can do to help.

XIV
Your Sex Life as a Film Title
A diversion for wet Wednesdays
*

'Sex on television can't hurt you,
unless you fall off.'

ANON.

In 1966, Charles F. Foley and Neil Rabens, two gentlemen with a nifty idea, patented a new game that required players to contort themselves on a large plastic mat covered in coloured circles. Anyone falling over was eliminated. Games company Milton Bradley launched the idea as Twister, 'the game that ties you up in knots', and it became a big hit after the cute and busty socialite Eva Gabor played it with Johnny Carson on the floor of the *Tonight Show*, in 1966. Suddenly demure young ladies and gentlemen found themselves intertwined in each other's apartments, enjoying a certain amount of inevitable bumping up against each other, and many new friendships were formed. Competing games companies enviously accused Milton Bradley of selling 'sex in a box', an accusation that can only have boosted sales.

But Twister is about as innocuous as that game where a circle of people pass an orange around under their chins. Nowadays, if you do an internet search for 'sex games', you will get 526 million results, covering everything from strip poker to something scary called spank the gimp. For the less adventurous I recommend a politer and funnier game suggested to me by my friend Keri. She proposed using a film title to describe your sex life and this struck me as a delightfully intellectual pursuit. Everybody's sex life has its own unique idiosyncrasies and there's a film for all tastes. Here are a few titles that occurred to me, but there are plenty left over for you to have a go with.

Above the Rim
Always Tell Your Wife
Amazing Dr. Clitterhouse, The
And Now For Something Completely Different
Any Which Way You Can
Are You Being Served?
Attack of the Killer Tomatoes
Bad Day at Black Rock
Bank Dick, The
Beaver, The
Black Hole, The
Black Joy
Better Late Than Never
Beauty and the Beast
Big
Bride of Frankenstein
Bullseye!
Can you Keep It Up For a Week?
Cockfighter
Come Blow Your Horn
Cover Her Face
Day the Earth Caught Fire, The
Deadwood
Deep Throat
Dirty Harry
Dr. Strangelove

Eating Raoul
Educating Rita
Endless Night
Enforcer, The
Enter the Void
Extremely Loud and Incredibly Close
Family Jewels, The
Fanny by Gaslight
Foul Play
Four Hundred Blows, The
Frenzy
Fun with Dick and Jane
Head
Having It All
Here We Go Round the Mulberry Bush
Hi, Mom!
Home Alone
It Happened One Night
It's Alive
Jerk, The
Keep It Up, Jack!
Knickers Ahoy!
Last Boy Scout, The
Lady and the Tramp
Lady Vanishes, The
Lethal Weapon

Let's Do It Again
Man Trouble
Man Who Knew Too Much,
 The
Moby Dick
Monkey Business
Mr Jolly Lives Next Door
Naked
Necessary Roughness
Never Give a Sucker an Even
 Break
Night After Night
Night of the Living Dead
No Deposit, No Return
Nob Hill
Noises Off
Norman . . . Is That You?
The Nude Bomb
Nothing in Common
Odd Couple, The
Out
Out of Order
Over Her Dead Body
Peeper
Pelvis
Penetrator, The
Percy's Progress
Perfectly Normal
Playtime
Pleasure Principle, The
Privates on Parade
Psycho
Reptile, The

Ring, The
Rise and Rise of Michael
 Rimmer, The
Rear Window
Rockets Galore
Rope
Rude Awakening
Ruggles of Red Gap
Skin Game, The
Scream
Screwballs
She's Gotta Have It
Shot in the Dark, A
Sideways
Smallest Show on Earth, The
Snatch
Something's Gotta Give
Tentacles
Terror by Night
Thing, The
Titfield Thunderbolt, The
Toy Story
Turn of the Screw, The
Up
Uranus
Victim
Violator, The
Wait Until Dark
When Willie Comes Marching
 Home
Which Way to the Front?
Whiffs
While Parents Sleep

Who Dares Wins
Whore
Why Me
Wild Women of Wongo
Willie Wonka and the
    Chocolate Factory
Wilt
Wind
Without a Clue
Wobblies, The

Woman in Flames, A
Wombling Free
Working Girl
World's Greatest Lover, The
Wrong Man, The
Young Man With a Horn
You're a Big Boy Now
Zorro, the Gay Blade

XV
WHEN THINGS GO WRONG
SEXUAL DYSFUNCTION IN A NUTSHELL

*

'I'm taking Viagra and drinking prune juice;
I don't know if I'm coming or going.'
RODNEY DANGERFIELD

Do you have restless genitals? Then you may be suffering from restless genital syndrome. This is not a line from a newspaper advertisement – restless genital syndrome is a real condition, originally known as persistent sexual arousal syndrome. Like many sexual conditions its name keeps changing and it is now generally called persistent genital arousal disorder, or PGAD, (see below).

These days everybody in glamour magazines and television commercials seems to be practically perfect in every way, just like Mary Poppins. All women look slim, gorgeous, intelligent and delightfully well bred; all men appear handsome, tall, witty, strong, mysterious, dominant and brave – with first-class teeth. But the idea that women are universally beautiful and bright, with fantastic hair and no wrinkles doesn't stand up when you have a look at the people queuing for the bus. Neither is there any truth in the notion that all men are Bugatti-driving six-foot-tall hunks who help old ladies across the road before arriving home with champagne to serenade their woman on the lute, cook a perfect soufflé and then make love all night with their blue-steel ten-inch penises.

Of course, this is not to say that ladies are all toothless Victorian washerwomen, nor that men are all cardigan-wearing myopic dullards with genitals like cashew nuts. But the situation for most people is a bit more ordinary than the pictures in magazines would have you believe. Dr Eric W. Corty, Associate Professor of Clinical Psychology and Abnormal Behavior at Pennsylvania State University, says that incessant exposure to the media's unreal sexual stereotypes create 'a situation ripe for disappointment and dissatisfaction', adding, 'We hope to dispel such fantasies and encourage men and women with realistic data . . . thus preventing sexual disappointments and dysfunctions.'

Though sexual dysfunction can be a physical problem, it is often the result of something else. Psychosexual therapist Dr Liz West told me that when things go wrong it's usually the relationship that's faulty. 'Most people with sex problems feel powerless and "stuck" but with better communication the sex will usually sort itself out', she explains. 'Men want a quick fix but success depends on the couple – getting the couple to talk to each other.' Sexual dysfunction covers a big field and Liz sees all kinds of problems. 'Men think women want things that they don't,' she says. 'They make assumptions about women without checking it out. Women want you to find out what they want – and negotiate it.'

Partner betweenness

One of the oddest-sounding maladies is 'partner betweenness' a condition revealed in a 2011 study of some 3,000 people, published in the *Journal of Sociology* by Professors Benjamin Cornwell and Edward Laumann. In their report they described a curious condition in middle-aged and older men, in which a woman knows her husband's friends better than he does. This, they said, leads to an increase in erectile dysfunction in the man. 'Men who experience partner betweenness in their joint relationships are more likely to have trouble getting or maintaining an erection,' the authors explained, 'and are also more likely to experience difficulty achieving orgasm during sex.' They summed up their theory in a forty-seven-word sentence: 'A man whose female partner has greater contact with some of his confidants than he does is about ninety-two per cent more likely to have trouble getting or maintaining an erection than a man who has greater access than his partner does to all of his confidants.'

Apparently, the men felt that their masculinity, autonomy and privacy had all been undermined. And who can blame them? What man wants to hear his wife say, 'I'm off down The Jolly Roger with your best mates Bill and Bob. Just leave my dinner in the oven – I'll probably be late.' Interesting though this research is, it is my humble opinion that the results are bleeding obvious.

Another strange problem is so-called 'sexsomnia'. The word is a conflation of 'sex' and 'insomnia', and the condition is also known as 'arousal parasomnia'. Sexomnia is identified by sexual activity during sleep, ranging from mild autoeroticism to sexual intercourse. The sexomniac is unaware of what he is doing and the condition is often accompanied by night terrors and bedwetting, so it's no joke. Many sufferers have a history of sleepwalking and some have sleepwalked before performing sex acts on strangers (so they say). In March 2009 the *News of the World* revealed that a sexomniac from York had been cleared of three rape charges in December 2005. When I tried to check details on the *News of the World* website I just got a page saying, 'Thank you & goodbye.' But I thought, if it was in the *News of the World*, it must be true.

On the physical side, there is a cornucopia of things that can, and do, go wrong. These range from the commonplace erectile dysfunction to a rare condition called diphallia. Here is a snapshot of some of the physical ailments, common and uncommon, that can crop up.

Persistent Genital Arousal Disorder

PGAD is the 'restless genitals' complaint I mentioned earlier. It was first recorded in women, in 2001, by Dr Sandra Leiblum, though some doctors now regard priapism (see below) as the same condition. Symptoms have been linked with something frightening-sounding called 'pudendal nerve entrapment' but, mercifully, restless genital syndrome is very rare and anaesthetic gels can help sufferers.

The effects of PGAD are a spontaneously occurring, uncontrollable and persistent genital arousal unconnected to feelings of sexual desire. Some might object that this is not a disorder so much as a lovely gift from the sex fairy, but sufferers find it an embarrassing nuisance and some have been prescribed antidepressants as a result.

Physical arousal can be intense in PGAD and go on for weeks at a time. Though orgasm can provide a relief, the symptoms may return suddenly, unpredictably and with a vengeance. Failure to relieve the symptoms of arousal frequently provokes wave after wave of spontaneous orgasms in women just as they are doing their makeup or pouring the vicar another cup of tea, and annoyingly inconvenient ejaculation in men at the bacon counter, petrol pump or job interview. This tends to hamper concentration, as you may well guess. Bus and train rides become hazardous, as vibrations aggravate the syndrome. Even mobile phones can set the condition off, confirming the suspicion of Scottish gentlemen that keeping your iPhone in your sporran is not best practice.

Frigidity and impotence

Problems with sexual arousal are a frequent difficulty, though loss of arousal is not quite the same thing as a loss of *desire* (wilting libido). Loss of sexual *arousal* was previously known as 'frigidity', in women, and 'impotence', in men but both these very descriptive terms have been abolished so as not to hurt people's feelings.

In a fit of pique, having had the word 'impotence' stolen from them, medics now sometimes refuse to call the affliction 'erectile dysfunction' and prefer their own amusing coinage, 'ascension deficit disorder', the visible signs of which are partial or total failure to get or keep an erection. About forty per cent of men suffer from some form of erectile dysfunction (ED), at least occasionally and the condition tends to feed on itself. Often the anxious man will be intensely scrutinized in his performance by a nauseatingly understanding, or unkindly amused woman, as he tries to get things to happen, like a snake charmer under the glare of the midday sun. No wonder the snake often remains asleep in his basket.

Dr Liz West explains that erectile dysfunction is one of the most common problems her clients report. 'The trouble is, men are penis-centred,' she says, 'and erections are very visible. Men think that if there's no erection they can't have sex. Women don't think like this. Erection problems are generally more about the relationship than the plumbing.'

Although anxiety and depression can provoke erectile dysfunction there are physical causes too. A man's erection depends on good blood supply to the penis and diseases that cause problems with the body's small blood vessels can result in the droopy-Joe effect. High blood pressure, obesity and heart disease can all cause problems, as can kidney disease, diabetes, and smoking and drinking (see 'brewers' droop' below). Surgical damage to the wonderfully named pelvic splanchnic nerves, which is a risk of prostate surgery, can also produce erectile problems, as can blood-pressure drugs, antipsychotics, antidepressants, sedatives and antacids. It's a wonder any babies are being born at all.

For years, surgical implants, either stiff bendables or soft inflatables, were the only treatments available for erectile dysfunction. But the introduction of Viagra in the 1990s (see below) vastly improved treatment. In the early days of Viagra, one enthusiastic patient accidentally killed himself with an overdose and the unfortunate funeral director couldn't shut the coffin. Nurses were then instructed to make patients swallow the pill slowly, but they all got stiff necks. Some of the many jokes Viagra spawned were even worse than this.

Brewer's droop
Brewer's droop is an age-old slang term for erectile dysfunction brought on by drinking alcohol. In *Macbeth*, the porter provides a delightful early seventeenth-century analysis of what is clearly this complaint.

> MACDUFF: Was it so late, friend, ere you went to bed, that you do lie so late?
> PORTER: 'Faith sir, we were carousing till the second cock; and drink, sir, is a great provoker of three things.
> MACDUFF: What three things does drink especially provoke?
> PORTER: Marry, sir, nose-painting, sleep, and urine. Lechery, sir, it provokes, and unprovokes; it provokes the desire, but it takes away the performance. Therefore, much drink may be said to be an equivocator with lechery: it makes him, and it mars him; it sets him on, and it takes him off; it persuades him, and disheartens him; makes him stand to, and not stand to; in conclusion, equivocates him in a sleep, and, giving him the lie, leaves him.

Shakespeare, it seems, was only too well aware of the problem.

Other drugs than alcohol are also a cause of brewer's droop and it's doubly likely in homosexual encounters, owing to the multiplication of penises. Tony Wendice, a man who in his twenties was an enthusiastic clubber, told me he was once dancing in The Shadow Lounge, a gay club in Soho, 'feeling young and beautiful', as he put it. Tony explained how the man he was dancing with suddenly pounced. 'There is always a sexual tension in a gay club,' he told me. 'It oozes sex; it's just there. He grabbed my belt and dragged me to the toilets, which were very dark, with a sparkling floor. There's a chap at the front giving you lollypops and making sure there's no drug-taking going on. Anyway, I was yanked into the cubicle and we rolled up a fiver and took a line of coke. Then we stripped naked and got down to business.' But all the trouble was for nothing as the cocaine's unwanted side effect was immediately apparent in Tony's new friend. 'He clambered on to the back of the loo seat but he couldn't get it up. I tried to do what I could but it was no use. So we politely got dressed and left. It was embarrassing.'

Whereas brewer's droop is a temporary disappointment, long-term alcohol abuse causes irreversible damage to the nerves of the penis, resulting in something called 'alcohol impotence', the symptoms of which are boozy showoffs with noses that look like brains, who are 'all talk and no action'.

Priapism
Priapism is the opposite of erectile dysfunction and is named after Greek fertility god Priapus, protector of livestock, gardens and male genitalia, who had a vast permanent erection (see chapter I). It is a painful condition, mainly affecting younger men, in which the penis becomes erect of its own free will, and stays that way for hours on end while you are just reading the *Metro* or cleaning out the garage. Priapism develops when blood is unable to drain from the penis and is a medical emergency requiring immediate treatment to avoid scarring and permanent loss of erectile function.

Orgasm problems
The absence of an orgasm after sexual excitement is called 'anorgasmia', who sounds a bit like one of Henry VIII's wives. It is far more common in women than it is in men, for whom it can

be especially frustrating. One cause of anorgasmia is addiction to opiates, particularly heroin. Another is antidepressants called selective serotonin reuptake inhibitors, which frequently delay or eliminate orgasm altogether. Taking antidepressants to treat depression and then getting depressed as a result of their depressing effects is surely the ultimate in pharmaceutical nuttiness.

Pain

Like anorgasmia, sexual pain disorders are generally a female problem and can sometimes be the result of having a clumsy great oaf go to work on you. The Latin term *impotentia coeundi* describes the general inability to insert the penis into the vagina. Although some fingers-and-thumbs sort of men might have trouble putting a carrot in a paddling pool there shouldn't really be a big problem here, not with a normal anatomy, anyway. Structural abnormalities of the penis like Peyronie's disease (also known as *Induratio penis plastica*) can make things difficult, though. The condition is marked by fibrous bands in the male organ, which result in a deformed-looking sort of banana-penis. Not yellow, of course.

Coital cephalalgia

Coital cephalalgia is a rare form of severe headache that starts at the base of the skull during sex. The pain can last from a few minutes to several days, sometimes worsening during intercourse or masturbation and at other times coming on suddenly at the moment of orgasm – so-called 'explosive headaches'. If you're getting coital cephalalgia, see your doctor, as unusual headaches can be a signal of something serious going on. Anyway, it must spoil things horribly in the boudoir.

Micropenis

Micropenis just means an unusually small penis, with a dorsal (top) length being 'at least 2.5 standard deviations smaller than the mean penis size'. I'm not sure what 2.5 standard deviations look like, but the thing sounds small.

Traumatic Masturbatory Syndrome

Yes, this is a real syndrome. At least Dr Lawrence Sank of the Center for Cognitive Therapy of Greater Washington thinks it's real, having come up with the name in 1998. Sank described Traumatic Masturbatory Syndrome (TMS) in an article in which he cited four male patients who complained of erectile dysfunction and anorgasmia. He said that their problems were the result of masturbating face down, which they did by rubbing their penises against their hand, the floor or whatever it was. Sank remarked that once he had retrained these men to masturbate face up, using the more customary penis-in-hand method, their erections and ejaculations returned to normal. You've got to hand it to him – as they said about the blind rent boy.

Diphallia

Diphallia is not a Welshman but a condition in which a man has two penises, usually side by side but sometimes at a distance from each other. Erection and ejaculation can be normal in both organs. The condition was first recorded in 1609 by a Swiss doctor named Johannes Jacob Wecker.

Sex addiction

Sex addiction is a new name for an old problem, once informally called 'womanizing' in men, and 'nymphomania' in women. It is a magnetic subject for headline writers and filmmakers and, in 2011, *Shame*, a British film about a sex addict, which contained rather a lot of naked sex, caused a bit of a stir. But it soon died down, as it always does.

Sex addiction is characterized by extreme sexual thoughts and behaviours that are out of the control of the 'sex addict', along with persistent unsuccessful efforts to stop. Sex addiction expert Patrick Carnes has come up with some 'core beliefs' that he says sex addicts share. These include the addict's belief that he or she is a bad, unworthy and unlovable person whose most important need is sex. These beliefs lead to the extreme sexual behaviour.

Walter Beardsley, who describes himself as a compulsive womanizer, told me he thinks there is no difference between 'womanizing' and 'sex addiction'. He said that sexual conquest is what he really wants but that, having successfully made the conquest, he finds that he doesn't really want the sex. 'I'm trying to fill an emptiness in myself. I'm completely fucked up sexually,' he explained helpfully.

The trouble is that there is no agreement among sexologists and others whether sex addiction, or so-called 'hypersexuality', is a true addiction or even a psychological condition at all. Whatever it is, it is certainly not a new phenomenon. In his 1968 memoir *My Father and Myself*, published a year after his death, J. R. Ackerley, an active homosexual who had been to bed with scores, if not hundreds of men, described his 'long pursuit of love through sex, out of which, in the end, I emerged as lonely as I began'. The pursuit of love through sex does not have a good record of success, being about as effective as a chocolate teapot.

Premature ejaculation
Premature ejaculation is a relatively common condition in which a man ejaculates earlier than he would prefer, or, more likely, earlier than his partner wants him to. As seventy-five per cent of men usually ejaculate within two minutes of penetration this means premature ejaculators are unbelievably quick off the mark. The problem is frequently psychological in nature and can be caused by anxiety, depression or unrealistic expectations about performance. J. R. Ackerley (see above), who continually suffered

from this 'nuisance', often had no time even to get his trousers off before ejaculation overtook him. In his memoir he remarked, 'A kiss then, the mere pressure of an embrace, if I got as far as that, was enough to finish me off . . .' If you can't get further than a smooch without 'spooging', as I understand it is known, you've got problems and might want to see someone about it.

Because sex problems are often in the head rather than the genitals, Masters and Johnson developed methods for treating premature ejaculation, impotence and female frigidity using two-week psychotherapy (talking) sessions. They claimed a success rate of about eighty per cent. If two weeks' chat can cure everything from impotence to sex addiction in nearly everyone, it ought to be on every sixth form curriculum in the country. It would be more use than Media Studies, anyway.

The disappearing G-Spot

The term 'Gräfenberg Spot', better known as the 'G-Spot', is a term that describes what is claimed to be an erogenous zone inside the vagina which, when stimulated, is said to lead to powerful sexual arousal, orgasms and, sometimes, female ejaculation. It is named after the German gynaecologist Ernst Gräfenberg (1881–1957), who developed the intrauterine device (IUD) and studied the female anatomy during orgasm (during the *woman* having an orgasm, not Gräfenberg). The subject became a topic of lively conversation after publication in 1982 of *The G-Spot and Other Recent Discoveries About Human Sexuality* by Alice Kahn Ladas and Beverly Whipple.

The announcement of this newly discovered spot led to much pipe sucking among sceptical medics, and after a bit they reached the consensus that there was no such thing. This created two camps, of pro- and anti-G-Spotters, and arguments grumbled on for years.

Then, in 2009, a team at King's College London reported that the G-Spot was very probably a figment of women's subjectivity. Their study, the biggest ever of its kind, appeared in the *Journal of Sexual Medicine* in 2010. It described how for fifteen years the team, led by Tim Spector, Professor of Genetic Epidemiology and Director of the Department of Twin Research, examined 1,800 women from identical and non-identical twin pairs. According to the researchers, if one identical twin reported having a G-Spot, the other ought to as well, but this did not happen. Co-author of the study, Swiss clinical psychologist Dr Andrea Burri, said that she believed it was irresponsible for people to claim the existence of a 'G-Spot' that had never been proved to exist and thereby put pressure on women who feared they lacked one.

But people continually insist on the existence of all kinds of things without any evidence, such as astrology, paranormal spoon bending and Bruce Forsyth having a full head of hair, while other people believe them. As might be imagined, Dr Beverly Whipple, co-author of the original bestselling G-Spot book, dismissed the findings.

The elderly
More money is spent today on Viagra and breast implants than on Alzheimer's research. In fifty years' time, there will be lots of old people walking about with pert bosoms and rock-hard erections a cat couldn't scratch but no earthly idea what they are supposed to do with them.

Actually all the jokes about old people and sex are wrong. Dr Patricia Bloom, Associate Professor of Geriatrics at the US Mount Sinai Medical Center, reports that not all old people are held together at either end by Dentafix and Anusol. She remarks that eighty-seven per cent of married men and eighty-nine per cent of married women between sixty and sixty-four years of age are sexually active. Among those over eighty, twenty-nine per cent of men and twenty-five per cent of women still have sex. 'Actually,' she says, 'many of my older patients often remark that the retirement and long-term care homes in which they live can sometimes seem like college dorms, and they're not just talking about social cliques and drinking alcohol.' Nonetheless, problems can, and do, creep up on your nether regions in old age, so a great deal of work has been put in to fixing problems such as erectile dysfunction.

The hard man

In a noteworthy piece of research in 1983, Professor Sir Giles Skey Brindley (fifty-seven), FRCP, FRS, GBE was to address members of the American Urological Association at their annual meeting in Las Vegas, gambling capital of the world. Described by Laurence Klotz, President of the Canadian Urology Association, as belonging 'in the pantheon of famous British eccentrics who have made spectacular contributions to science', Brindley is a neurophysiologist, musicologist, pole-vaulter, marathon runner, composer and cross-country skier. He has invented a musical instrument called the 'logical bassoon' and composed various pieces featuring the instrument, including *Variations on a Theme by Schoenberg*. He is also an expert on penises that have lost their oomph.

On the day of his lecture, Brindley entered the auditorium where he was to speak on the relatively bland-sounding subject of erectile dysfunction. The talk seemed well enough attended and the audience members looked on in anticipation of an unexpected treat from the inventive professor. Many of the urologists were on their way to a black-tie reception and had brought along their wives. Pearls and bow ties were in abundance and couples were sitting in full evening regalia.

Professor Brindley, who had seemed uncharacteristically fidgety in the lift before the lecture, duly mounted the podium and began his talk with a few unremarkable slides. Then suddenly, and without warning, the professor announced that, in his hotel room before the presentation, he had injected himself in the penis with a long-acting vasodilatory drug. This was nothing to him: he had already experimentally injected his penis with thirty-three other drugs (at different times) but he claimed that this one caused long-lasting erections. It was a revolutionary announcement, as all erectile dysfunction had previously been treated with penile implants. Many in the audience were sceptical, so to persuade them of the truth of his seminal announcement Brindley dropped his trousers and pants, revealing, as one person recalled, a 'long, clearly erect penis'.

The sense of drama in the room was described as 'palpable'. People were agog as, trying not to catch their wives' eyes, the black-tied urologists shifted uncomfortably in their seats. Everyone seemed to have stopped breathing and an eerie hush hung over the room as Brindley announced, 'I'd like to give some of the audience the opportunity to confirm the degree of tumescence.' There were gasps, then, without more ado, and under the quiet whirr of the air conditioning, he waddled down the stairs into the auditorium, his erection wagging in front of him like the tiller of a narrowboat in a stiff breeze.

The professor shuffled towards several discombobulated urologists in the front row, pants around his knees, but screams from a few of the ballgowned ladies obliged him to pull up his trousers and return to the podium.

Nonetheless he had made a distinct impression and achieved a first (in more than one way), establishing that a long-lasting erection could be produced with the injection of a drug. It looked as if penile implants could be on the way out.

An unembarrassed Brindley published his findings a few months later, launching a new, successful and now long-standing research project in the field of erectile dysfunction.

The little blue pill

With men living to a greater and greater age, research into the problems of the old are becoming increasingly well funded by gigantic pharmaceutical companies. Being so common, cardio-vascular disease is an area of great interest. Less than ten years after Professor Brindley's audacious revelations, the multinational pharmaceutical firm Pfizer (rhymes with Tizer) was researching sildenafil citrate, a new drug for treating angina (that's the chest pain, not the thing they wrote the monologues about). The drug had been a bit of a let-down in trials and wasn't providing much relief for the heart patients who were swallowing it. However, some previously impotent subjects were reporting a strange and welcome side effect – they were getting erections.

Immediately Pfizer's ears pricked up and by 1995 the drug was showing improved erectile function even in men with spinal cord damage. The company's shareholders were cock-a-hoop and started to dribble in anticipation of gigantic sales income. By this time the drug had a commercial name, Viagra.

Research continued apace and the marketing teams got into gear. In 1997, having been politely asked, the Vatican reportedly gave Viagra its imprimatur, though there is no evidence that the Pope actually tried the stuff himself – or *needed* to. The drug was approved for sale in the US the following year, making it the first effective oral treatment for erectile dysfunction. Viagra was an immediate and huge financial success, making a profit of $411 million in the first three months of its release. It was a win–win situation, Pfizer were laughing all the way to the bank, while thousands of previously disappointed and disappointing men no longer had to try to shoot pool with a rope.

XVI
DIRTY BOOKS, 1
A HISTORY SEXUAL LITERATURE

*

'Love looks not with the eyes, but with the mind.'

WILLIAM SHAKESPEARE

—

The most powerful sexual organ is the one hanging between your ears, and much effort has been spent over the years to stimulate this erogenous zone by perfecting the art of erotic or pornographic literature.

Ex-porn star, now feminist, Gloria Leonard once said, 'The difference between pornography and erotica is lighting.' In literature, the 'lighting' is supplied by the author. In porn, taboos, four-letter words and fetishes run riot. The use of short sentences, blunt sexual terms and a dearth of adjectives is often a mark of frankly pornographic and 'obscene' books, such as *My Secret Life* (see below). Yet the erotic and the pornographic remain cheerful bedfellows. A softer, more descriptive literary style belongs to 'erotica', such as *Fanny Hill* (see below), though to many, it's all 'smut'. Both literary styles contrast with 'romance novels', such as those famously published by Mills and Boon, where gooey euphemism is king.

Some of the earliest erotic books were the first sex manuals, such as the Indian *Kama Sutra* and *The Perfumed Garden*, a sixteenth-century Arabic work. As well as being practical how-to books, these volumes were often beautifully written.

Dirty books have been going a long time in the West too, in fact since the beginning of printing, in 1440. Pietro Aretino

(1492–1556), an influential Italian satirist and pornographer, is commonly said to have invented 'literate pornography'. He is notorious for his ribald tales set in brothels, and his racy *Sonetti Lussuriosi* (Lust Sonnets) described various sexual acts, and were illustrated with delightfully pornographic engravings, causing such affront to the Church and the Establishment that he had to leave Rome in a hurry.

The twentieth century produced several erotic classics, such as Guillaume Apollinaire's *Les onze mille verges* (1907), politely translated as *The Eleven Thousand Rods*, which was partly inspired by de Sade. But it is nothing compared to the memoirs of the creepy Edith Cadivec, an Austrian teacher convicted in 1924 for sexually abusing underage girls, whose two bestselling books, *Confessions and Experiences*, and *Eros: the Meaning of My Life* (published together in 1930–1), are seen by some as classics of erotic literature.

Greek and Roman erotica

Ancient Greece and Rome produced plenty of erotic literature, including poetry. Sappho of Lesbos, Catullus and Ovid, best remembered for his voluminous outpourings of erotic verse, are all still published, while Giovanni Boccaccio's handwritten *Decameron* (1353), all about lecherous monks seducing nuns, may be found in your local library next to the large-print Dorothy L. Sayers. The *Decameron* so upset people that English magistrates were still having it pulped in 1958. Another erotic scorcher was *The Tale of Two Lovers* (1444) by a chap named Aeneas Sylvius Piccolomini, which made it on to the fifteenth century's bestseller lists. Then its author went and spoiled the marketing plan by becoming Pope Pius II.

During the Renaissance many rude poems were privately circulated, and even Shakespeare got in on the racket, but his saucy verses, such as *Venus and Adonis*, escaped pulping and are now set texts, mainly, I suppose, because he couched them in fragrant euphemism.

Writing in *Fair of Speech: The Uses of Euphemism* (1985), Joseph Epstein says there are 'times and places where it will not do to call a spade a spade, let alone other things other things, and sex is surely one of them'. He says that without euphemism sex is 'chilling, even loathsome'. He may have a point, but in pornography calling a spade a 'long-handled digging implement' doesn't really do the trick.

'The Merry Gang'

Restoration rake John Wilmot, Earl of Rochester (1647–80), wrote fantastically obscene poems. Rochester was a drunken wit, and member of a group of naughty boys known as the Merry Gang. His charming poem, *A Ramble in St. James's Park,* starts off like this,

> Much Wine had past, with grave Discourse,
> Of who Fucks who, and who do's worse;
> Such as you usually do hear
> From them that Diet at the *Bear*;
> When I, who still take care to see
> Drunk'nness Reliev'd by Letchery,
> Went out into St. *James*'s Park,
> To cool my Head, and fire my Heart;
> But though St. *James* has the Honour ont!
> 'Tis Consecrate to *Prick* and *Cunt.*

Rochester also wrote *The Quintessence of Debauchery* (1684), a play in which the quaintly named Bolloxinion, King of Sodom, authorizes 'that buggery may be used o'er all the land, so cunt be not abused'. His poems were never read on *Jackanory* and he died at the age of thirty-three, it is presumed from VD and his vast intake of alcohol.

Other toff poets and members of the Merry Gang also took pleasure in the vulgar tongue, as if letting their posh hair down. These included dramatist Sir Charles Sedley (who was once tried for a gross breach of public decency in Covent Garden) and dodgy poet Charles Sackville, the somewhat excessive 6th Earl of Dorset.

The eighteenth century

In 1763, a collection of four erotic poems attributed to the radical journalist John Wilkes, entitled *An Essay on Woman*, was published in England. The verses include a take-off of Pope's *A Dying Christian to his Soul*, called *The Dying Lover to his Prick*. These poems were pronounced obscene and blasphemous after being read out in the House of Lords, the only time such filth has been performed from the red benches, which seems a bit of a shame. The nearest anyone might have come was in 2011, when the delightful Lady Trumpington gave Lord King the traditional two-finger salute on telly, when he implied that she was looking 'pretty old'.

Bawdy songs also appealed to Robert Burns (1759–96), the Bard of Ayrshire, who was a great collector of old Scottish folk ditties, published as *The Merry Muses of Caledonia*. He wrote a song alarmingly entitled 'Cock Up Your Beaver' – which is actually quite innocuous, being about a sort of hat. French philosopher Diderot's *Les Bijoux indiscrets* (1747) even tells of a magic ring which causes ladies' pudenda to relate their sexual histories. It was, perhaps, the *Vagina Monologues* of its time.

Giacomo Girolamo Casanova de Seingalt's *Histoire de ma vie* (*My Life Story*) endlessly reports how brilliant he was in the seduction department. Indeed, without his own boasts he might now be forgotten. At the end of the century the Marquis de Sade broadened the field a bit by writing books containing descriptions of sadism, although it wasn't called that then, obviously. During this period, the novel was taking hold as a literary form in England

and the pornographic novel was, naturally, hard on its heels. One of the first, and now the most famous, was *Fanny Hill* (1748) by John Cleland (see below).

Victorian values

The quality of erotic fiction sank to something of a low during the Victorian period. Obvious titles such as *My Lustful Adventures*, by the conspicuously named 'Ramrod', were ground out by the pound and unsubtle sexual 'memoirs' became popular. Of these, Edward Sellon's *The Ups and Downs of Life* (1867) was one of the less sophisticated, and the notoriously long *My Secret Life* by 'Walter' (see below), was undoubtedly the filthiest.

Taboos were now the lifeblood of porn. The erotic novella *Venus in Furs* (1870) by the Austrian author Leopold von Sacher-Masoch dealt with what came to be known as 'masochism', and pioneering gay erotica made its appearance in the shape of *The Sins of the Cities of the Plain* (1881). This volume featured as characters a pair of real transvestites: Earnest Boulton, who was known to friends as 'Stella', and Frederick William Park, who laboured under the name 'Fanny'. These two were often mistaken for women as they trolled round London in drag. In *The Sins of the Cities* the transvestite narrator tells how he meets Boulton and Park and spends the night with them, 'all dressed as ladies', in their rooms in Eaton Square (see Lord Boothby, chapter XI). A court case, in which the two were accused of 'unnatural practices' in a dark alleyway, involved Lord Arthur Pelham-Clinton (1840–70), who had once lived with 'Stella', as his 'husband'.

Flagellation

Charles Carrington (1867–1921), who operated his literary business out of Paris for legal reasons was the proud publisher of *Raped on the Railway: a True Story of a Lady who was first ravished and then flagellated on the Scotch Express* (1894). This failed to win the Nobel Prize for Literature, and the lumpy title left little to the imagination. Erotic flagellation was big with the Victorians. *Early Experiences of A Young Flagellant* (1876) by one Rosa Coote was a book typical of the genre. The subject was covered in verse too. Decadent poet Algernon Charles Swinburne (1837–1909) was a great churner-out of pornographic verse on this subject. Some of Swinburne's dirty flogging poetry appeared anonymously in the wittily titled *Whippingham Papers* (c. 1888), and his poem *The Flogging Block by Rufus Rodworthy* carries the legend, 'annotated by Barebum Birchingly'. Now it might be true that young Algernon was good with a rhyme, but he plainly wasn't so hot when it came to funny names. *The Rodiad* (Anon.) was another flogging poem of the time, and a year before his death John Camden Hotten (1832–73), compiler of *A dictionary of modern slang, cant, and vulgar words*, wrote a comic flagellation opera called *Lady Bumtickler's Revels*. Sophisticated it wasn't.

The subject of erotic whipping, spanking and beating has been a hot favourite for centuries. An early representation of sexual flagellation appears on a sixth-century BCE Etruscan tomb, the *Tomba della Fustigazione* (the Flogging Tomb). Twentieth-century fans of the sport included T. E. Lawrence (Lawrence of Arabia), theatre critic Kenneth Tynan and *Rumpole of the Bailey* author John Mortimer. Judging by numerous websites devoted to the subject, the practice is still a goer today. Hardly surprisingly, it is widely known as the 'English vice' and in recent times several English celebrities have appeared in the papers, exposed, very unfairly, as enthusiasts.

The limerick

One of the most delightful art forms is the rude limerick, and the nineteenth and twentieth centuries saw the nicest examples of the anonymous art. The better rude limericks avoid coarseness and the best are truly ingenious. W. H. Auden, Kingsley Amis and others were all great fans of this form, which is often sneered at, sometimes rightly, as, along with the good, there are many bad examples. Here are three good ones.

> There was a young lady of Kew
> Who remarked, as the Curate withdrew,
> 'The Vicar is quicker
> And slicker and thicker
> And longer and stronger than you.'

> There was a young girl of Madras
> Who had a magnificent ass;
> Not what you think,
> Soft, round and pink,
> It was grey, had long ears and ate grass.

> There was a young lady of Exeter
> So pretty the men craned their necks at her.
> But some, more depraved,
> Went much further and waved
> The distinguishing marks of their sex at her.

The Irish

The Irish were also to play a part in rude writing during the twentieth century. Erotic publishing was by now a business like any other – though still illegal. Modernist author James Joyce is famous for his novel *Ulysses* (1922), the story of a day in the life of a chap called Leopold Bloom. Joyce chose 16 June 1904 as the date in question because it was the day of his first tryst with his future wife, the alluringly named Nora Barnacle. The final chapter of *Ulysses* consists of a bluntly sexual internal monologue by Molly, Leopold Bloom's wife – a character apparently based on Nora. The frankness of this passage upset people, but what upset me were the eight vast 'sentences' used to express it, one of which is 4,391 words long, with only two full stops. Joyce used to send pornographic letters to Ms Barnacle, whom he called his 'dirty little girl', saying things like, '[I] pulled myself off twice', and asking her to smack, whip or flog him. His romantic streak really came out, though, in pronouncements such as, 'It is wonderful to fuck a farting woman . . .'

Frank Harris (1856–1931) was another Irish-born (though later American) writer and editor. He is best remembered for his long memoir *My Life and Loves* (1922–27, see below), which was banned for its sexual explicitness. Other Irish authors were more circumspect, though W. B. Yeats, who mainly confined himself to the esoteric, did once turn out a poem with the arresting title of *Fanny Power*. This sounds like a feminist slogan, but is actually about a girl waking to the sound of 'two cocks', and her lover knocking at her door.

Lady Chatterley's Lover

'But what about *Lady Chatterley's Lover*?' I hear you cry. First printed privately in Italy in 1928, because it was too rude to be published in the UK, *Lady Chatterley's Lover* became infamous for its graphic descriptions of sex, including a couple of (then) unprintably blunt four-letter words. Another shocking thing for the British, most of whom had never read the book but liked to splutter anyway, was the relationship it explored between a working-class man and an aristocratic woman. This union may have been based on a love affair that the sex-maniac society hostess Lady Ottoline Morrell (known as Lady Utterly Immoral) had with a young stonemason called 'Tiger' when he came to carve plinths in her garden. *Lady Chatterley's Lover* was finally published in Britain in 1960, when it caused quite a squall (see more about this in chapter XVII).

The Girls of Radcliff Hall

During the 1930s the composer, painter, novelist and 'aesthete' Gerald Hugh Tyrwhitt-Wilson, 14th Baron Berners (1883–1950) had an idea, and wrote a rude story under the female pseudonym 'Adela Quebec'. Entitled *The Girls of Radcliff Hall*, the story featured Lord Berners and his 'artistic' friends portrayed as lesbian schoolgirls. This jape was typical of Berners, who, as a boy, had thrown his mother's dog out of the window to teach it to fly. He was sent to boarding school for a short time to sort himself out but instead began a romance with a school chum. This ended in tears when Berners accidentally vomited on the unfortunate boy.

Anyway, among the 'artistic' friends he included in *The Girls of Radcliff Hall* were such famous names as Cecil Beaton and Oliver Messel. Cecil Beaton was said to have tried to have all copies destroyed. One person who seems not to have complained about *The Girls of Radcliff Hall* was Radclyffe Hall (1880–1943), a lesbian writer who was the butt of Berners' wit. Radclyffe Hall is herself best remembered for her lesbian novel *The Well of Loneliness* (1928), a story about a woman named 'Stephen', which the editor of the *Sunday Express* gave a rather poor review. 'I would rather give a healthy boy or a healthy girl a phial of prussic acid than this novel,' he said. They didn't use this quote on the back cover. Perhaps he should have tried reading one of Lord Berners' novels instead: *Romance of a Nose*, say.

In later life Berners kept a giraffe as a companion, dyed pigeons different colours and reportedly attached a notice to the 100-foot viewing tower of his house reading, 'Members of the public committing suicide from this tower do so at their own risk.'

Tropic of Cancer

Henry Miller's novel *Tropic of Cancer* (1934) was first published by the Obelisk Press in Paris but was not published in the US until 1961. Even then it caused a stink because of its frank sexuality, and its publisher was prosecuted for obscenity. Miller followed up with a sequel, *Tropic of Capricorn* (Paris, 1938), which also got into trouble in the US. It was not until 1964 that the US Supreme Court decided these books were not obscene. Indeed, they are now seen as works of great literary importance.

The French

The French were decades ahead of the British and the Americans in their openness to sex in books. In 1954, Pauline Réage's sadomasochistic erotic novel *Histoire d'O* (*The Story of O*) was published in France, where it became a huge hit, causing much guessing as to the true identity of its author. In fact the book was by Anne Desclos (1907–98), a French journalist whose boss, Jean Paulhan, was also her lover. He had challenged her with the observation that no woman could write an erotic novel. Taking the bait, the occasionally bisexual Desclos wrote a graphic sadomasochistic sex story. When it was published, it was so fruity that some doubted that it had really been written by a woman. Desclos kept quiet for forty years, only admitting her authorship to the *New Yorker* in the nineties. Graham Greene called *The Story of O*, 'a rare thing, a pornographic book well written and without a trace of obscenity'. It was French good taste again.

One of the best-known authors of non-obscene high-class female erotica was the French-Cuban Anaïs Nin. She had begun writing pornographic stories in the 1940s for a man she amusingly referred to as a 'collector'. This was a dollar-a-page moneymaking exercise, but in the early seventies Nin agreed to her writings being published. Her books, *Delta of Venus* (1940s) and *Little Birds* (1979), were very well received by literary critics and heavy breathers alike, which is a hard one to pull off.

Lolita

Publishers often found themselves torn between the obvious

commercial potential of an erotic or pornographic title and the probable difficulties of publishing it. Vladimir Nabokov's *Lolita*, the story of a middle-aged professor who becomes sexually involved with a twelve-year-old girl, was turned down by several publishers in America, who regarded the subject as radioactive poison.

Nabokov had intended publishing *Lolita* under the nom de plume 'Vivian Darkbloom', which anagram fans would have had little trouble with, but it was finally published under his own name in 1955, by Olympia Press, a Parisian publisher of rubbishy porn. The title received few reviews until Graham Greene recommended it, despite its liberal sprinkling of typographical errors. The editor of the *Sunday Express* got hold of a copy and reviewed it as 'the filthiest book I have ever read'. One wonders how many filthy books he did read. If it was lots, then why? If it was hardly any, then his review was meaningless.

Although the novel has erotic themes, it did not deserve its instant reputation as 'sheer unrestrained pornography'. In any case, the book was banned in the UK but, as usual, all the fuss just made it highly desirable and the first American edition (1958) sold 100,000 copies in its first three weeks. Moreover, it has since been recognized as a work of high literary merit.

Harold Robbins

Whether the work of Harold Robbins (1916–97) can be regarded as being of high literary merit is a moot question, though he is certainly the most financially successful author of erotic fiction ever. Indeed, he is arguably the most successful author of *anything* ever (apart from the Bible, that is). The graphic sex scenes in his first book, *Never Love a Stranger* (1948), outraged some people, and his work was derided by many. In an episode of *Fawlty Towers* Basil Fawlty calls Robbins' books 'pornographic muzak', but the fans kept buying. In March 1965, he had three novels on the

British paperback bestseller list. He sold something like 750 million copies, and earned about $50 million while he was alive. He owned several homes, two yachts and fourteen cars, including a white Rolls-Royce. His valuable art collection contained paintings by Picasso but also by Bernard Buffet, a terrible painter of clowns and facile 'erotic art', which tells you something.

Naked Came the Stranger

Newsday columnist Mike McGrady was such a non-fan of the 'Big Money' books in the bestseller lists that in 1969 he decided to expose these vulgar paperbacks as trash. He asked twenty-four colleagues each to write one formulaic chapter of a Harold-Robbins-type novel. His rules: (1) everything they wrote should lack all literary merit but contain a lot of boring sex, (2) the prose must drip with cliché and the story be chaotically disorganized, (3) every character should be 'deeply shallow'. Concealing his writers' identities behind the sexy nom de plume 'Penelope Ashe', McGrady gave his book the pretentious title, *Naked Came the Stranger*. This sounded rather like the title of Robbins' first book, *Never Love a Stranger*. The plot, such as it turned out to be, centres on a suburban housewife, Gillian Blake, who revenges herself against her unfaithful husband by fornicating a channel through the men of Long Island. Naturally enough, most of the book is taken up with descriptions of Mrs Blake's bed hopping, including the unlikely 'curing' of a token gay man's homosexuality under the unstoppable influence of her stupendous breasts. Published under a lurid cover, the novel became an enormous hit, zooming into the *New York Times* bestseller list. A highly successful truly terrible film followed in 1975.

Portnoy's Complaint

Another bad film was *Portnoy's Complaint* (1972), which was adapted from the successful and controversial 1969 novel of the same name by Philip Roth. The novel featured explicit and detailed sex scenes including masturbation with a piece of raw liver. *Portnoy's Complaint* is in the form of a monologue by a young sex-obsessed Jewish patient, Alexander Portnoy, to his psychoanalyst, Dr Spielvogel (literally, 'game bird'). Roth said that the format allowed him to use 'intimate, shameful detail, and coarse, abusive language' that might otherwise have been 'pornographic, exhibitionistic, and nothing but obscene'. Despite this, some US libraries banned the book, though customers flocked to the tills.

Sexual intercourse cordon bleu

In 1972, the same year that *Portnoy's Complaint* was emptying the cinemas, *The Joy of Sex: A Gourmet Guide to Lovemaking* hit the bookshops. It was written by the reassuringly named Alex Comfort, MB Bchir, PhD, DSc (1920–2000), a British anarchist, 'aggressive anti-militarist', sex fan, doctor and author who, when young, had lost four fingers from his left hand in an accident.

Comfort authored several books, and occasionally wrote under the pseudonym Obadiah Hornbrooke, a name guaranteed not to draw attention to itself. He decided that his new book *The Joy of Sex: A Gourmet Guide to Lovemaking* was to be less clinical than other sex manuals of the time, and more down to earth. Although this was an instruction manual, the message was that sex, and sexual experiment, could be fun. The 'Cordon Bleu sex' idea was Comfort's. 'It's hard to make mayonnaise by trial and error,' he wrote, and his section headings included such appetizing morsels as 'starters' and 'main courses'. Comfort had taken the food idea from a fantastically successful American cookery book called *Joy of Cooking*, which has been in print since 1936, selling more than 18 million copies to date, though *The Joy of Sex* did not go as far as including post-prandial cigars, nor the question, 'Shall we join the ladies?'

Comfort wrote the book quickly, but managed to give some sage advice to his readers, such as, 'Plan your menus. Nobody wants a seven-course meal every time.' Even to the grumpy British man, who assumed he knew exactly what he was doing when it came to sex, this was a good tip. The book featured a variety of positions for sexual intercourse and a few sexual practices such as oral sex, bondage and swinging, which did not feature in sex manuals of the time. The usual suppliers of such material were dingy shops with yellow plastic covering their windows, which could usually provide whatever was required from under their counters. *The Joy of Sex* brought such activities into the mainstream.

What Alex Comfort did not say was that he himself was an enthusiastic participant in swinging parties in the USA, where he was known as a bit of a lurker, often to be spotted sitting voyeuristically in the shadows, his lonely left thumb sticking out in front of him like a peg.

The Joy of Sex became an immediate hit, notable for its distinctive black-and-white illustrations. These had been done by an illustrator named Chris Foss whose stock in trade was science-fiction book covers depicting vast, gaudily coloured spaceships and alien cities. His tasteful sex illustrations were a delightful contrast, though some of the looming genitalia were occasionally suggestive of spacecraft executing docking manoeuvres.

The illustrations depicting numerous positions for sexual intercourse had been one of the proposed book's main challenges, and the publishers were being very careful. Only the previous year, the editors of the satirical *Oz* magazine had been found guilty of obscenity for publishing a pornographic story featuring Rupert Bear. But, relying on the legal argument previously used success-fully to defend *Lady Chatterley's Lover*, Peter Kindersley, the art director of *The Joy of Sex*, decided that artistic illustrations of quality would protect the publishers from prosecution.

'We were a bit nervous when we took this on', Chris Foss told the BBC in 2012. 'The publisher had to write a contract which confirmed that they would pay our defence if some old fart decided to make an issue out of it.' Comfort too was anxious not to be struck off the medical register and claimed at first just to be the editor of the manuscript, which, he said, had been supplied to him by an anonymous couple. Nonetheless he enthusiastically accepted the royalties, when they began to flow in.

Peter Kindersley finally decided to use tasteful line illustrations based on photographs, and his first stop for models was Soho, London's red light district. This proved a disaster. Though willing, these hard-nosed characters were used to negotiating with clients and would suddenly break off to demand extra money halfway through a session. 'It was just complete chaos,' remembered Kindersley.

The book's colour illustrator, Charles Raymond, then had a brainwave – he volunteered to model the sex positions himself, alongside his German wife, Edeltraud. Edeltraud agreed, and so it happened. During a frenzied two-day sex marathon in Chris Foss's Fulham studio, Charles and Edeltraud disrobed, consulted the manuscript, took up position and got cracking, while Foss focused his lens, wiped off the steam and took the photographs.

As a result of the miners' strike, power cuts would frequently interrupt the shoot, cloaking the studio in darkness. Foss also recalled that the couple would occasionally get a bit carried away, and instead of just posing would go into action for real. 'We'd say, "Charlie, we've only got another twenty minutes," and he'd say, "Oh I'm terribly sorry," and he'd go off to prepare himself to perform again, and Edeltraud would go, "Charles, Charles, please, please come on, we only have ten minutes, please two more positions."'

Peter Kindersley remembered that Alex Comfort was impressed with the photographs because, 'it wasn't a cooked-up thing'. Foss agreed, 'I think the fact that they were in love had something to do with it.' Foss used selected pictures to create his line drawings, which today have a charming period feel. Much of the flavour of the seventies is conjured up by Charles Raymond's long hair and wavy beard.

To Alex Comfort's dismay, *The Joy of Sex* became his most famous book, overshadowing his other work, selling many millions of copies, staying for years on the bestseller lists and earning him $3 million (which he didn't complain about). The book also made him a household name and, Like Alfred Kinsey before him, he swiftly became known as 'Dr Sex'.

The Joy of Sex was not to everyone's taste, however. All that long hair put off *Playboy* magazine, who turned the book down.

Oops!

Despite the commercial astuteness of many publishers of sex books, some naivety persisted amongst a few, even into the twentieth century. None of the real books in the following list were intended to be pornographic, or rude in any way, they just sound it.

Erections on Allotments
Scouts in Bondage
The History of Lesbian Hair
Invisible Dick
Games to Play with Your Pussy
The Attractive Child
Natural Bust Enlargement with Total Mind Power
Gay Story Book
Play With Your Own Marbles
The Day Amanda Came
Willie's Ordeal
The Big Book of Lesbian Horse Stories

How Nell Scored
Masturbation in the American Catholic Church
Shag the Pony (for children)

The Internet

At the end of the twentieth century, the Internet began cutting serious inroads into the dirty book trade. The trend continues apace in the twenty-first century with Internet porn downloadable at the touch of a key. Much of it is now effectively free, and on such sites as Alt Sex Stories Text Repository (asstr.org), there are acres of downloadable smut, written by amateurs. In nearly every case, this shows.

But erotic books are still making an impression and prostitution continues to be a popular subject. In 2005, *The Intimate Adventures of a London Call Girl* became a top ten bestseller. Written under the pseudonym 'Belle de Jour', the book was based on a weblog recording the daily doings of a London call girl. The blog had been written pseudonymously by research scientist Dr Brooke Magnanti who, while finishing her PhD, had made a bit of cash doing sex work in London. The book showed that there is no reason a serious scientist cannot also be a call girl and write literate erotica. Dr Magnanti became a contributor to the online magazine *Freedom in a Puritan Age*, and continues to write for print and on her blogs.

In 2011, British author E. L. James had a worldwide smash hit with her erotic novel *Fifty Shades of Grey*. It is the fastest-selling paperback ever in the UK, but critical reception has been cool. The *Telegraph* called it 'treacly cliché'. Harold Robbins eat your heart out.

Whether dirty books are hindered by censorship is an interesting question. Some of the most successful dirty books have been given a huge publicity boost after being banned. You can check out a few of these in the next chapter.

XVII
Cut That Out!
Censorship – a brief unexpurgated history

*

'If you can't say fuck,
you can't say, fuck the government.'
LENNY BRUCE

Psychologists say that those who cannot control their emotions try instead to control the behaviour of those who are upsetting them. The trouble is that a censor is like is a man with a hammer, looking for nails to hit. When he runs out of nails he is liable to hammer anything he can find.

In England, erotic and pornographic publications were originally the responsibility of the Church courts. After the sixteenth-century English Reformation the Crown took more control, licensing every printed book. They say that obscenity is whatever gives the judge an erection, and the first conviction for obscenity in England was in 1727, when Edmund Curll was fined for the publication of *Venus in the Cloister*, or *The Nun in her Smock*, the title of which gives a good idea of its content.

Ten years later, the Licensing Act 1737 made the senior official of the Royal Household – the Lord Chamberlain – responsible for stopping the performance of any new play he didn't personally care for. Theatre owners found themselves in the uncomfortable position of laying themselves open to prosecution if they put on a play that the Lord Chamberlain hadn't seen and okayed beforehand. The Theatres Act 1968 finally got rid of this daft rule, but the first London performance of the musical *Hair* only just scraped through. Having been refused a licence, it was held up until the act had been passed.

The world's first law criminalizing pornography was the Obscene Publications Act 1857, which made the sale of obscene material an offence in Britain (except in Scotland), giving the courts power to seize and destroy offending material. One shortcoming of the act was that it failed to define 'obscene', leaving the courts with a terrible headache for many decades to come.

In 1868 Lord Chief Justice Sir Alexander Cockburn decided that the test of obscenity was whether the book, or whatever it was, tended 'to deprave and corrupt those whose minds are open to such immoral influences . . .' regardless of its artistic or literary merit. This showed nicely the Victorian attitude that porn was OK for some (the well-off and educated) but harmful for others (the great unwashed). What exactly they meant by 'deprave and corrupt' was not spelled out so it didn't really put a stop to arguments.

The UK has less of this kind of nonsense now than it used to, although it is running to keep up with other more groovy European nations. Interestingly, the USA has more laws governing sexual behaviour than all the countries of Europe put together.

One of the UK's most charming offshoots of its one-time obsession with censorship is the Secretum of the British Museum. Also known as Room 55 and Cupboard 55, the Secretum was a locked cabinet in the Department of Medieval and Later Antiquities. It originally contained the collection of ancient erotica donated by George Witt (1804–69), doctor and collector of phallic antiquities in 1865, consisting of 434 diverse objects described as 'Symbols of the Early Worship of Mankind', many of which were just phalluses.

Cupboard 55 was inaccessible by the public for years but in the thirties, many of the erotic exhibits began to be dispersed around the museum and integrated into their respective cultural collections. One of the most interesting aspects of these items is that, though the claim was that they had been made by artisans from ancient cultures, many of them were just Victorian fakes.

Some banned books

In 1999 an American newspaper reported that its local high school had told children that they must get special permission before they could read three very shocking plays by a long-haired English playwright. The corrupting titles of these works were *Hamlet*, *Macbeth* and *King Lear*, all by that disgusting pervert, William Shakespeare. Three years earlier, another of his filthy works, *Twelfth Night*, was pulled by a New Hampshire school, falling foul of the school board's Prohibition of Alternative Lifestyle Instruction Act. Mark Twain said, 'In the first place, God made idiots. That was for practice. Then he made school boards.' I suppose that the boards which banned *Twelfth Night* and *Hamlet* had read and seen neither but had been told they contained rude words. Here is the material that I suspect might have terrified them.

In *Twelth Night* Malvolio is examining the handwriting of a love letter to see if it has been written by his lady.

> MALVOLIO: By my life, this is my lady's hand these be her very C's, her U's and her T's and thus makes she her great P's. It is, in contempt of question, her hand.

In performance, 'and her T's' would sound like 'N her T's', thus spelling out 'cunt'. Her 'great P's' is a vulgarity as easily understood by Elizabethan audiences as by the modern schoolboy.

Shakespeare's reference to the C-word appears also in *Hamlet*, when the prince is chatting up the luscious Ophelia. I've italicized the word that probably upset the school board.

HAMLET: Lady, shall I lie in your lap?

OPHELIA: No, my lord.

HAMLET: I mean, my head upon your lap?

OPHELIA: Ay, my lord.

HAMLET: Do you think I meant *country* matters?

OPHELIA: I think nothing, my lord.

HAMLET: That's a fair thought to lie between a maid's legs.

OPHELIA: What is, my lord?

HAMLET   Nothing.

The idea that banning some of the greatest plays ever written because they contained a rude word doesn't seem to have struck the school boards as nutty. The trouble is, people will try banning anything if society is permissive enough to let them.

FANNY HILL

In the nineteenth century the publication and sale of pornography and erotica, whether written or pictorial, were outlawed in the UK. *Fanny Hill* by John Cleland (see chapter XVIII), first published in England in 1748 is possibly the most banned book in history.

The novel was published in two instalments but it was only in 1749, a year after the first part was published, that Cleland was charged with corrupting the king's subjects. He regretted all the fuss and renounced the novel, which was then officially withdrawn. The book eventually reached the United States, where it was banned for obscenity in 1821. Not until 1963, after the failure of the British obscenity trial of *Lady Chatterley's Lover* in 1960, was an unexpurgated edition of *Fanny Hill* published.

LADY CHATTERLEY'S LOVER

In 1959, Penguin Books had issued a complete and unexpurgated edition of D. H. Lawrence's *Lady Chatterley's Lover*. The pages of the book were sprinkled with the word 'fuck', a word first recorded in a poem written some time before 1500, but considered unprintable by the Establishment. Even more shocking was the word 'cunt', which has been around since at least the thirteenth century but which has a mysterious – almost magical – power to make people gasp. The book sold out.

Penguin were taken to court under the Obscene Publications Act of 1959 but the publishers saw their chance to test the new defence that a book was not obscene if it was of literary merit. At the trial, prosecutor Mervyn Griffith-Jones asked whether the book was one 'you would wish your wife or servants to read?' revealing himself to be a bit out of touch with ordinary mortals, some of whom might have been on the jury. Various academics and august literary critics, including E. M. Forster and Richard Hoggart spoke up for *Lady Chatterley's Lover* and the publisher was found not guilty by the jury of unshocked men and women.

In later prosecutions of literary erotica, even pornographic works of no literary merit were allowed through, and these days almost anything, excluding violent or paedophile pornography, goes. Here are a few stupidly banned books that came a cropper over the years.

- *Candide* by Voltaire: seized by US Customs in 1930 for obscenity.
- *Brave New World* by Aldous Huxley: banned in Ireland in 1932, because of references to sexual promiscuity.
- *The Diary of Anne Frank* by Anne Frank: banned from schools in Virginia, after complaints about 'sexual themes'.
- *Phallus in Wonderland*: in 1966, W. H. Smith's banned Gavin Ewart's long erotic poem, which was already thirty-three years old.
- *Lolita* by Vladimir Nabokov: banned in France, the UK,

Argentina, New Zealand and South Africa on grounds of obscenity. A famous edition later appeared showing a girl on the cover, sucking a lollypop.

- *Madame Bovary* by Gustave Flaubert: generally agreed to be a classic work of literature. Flaubert was prosecuted for offences against public morals.
- *Ulysses* by James Joyce: banned in the UK during the 1930s, and in the US, for its sexual content. I got to page six. Twice. Shan't bother again.
- *The Well of Loneliness* by Radclyffe Hall: banned in the UK in 1928 for its homosexual theme.

Dirty films

Hollywood films made between 1930 and 1968 all came under the Motion Picture Production Code, a set of censorship guidelines popularly known as the Hays Code, after Hollywood's big-cheese censor of the time, Will H. Hays. The Hays Code contained a delightful list of dangerous and forbidden subjects including 'impure love' and 'dancing'. Here are a few:

- Any licentious or suggestive nudity;
- White slavery [i.e. sex slavery];
- Any inference of sex perversion;
- Miscegenation;
- Sex hygiene and venereal diseases;
- The sale of women, or of a woman selling her virtue;
- Rape or attempted rape;
- Deliberate seduction;
- Excessive or lustful kissing.

Deep Throat (1972) was one of the first pornographic films to feature an actual plot and non-cardboard characters. Despite being banned in some places, it entered the mainstream and chalked up the highest budget-to-box-office ratio ever, costing $22,000 to make and pulling in an astonishing $100 million.

Surprisingly few films have actually been banned but there are a few that were felt to be a bit much, over the years. Here are some of them.

- In 1917 a family-planning film called *Birth Control* was banned in the USA, 'in the interest of morality, decency, and public safety and welfare'.

- *I Am Curious (Yellow)* is a 1967 Swedish drama called *Jag är nyfiken – en film i gult* in the original, in which there is much nudity and (pretend) sexual intercourse. In one controversial scene, the heroine kisses her boyfriend's (flaccid) penis. These days, there would be howls of protest, not at the obscenity but the apparent erectile dysfunction. The film was banned in 1969 in Massachusetts for being pornographic but was later declared non-obscene and unbanned. What great publicity.

- Unlike *I Am Curious (Yellow)*, *Cocksucker Blues* has remained banned since 1973. It is a documentary of the Rolling Stones' 1972 US tour, and features the boys taking drugs and having sex with people. When the band, who had commissioned the film, regained consciousness and saw it for the first time, they came to the mature conclusion that its content might conceivably embarrass them. The film may therefore not be legally shown unless director Robert Frank is physically present.

XVIII
Dirty Books, 2

An anthology of sexual literature

*

'Sex is a three-letter word which needs some old-fashioned
four-letter words to convey its full meaning.'

ANON.

'To the man who loves art for its own sake it is frequently in its least important and lowliest manifestations that the keenest pleasure is to be derived.' So said Sherlock Holmes, and good pornographic writing is a nice illustration of his point. In this section you can read four carefully selected extracts from some renowned, not to say notorious, sex books. There's everything here from saucy erotica to salty lowbrow memoirs. All of these works possess some literary merit and have survived in print to this day, but only two, *Fanny Hill* and *My Life and Loves*, appear to have been written in order to titillate the reader. *The Perfumed Garden* is educational and *My Secret Life* is a starkly candid auto-biographical diary of prodigious sexual enterprise.

Fanny Hill by John Cleland

First published in England in 1748, John Cleland's *Memoirs of a Woman of Pleasure*, or *Fanny Hill* as it is more popularly known, is the first published piece of English prose pornography, and the first recorded erotic novel.

Cleland composed the book while he was in debtor's prison in London. Following publication he was arrested and the book officially withdrawn for more than a hundred years. Banning books makes them very marketable commodities and *Fanny Hill* continued selling well in unofficial editions but was not officially published in full until the 1960s.

Though written by a man, *Fanny Hill* adopts the point of view of a woman. It contains various taboo subjects, including flagellation (almost compulsory in British porn from then on) and a notorious sodomy scene, which disappeared from later editions. Fanny also seems to be overly impressed by penis size, and goes on about it at length. Because of all this, some critics have suggested that the unmarried ex-public schoolboy Cleland was homosexual.

From the outset *Fanny Hill* reads like a proper book and its sentences are beautifully composed, if long. Its second sentence contains 134 words. In contrast to *My Secret Life* (see below), which resembles nothing so much as a pathologist's unvarnished autopsy report, Cleland's artistic euphemism leaves something to the reader's imagination. It is the difference between the delightful window display of a Parisian patisserie and the sights and smells of an East End butcher's shop.

Here's a bit of *Fanny Hill,* from the second part, entitled *Letter the Second:*

> One morning then, that both Mrs. Cole and Emily were gone out for the day, and only Louisa and I (not to mention the house-maid) were left in charge of the house, whilst we were loitering away the time, in looking through the shop windows, the son of a poor woman, who earned very hard bread indeed by mending of stockings, in a stall in the neighbourhood, offer'd us some nosegays, ring'd round a small basket; by selling of which the poor boy eked out his mother's maintenance of them both: nor was he fit for any other way of livelihood, since he was not only a perfect

changeling, or idiot, but stammer'd so that there was no understanding even those sounds his halfdozen, at most, animal ideas prompted him to utter.

The boys and servants in the neighbourhood had given him the nickname of *good-natured Dick*, from the soft simpleton's doing every thing he was bid at the first word, and from his naturally having no turn to mischief; then, by the way, he was perfectly well made, stout, clean-limb'd, tall of his age, as strong as a horse, and, withal, pretty featur'd; so that he was not, absolutely, such a figure to be snuffled at neither, if your nicety could, in favour of such essentials, have dispens'd with a face unwashed, hair tangled for want of combing, and so ragged a plight, that he might have disputed points of shew with e'er a heathen philosopher of them all.

This boy we had often seen, and bought his flowers, out of pure compassion, and nothing more; but just at this time as he stood presenting us his basket, a sudden whim, a start of wayward fancy, seized Louisa; and, without consulting me, she calls him in, and beginning to examine his nosegays, culls out two, one for herself, another for me, and pulling out half a crown, very currently gives it him to change, as if she had really expected he could have changed it: but the boy, scratching his head, made his signs explaining his inability in place of words, which he could not, with all his struggling, articulate.

Louisa, at this, says: 'Well, my lad, come up-stairs with me, and I will give you your due,' winking at the same time to me, and beckoning me to accompany her, which I did, securing first the street-door, that by this means, together with the shop, became wholly the care of the faithful house-maid.

As we went up, Louisa whispered me that she had

conceived a strange longing to be satisfy'd, whether the general rule held good with regard to this changeling, and how far nature had made him amends, in her best bodily gifts, for her denial of the sublimer intellectual ones; begging, at the same time, my assistance in procuring her this satisfaction. A want of complaisance was never my vice, and I was so far from opposing this extravagant frolic, that now, bit with the same maggot, and my curiosity conspiring with hers, I enter'd plump into it, on my own account.

Consequently, soon as we came into Louisa's bed-chamber, whilst she was amusing him with picking out his nosegays, I undertook the lead, and began the attack. As it was not then very material to keep much measures with a mere natural, I made presently free with him, though at my first motion of meddling, his surprise and confusion made him receive my advances but awkwardly: nay, insomuch that he bashfully shy'd, and shy'd back a little; till encouraging him with my eyes, plucking him playfully by the hair, sleeking his cheeks, and forwarding my point by a number of little wantonnesses, I soon turn'd him familiar, and gave nature her sweetest alarm: so that arous'd, and beginning to feel himself, we could, amidst all the innocent laugh and grin I had provoked him into, perceive the fire lighting in his eyes, and, diffusing over his cheeks, blend its glow with that of his blushes. The emotion in short of animal pleasure glar'd distinctly in the simpleton's countenance; yet struck with the novelty of the scene, he did not know which way to look or move; but tame, passive, simpering, with his mouth half open, in stupid rapture, stood and tractably suffer'd me to do what I pleased with him. His basket was dropt out of his hands, which Louisa took care of.

I had now, through more than one rent, discovered and felt his thighs, the skin of which seemed the smoother and fairer for the coarseness, and even dirt of his dress, as the teeth of Negroes seem the whiter for the surrounded black; and poor indeed of habit, poor of understanding, he was, however, abundantly rich in personal treasures, such as flesh, firm, plump, and replete with the juices of youth, and robust well-knit limbs. My fingers too had now got within reach of the true, the genuine sensitive plant, which, instead of shrinking from the touch, joys to meet it, and swells and vegetates under it: mine pleasingly informed me that matters were so ripe for the discovery we meditated, that they were too mighty for the confinement they were ready to break. A waistband that I unskewer'd, and a rag of a shirt that I removed, and which could not have cover'd a quarter of it, revealed the whole of the idiot's standard of distinction, erect, in full pride and display: but such a one! It was positively of so tremendous a size, that prepared as we were to see something extraordinary, it still, out of measure, surpass'd our expectation, and astonish'd even me, who had not been used to trade in trifles. In fine, it might have answered very well the making a skew of; its enormous head seemed, in hue and size, not unlike a common sheep's heart; then you might have troll'd dice securely along the broad back of the body of it; the length of it too was prodigious; then the rich appendage of the treasure-bag beneath, large in proportion, gather'd and crisp'd up round in shallow furrows, helped to fill the eye, and complete the proof of his being a natural, not quite in vain; since it was full manifest that he inherited, and largely too, the prerogative of majesty which distinguishes that otherwise most unfortunate condition, and gave rise to the vulgar saying 'That a fool's bauble is a lady's playfellow.' Not wholly without reason: for, generally speaking, it is in love as it is in war, where the longest weapon carries it. Nature, in short, had done so much for him in those parts, that she perhaps held herself acquitted in doing so little for his head.

For my part, who had sincerely no intention to push the joke further than simply satisfying my curiosity with the sight of it alone, I was content, in spite of the temptation that star'd me in the face, with having raised a maypole for another to hang a garland on: for, by this time, easily reading Louisa's desires in her wishful eyes, I acted the commodious part, and made her, who sought no better sport, significant terms of encouragement to go through-stitch with her adventure; intimating too that I would stay and see fair play: in which, indeed, I had in view to humour a new-born curiosity, to observe what appearances active nature would put on in a natural, in the course of this her darling operation.

Louisa, whose appetite was up, and who, like the industrious bee, was, it seems, not above gathering the sweet of so rare a flower, tho' she found it planted on a dunghill, was but too readily disposed to take the benefit of my cession. Urg'd then strongly by her own desires, and embolden'd by me, she presently determined to risk a trial of parts with the idiot, who was by this time nobly inflam'd for her purpose, by all the irritation we had used to put the principles of pleasure effectually into motion, and to wind up the springs of its organ to their supreme pitch; and it stood accordingly stiff and straining, ready to burst with the blood and spirits that swelled it . . . to a bulk! No! I shall never forget it.

Louisa then, taking and holding the fine handle that so invitingly offer'd itself, led the ductile youth, by that mastertool of his, as she stept backward towards the bed; which he joyfully gave way to, under the incitations of instinct, and palpably deliver'd up to the goad of desire.

Stopped then by the bed, she took the fall she lov'd, and

leaned to the most, gently backward upon it, still holding fast what she held, and taking care to give her clothes a convenient toss up, so that her thighs duly disclos'd, and elevated, laid open all the outward prospect of the treasury of love: the rose-lipt overture presenting the cock-pit so fair, that it was not in nature even for a natural to miss it. Nor did he: for Louisa, fully bent on grappling with it, and impatient of dalliance or delay, directed faithfully the point of the battering-piece, and bounded up with a rage of so voracious appetite, to meet and favour the thrust of insertion, that the fierce activity on both sides effected it with such pain of distention, that Louisa cry'd out violently, that she was hurt beyond bearing, that she was killed. But it was too late: the storm was up, and force was on her to give way to it; for now the man-machine, strongly work'd upon by the sensual passion, felt so manfully his advantages and superiority, felt withal the sting of pleasure so intolerable, that maddening with it, his joys began to assume a character of furiousness, which made me tremble for the too tender Louisa. He seemed, at this juncture, greater than himself; his countenance, before so void of meaning, or expression, now grew big with the importance of the act he was upon. In short, it was not now that he was to be play'd the fool with. But, what is pleasant enough, I myself was aw'd into a sort of respect for him, by the comely terrors his motions dressed him in: his eyes shooting sparks of fire; his face glowing with ardours that gave another life to it; his teeth churning; his whole frame agitated with a raging ungovernable impetuosity: all sensibly betraying the formidable fierceness with which the genial instinct acted upon him. Butting then and goring all before him, and mad and wild like an over-driven steer, he ploughs up the tender furrow all insensible to Louisa's complaints; nothing can stop, nothing can keep out a fury like his: with which, having once got its head in, its blind rage soon made way for the rest, piercing, rending, and breaking open all obstruction. The torn, split, wounded girl cries, struggles, invokes me to her rescue, and endeavours to get from under the young savage, or shake him off, but alas! in vain: her breath, might as soon have still'd or stemm'd a storm in winter, as all her strength have quell'd his rough assault, or put him out of his course. And indeed, all her efforts and struggles were manag'd with such disorder, that they serv'd rather to entangle, and fold her the faster in the twine of his boisterous arms; so that she was tied to the stake, and oblig'd to fight the match out, if she died for it. For his part, instinct-ridden as he was, the expressions of his animal passion, partaking something of ferocity, were rather worrying than kisses, intermix'd with eager ravenous love-bites on her cheeks and neck, the prints of which did not wear out for some days after.

My Secret Life, by 'Walter'

Banned for nearly 100 years *My Secret Life* by the pseudonymous 'Walter' is the sexual memoir of a Victorian gentleman. The first thing you notice about this work is that it is more than a million words long. Published in *eleven* volumes, *My Secret Life* was privately printed over a period of seven years, starting with just twenty-five copies some time around 1888, the year bicycles were introduced on to British roads.

The book's first uncensored US publication was in 1966, but even as late as 1969 a British printer got two years in prison for reprinting it in the UK. It was not until 1995 that the work was finally published without legal trouble.

My Secret Life is written with a detached, almost third-person objectivity, and seemingly with no attempt to titillate. 'Walter's compulsive sexual encounters are almost exclusively with unglamorous prostitutes, or servants, which is typically Victorian. Unlike *Fanny Hill*, the text is all over the place, and its repetitive and straightforward qualities become tiresome very fast. Though it is full of events, it is a bore to read more than a few pages of it. The narrative lacks the lightness of touch of *Fanny Hill*, and, unlike Frank Harris's *My Life and Loves*, the bleak style does not even attempt to make an attractive hero of the author.

'Walter's' descriptions resemble a private detective's routine report on a suspect: systematic, unemotional and unshaded by tenderness or euphemism. The sexual bluntness is unwavering, even by today's standards. 'Walter' is a man who does indeed call a spade a spade; and his sex drive seems equalled only by his compulsion to tell us about the mechanics in every last lurid detail. Reading this stuff is like staring into a bright blue sky. This is not to say that it is *badly* written: 'a building of Swiss type appeared on a little eminence about a hundred feet from the river' is rather nice, for example, and the million words are fascinating as an example of pornographic Victoriana.

'Walter's' true identity is still debated. He may well have been Henry Spencer Ashbee (1834–1900), a Victorian porn aficionado and Cervantes expert who composed a vast bibliography of filthy literature, under the rude pseudonym Pisanus Fraxi, a blunt pun on a Latin version of his real name: 'Fraxinus' (ash) and 'Apis' (bee). Ashbee amassed thousands of volumes of erotica, which are now in the British Library (except for the six boxes of 'offensive matter which is of no value or interest', which they simply burnt). Among Ashbee's sex-mad friends were some of the usual suspects: Algernon Charles Swinburne, Richard Monckton Milnes (Baron Houghton), who kept pestering Florence Nightingale for a bit of a snog, and Sir Richard Burton.

'Walter' appears to be what would today be called a 'sex addict', and you get the feeling that there's something wrong 'upstairs'. It seems such a waste of time, all that relentless sex, and all that writing about it. I mean, what about the rest of life? If this is his *secret* life, how dull must his public life have been?

In photographs, Ashbee senior wears a somewhat rumpled beard and a buttoned-up suit that suggests gravy stains. It's a wonder he managed to have as much sex as he claimed to. He was curiously conservative in his opinions (apart from sex, that is) and his suffragette wife got on his nerves, as he must surely have got on hers. His relationship with his son, Charles, who was a contrast to his father, being a homosexual socialist, was not good either and the pair became estranged.

The following excerpt is from volume 10 of *My Secret Life*, which opens in the style of the time with a brief list of the charming subjects covered including 'Crabs', 'Exhibition of wet quims', 'At a Swiss village', 'Invitation to anus', 'Clapped' and 'Outside a metropolitan railway station'. One interesting thing about *My Secret Life* is the slang usage that survives today, with everything here from 'randy' to 'bum' to 'grope'. For those less-well-known words, here is a brief glossary.

> demirep: a woman of suspicious chastity (demi-reputation)
> motte: pubic mound
> pego: the penis
> quim: the female genitalia

From *My Secret Life* by 'Walter', vol. 10, chapter II:

> I found to my annoyance one hot morning that crabs had assailed me, had lodged in motte, bum furrow, anus, and the wrinkles of my scrotum. It's impossible to say where I got these irritators of the genitals, having varied recently my amours, and a night or two before had revelled in three cunts yet warm and lubricated by other pricks. I keep mine in the ladies till it will remain no longer, luxuriating in their

lubricious baths, giving great chance to these parasites of changing their abode, and I have escaped them well I think. The annihilation of the crustacea took quite ten days, and caused me much inconvenience. In the month of September I was at the little village of **** in Switzerland. There was [then] a little building called a casino, to which people went to read the journals situated in small grounds filled with trees and large shrubs. It was a dull, muggy afternoon, and had been raining hard when I wandered there just before the *table d'hote*. Few people were out, and walking by herself, quite on the outskirts of the grounds, was a well-grown woman seemingly about twenty-five or more years old, dressed very nicely in dark silk. She never approached the building and I got curious about her, passed and repassed her looking in her face, wondering whether she was of easy virtue or not. She looked at me in return but quite in a casual way, without the least indication of the demirep about her. For all that, as I passed a desire for the woman came over me, and a voluptuous thrill passed through my pego. I had been some days at the place and had never noticed the lady there before, tho I must have seen nearly all the visitors there.

I dined, not thinking any more about her. Soon after, it being quite dark, going towards the casino to read I saw her somewhat nearer the casino than before, but well away from all light and still walking alone. At once I guessed she was a free lover. My dinner had warmed, my pego began to get rebellious for it had not touched strange cunt for nearly two months, and I went towards her. Seeing that, she went further off quite into the dark under some trees and stopped. Next minute I was by her side and heard I could go home with her. We spoke in French, but I don't think she was a Frenchwoman.

She had told me where her lodging was and I agreed to

follow her. She went away by a path I'd not traversed, crossed a wooden trembling bridge over the roaring rushing river, and was soon away from all street lights and human habitation as far as I could see. The road lay alongside the river, it was pitch dark, and at first I kept her just in sight, but as it was much further than I'd expected I got uncomfortable, as it was a spot where a knock on the head could very easily be given, and a body pitched into the river within a few yards of our path would have been thirty miles off before next morning, and had I screamed, the roar of the torrent would have drowned my voice, so I went up to her and said I could go no further. She said we were close by her dwelling and again we walked on.

When I first followed her I wanted to grope her, but she refused it. I got however one hand upon her thigh, the crisp hair of her quim touched my finger, and the feel of her tho slight and but for an instant only, made me thoroughly randy. As I followed her, I thought of her make and possible perfections, as I usually do when I follow a woman. From her walk I guessed she'd good limbs and a fat bum, my cock stood rigidly, pleasurably, and directly I'd crossed the bridge, with one of my old erotic whims I pulled it out of my trowsers, and went along with it sticking out naked. The lewedness of the act pleased me much, absurd as it seems. Hearing someone or something approaching, hastily I tucked it in, but it was only a donkey, I fancy tethered. Then as the distance increased and I grew anxious, my John Thomas drooped, and remained so till she stopped, when desire rose again. There was a huge piece of rock close by there, and I suggested an up-righter against it, but she wouldn't hear of such a thing. On we went now side by side. I was about to refuse going further, when a building of Swiss type appeared on a little eminence about a hundred feet from the river. The light in two windows gladdened me, tho I didn't like to be in that lonely spot with a stranger at that time of night. There was seemingly a balcony all round it as is customary in those chalets. A big man, who was, as well as I could see in the darkness, sitting aginst the steps leading up to it, was smoking a pipe, and apparently took no notice of us, yet I didn't like his being there. Up the steps she went, I following on to the balcony, from which she opened a door into a large bedroom, meanly and coarsely furnished, tho there was everything needed for convenience, and a large common lamp alight. I complained that the light was not enough, whereon without reply she sought and lighted a candle. It was an angle room with windows on two sides, on one side only were short white curtains. The gaunt, naked look of the place, and the noise made by our feet on the naked wooden floor, the complete silence she observed, the gloom seen thro the uncurtained windows, and the roar of the river, I confess made me most uncomfortable – I wished I hadn't come and resolved to pay her and leave.

'What shall I do?' said she, taking off her bonnet. They were the first words she'd uttered in the room. 'Let me feel your cunt and then I'll go,' said I. 'I'll take off my things first,' and she began to undress herself quickly. Her face was very handsome, she had dark hair and luminous dark eyes, and as she pulled off her gown she showed such a fine pair of arms that I forgot my fears, touched them, and then let her strip to her chemise. She sat down and piddled, then washed her quim, then pulled her stockings well up under her garters, and disclosed a very handsome form with thick bushes of dark hair in her armpits. Then to my question she said she was twenty-five.

Then I wanted to see her quim more plainly, but she resisted that a little, nor would she let me bring the light to it. She didn't like to be looked at 'in that vulgar way.' She'd unbuttoned my trowsers and got my prick out, and as soon as it was in her hand said, '*Aha – baisez moi, cheri*' and lain down on the bed, but somehow a feeling came over me that I'd better not have her, said I wouldn't, put down her money, and said I'd leave. 'Oh! come all this way without kissing me? that you shan't.' Getting off the bed she came to me, put the money first into a drawer, then throwing an arm round me kissed me and felt my cock. 'Are you quite well? if you're not quite sure, if there are any of your monthlies about, tell me, you've got the money, and I am quite content.'

She was perfectly well, she replied. 'Kiss me – come – you've paid me – is it likely I'd let you do it if I wasn't well? Oh – kiss me, come take off your things, you're a fine man, you've made me want it so, *baisez moi, cheri*' and laying down she lifted her chemise to her armpits. I saw a fine bust, large thighs, a dark haired motte, desire returned, I threw off coat and waistcoat, with my trowsers on mounted her and in a few minutes had filled her quim with sperm. She enjoyed the embrace as much as I had [. . .]

Two days after I had a clap. Incensed, I was fool enough to go to the chalet [. . .] I had been sitting on a wet stone the day before, which might have irritated my bladder. I hoped it was so. 'Pogh,' said the doctor. 'It's not caused by a cold wet stone, but a hot wet something else.'

The Perfumed Garden **translated by Sir Richard Burton**
Captain Sir Richard Francis Burton, KCMG FRGS (1821–90) was a British explorer, ethnologist, spy, fencer and diplomat. He had travelled all over the world and reportedly spoke twenty-nine languages but could probably only say 'yes', 'no', and 'hello' in some of them. He had a frightening face in photographs and was feared by some who knew him. Burton was a prolific author and

scholar and wrote about everything from falconry to sexual practices. He made an unexpurgated translation of *One Thousand and One Nights* and published the *Kama Sutra* in English. His translation of a fifteenth-century Islamic sex manual, *The Perfumed Garden of Sensual Delight* (*al-rawd al-'âtir fi nuzhati'l khâtir*) described as 'a manual of Arabian erotology', became widely known in 1886. Burton said it presented 'lascivious and obscene matters' in a serious way. Chapter titles include:

- *The Sundry Names given to the Sexual Parts of Men*
- *Concerning the Organs of Generation of Animals*
- *On the Deceits and Treacheries of Women*
- *Concerning the Causes of Impotence in Men*
- *Prescriptions for increasing the Dimensions of small Members, and for making them splendid*

Here are a couple of extracts from *The Perfumed Garden*:

CHAPTER VI
Concerning Everything That Is Favourable to the Act of Coition

Know, O Vizir (God be good to you!), if you would have a pleasant coition, which ought to give an equal share of happiness to the two combatants and be satisfactory to both, you must first of all toy with the woman, excite her with kisses, by nibbling and sucking her lips, by caressing her neck and cheeks. Turn her over in bed, now on her back, now on her stomach, till you see by her eyes that the time for pleasure is near, as I have mentioned in the preceding chapter, and certainly I have not been sparing with my observations thereupon.

Then when you observe the lips of a woman to tremble and get red, and her eyes to become languishing, and her sighs to become quicker, know that she is hot for coition, then get between her thighs, so that your member can enter into her vagina. If you have followed my advice, you will have both a pleasant coition, which will give you the greatest satisfaction, and leave to you a delicious remembrance.

Someone has said:

'If you desire the coition, place the woman on the ground, cling closely to her bosom, with her lips close to yours; then clasp her to you, suck her breath, bite her; kiss her breasts, her stomach, her flanks, press her close in your arms, so as to make her faint with pleasure; when you see her so far gone, then push your member into her. If you have done as I said, the enjoyment will come to both of you simultaneously. This it is which makes the pleasure of the woman so sweet. But if you neglect my advice the woman will not be satisfied and you will not have procured her any pleasure.'

The coition being finished, do not get up at once, but come down softly on her right side, and if she has conceived, she will bear a male child, if it please God on high!

Sages and Savants (may God grant to all his forgiveness!) have said:

'If anyone placing his hand upon the vulva of a woman that is with child pronounces the following words. "In the name of God! may he grant salutation and mercy to his Prophet (salutation and mercy be with him). Oh! my God! I pray thee in the name of the Prophet to let a boy issue from this conception," it will come to pass by the will of God, and in consideration for our lord Mohammed (the salutation and grace of God be with him), the woman will be delivered of a boy.'

Do not drink rainwater directly after copulation, because this beverage weakens the kidneys.

If you want to repeat the coition, perfume yourself with

sweet scents, then close with the woman, and you will arrive at a happy result.

Do not let the woman perform the act of coition mounted upon you, for fear that in that position some drops of her seminal fluid might enter the canal of your *verge* [dick] and cause a sharp uretritis.

Do not work hard directly after coition; this might affect your health badly, but go to rest for some time.

Do not wash your *verge* directly after having withdrawn it from the vagina of the woman; until the irritation has gone down somewhat; then wash it and its opening carefully. Otherwise, do not wash your member frequently. Do not leave the vulva directly after the emission, as this may cause canker [. . .]

CHAPTER XVIII

Prescription For Increasing the Dimensions of Small Members and For Making Them Splendid

Know, O Vizir (God be good to you!), that this chapter which treats of the size of the virile member, is of the first importance both for men and women. For the men, because from a large and vigorous member there spring the affection and love of the women; for the women, because it is by such members that their amorous passions get appeased, and the greatest pleasure is procured for them. This is evident from the fact that many men, solely by reason of their insignificant member, are, as far as the coition is concerned, objects of aversion to the women, who likewise entertain the same sentiment with regard to those whose members are soft, nerveless, and relaxed. Their whole happiness consists in the use of robust and strong members.

A man, therefore, with a small member, who wants to

make it grand or fortify it for the coitus, must rub it before the copulation with tepid water, until it gets red and extended by the blood flowing into it, in consequence of the heat; he must then anoint it with a mixture of honey and ginger, rubbing it in sedulously. Then let him join the woman; he will procure for her such pleasure that she objects to him getting off her again.

Another remedy consists in a compound made of a moderate quantity of pepper, lavender, galanga, and musk, reduced to powder, sifted and mixed up with honey and preserved ginger. The member, after having been first washed in warm water, is then vigorously rubbed with the mixture; it will then grow large and brawny, and afford to the woman a marvellous feeling of voluptuousness.

A third remedy is the following: wash the member in warm water until it becomes red, and enters into erection. Then take a piece of soft leather, upon which spread hot pitch, and envelop the member with it. It will not be long before the member raises its head, trembling with passion. The leather is to be left on until the pitch grows cold, and the member is again in a state of repose. This operation, several times repeated, will have the effect of making the member strong and thick.

A fourth remedy is based upon the use made of leeches, but only of such as live in water [sic]. You put as many of them into a bottle as can be got in, and then fill it up with oil. Then expose the bottle to the sun, until the heat of the same has effected a complete mixture. Then, with the fluid thus obtained the member is to be rubbed several consecutive days, and it will, by being thus treated, become of a good size and of full dimensions.

For another procedure I will here note the use of an ass's member. Procure one and boil it, together with onions and a large quantity of corn. With this dish feed fowls, which you eat afterwards. One can also macerate the ass's *verge* with oil, and use the fluid thus obtained afterwards for anointing one's member with it, and drinking of it.

Another way is to bruise leeches with oil, and rub the *verge* with this ointment; or, if it is preferred, the leeches may be put into a bottle, and, thus enclosed, buried in a warm dunghill until they are dissolved into a coherent mass and form a sort of liniment, which is used for repeatedly anointing the member. The member is certain to greatly benefit by this.

One may likewise take rosin and wax, mixed with tubipore, asphodel, and cobbler's glue, with which mixture rub the member, and the result will be that its dimensions will be enlarged.

The efficacy of all these remedies is well known, and I have tested them.

And if you believe that, you'll believe *anything*. Good luck tracking down some cobbler's glue.

My Life and Loves by Frank Harris

Born on Valentine's Day, Frank Harris (1856–1931) was a pushy and aggressive Irish-born American writer and editor with big ears, a short temper and a dashing handlebar moustache. He ran away from school as a youth and travelled to the USA, where he studied at the University of Kansas. On returning to England, he became editor of the *Evening News* and moved among the literati and glitterati of his time. He counted Oscar Wilde, H. G. Wells and George Bernard Shaw amongst his friends.

Harris's most famous work is his explicit memoir *My Life and Loves*, which he wrote in his sixties and published privately in Berlin between 1922 and 1927. The four-volume work is well written and is illustrated with delightful drawings and photographs of naked women. Along with a record of larger events, such as the Great Chicago Fire of October 1871, it contains explicit descriptions of Harris's sexual shenanigans. Unlike *My Secret Life*, however, *My Life and Loves* bears the characteristic hallmarks of fiction, or hyperbole anyway. As well as his sexual adventures, Harris records tittle-tattle – sometimes rather unflattering tittle-tattle – about the sex lives of the rich and famous. One is left with the impression that while the self-important author was a brilliant Don Juan, nobody else quite cut the mustard in this department.

This excerpt from *My Life and Loves* records an occasion when Harris was working as a young man in America. The word 'ill', used at the end of the piece, was a longstanding euphemism for what today a chap might call 'being up on blocks', that is to say 'having a menstrual period'.

That same morning Willie recommended to me a pension kept by a Mrs. Gregory, an Englishwoman, the wife of an old Baptist clergyman, who would take good care of me for four dollars a week. Immediately I went with him to see her and was delighted to find that she lived only about a hundred yards from Mrs. Mayhew on the opposite side of the street. Mrs. Gregory was a large, motherly woman evidently a lady, who had founded this boarding-house to provide for a rather feckless husband and two children, a big pretty girl, Kate and a lad, a couple of years younger. Mrs. Gregory was delighted with my English accent, I believe, and showed me special favor at once by giving me a large outside room with its own entrance and steps into the garden.

In an hour I had paid my bill at the Eldridge House and had moved in: I showed a shred of prudence by making Willie promise Mrs. Gregory that he would turn up each

Saturday with the five dollars for my board; the dollar extra was for the big room.

In due course I shall tell how he kept his promise and discharged his debt to me. For the moment everything was easily, happily settled. I went out and ordered a decent suit of ordinary tweeds and dressed myself up in my best blue suit to call upon Mrs. Mayhew after lunch. The clock crawled but on the stroke of three, I was at her door: a colored maid admitted me.

'Mrs. Mayhew', she said in her pretty singing voice, 'will be down right soon: I'll go call Miss Lily.'

In five minutes Miss Lily appeared, a dark slip of a girl with shining black hair, wide laughing mouth, temperamental thick red lips and grey eyes fringed with black lashes: she had hardly time to speak to me when Mrs. Mayhew came in: 'I hope you two'll be great friends,' she said prettily; 'you're both about the same age,' she added.

In a few minutes Miss Lily was playing a waltz on the Steinway and with my arm round the slight, flexible waist of my inamorata I was trying to waltz. But alas! after a turn or two I became giddy and in spite of all my resolution had to admit that I should never be able to dance.

'You have got very pale', Mrs. Mayhew said, 'you must sit down on the sofa a little while.' Slowly the giddiness left me: before I had entirely recovered Miss Lily with kindly words of sympathy had gone home and Mrs. Mayhew brought me in a cup of excellent coffee: I drank it down and was well at once.

'You should go in and lie down,' said Mrs. Mayhew still full of pity, 'see,' and she opened a door, 'there's the guest bedroom all ready.' I saw my chance and went over to her: 'if you'd come too,' I whispered and then, 'the coffee has made me quite well: won't you, Lorna, give me a kiss? You

don't know how often I said your name last night, you dear!'
and in a moment I had again taken her face and put my lips
on hers. She gave me her lips this time and my kiss became
a caress; but in a little while she drew away and said, 'let's sit
and talk, I want to know all you are doing.' So I seated myself
beside her on the sofa and told her all my news. She thought
I would be comfortable with the Gregorys. 'Mrs. Gregory is
a good woman,' she added, 'and I hear the girl's engaged to
a cousin: do you think her pretty?'

'I think no one pretty but you, Lorna,' I said and I pressed
her head down on the arm of the sofa and kissed her. Her
lips grew hot: I was certain. At once I put my hand down on
her sex; she struggled a little at first, which I took care should
bring our bodies closer and when she ceased struggling I put
my hands up her dress and began caressing her sex: it was hot
and wet, as I knew it would be, and opened readily.

But in another moment she took the lead: 'Some one
might find us here,' she whispered, 'I've let the maid go:
come up to my bedroom' and she took me upstairs. I begged
her to undress: I wanted to see her figure; but she only said,
'I have no corsets on, I don't often wear them in the house.
Are you sure you love me, dear!' 'You know I do!' was my
answer. The next moment I lifted her on to the bed, drew
up her clothes, opened her legs and was in her. There was no
difficulty and in a moment or two I came; but went right on
poking passionately; in a few minutes her breath went and
came quickly and her eyes fluttered and she met my thrusts
with sighs and nippings of her sex. My second orgasm took
some time and all the while Lorna became more and more
responsive, till suddenly she put her hands on my bottom
and drew me to her forcibly while she moved her sex up and
down awkwardly to meet my thrusts with a passion I had
hardly imagined. Again and again I came and the longer the

play lasted, the wilder was her excitement and delight. She kissed me hotly foraging and thrusting her tongue into my mouth. Finally she pulled up her chemise to get me further into her and at length with little sobs she suddenly got hysterical and panting wildly, burst into a storm of tears.

That stopped me: I withdrew my sex and took her in my arms and kissed her; at first she clung to me with choking sighs and streaming eyes, but as soon as she had won a little control, I went to the toilette and brought her a sponge of cold water and bathed her face and gave her some water to drink – that quieted her. But she would not let me leave her even to arrange my clothes.

'Oh, you great, strong dear,' she cried, with her arms clasping me, 'oh, who would have believed such intense pleasure possible: I never felt anything like it before: how could you keep on so long! Oh; how I love you, you wonder and delight!'

'I am all yours,' she added gravely, 'you shall do what you like with me: I am your mistress, your slave, your plaything and you are my God and my love! Oh, Darling! oh!'

There was a pause while I smiled at her extravagant praise, then suddenly she sat up and got out of bed: 'You wanted to see my figure,' she exclaimed, 'here it is, I can deny you nothing; I only hope it may please you' and in a moment or two she showed herself nude from head to stocking.

As I had guessed, her figure was slight and lissom, with narrow hips but she had a great bush of hair on her Mount of Venus and her breasts were not so round and firm as Jessie's: still she was very pretty and well formed with the fines attaches (slender wrists and ankles) which the French are so apt to over-estimate. They think that small bones indicate a small sex; but I have found that the exceptions are very numerous, even if there is any such rule.

After I had kissed her breasts and navel, and praised her figure, she disappeared in the bathroom but was soon with me again on the sofa which we had left an hour or so before.

'Do you know' she began, 'my husband assured me that only the strongest young man could go twice with a woman in one day? I believed him; aren't we women fools! You must have come a dozen times?'

'Not half that number,' I replied smiling.

'Aren't you tired?' was her next question, 'even I have a little headache' she added: 'I never was so wrought up: at the end it was too intense: but you must be tired out.' 'No,' I replied, 'I feel no fatigue, indeed I feel the better for our joy ride!'

'But surely you're an exception,' she went on; 'most men have finished in one short spasm and leave the woman utterly unsatisfied, just excited and no more.'

'Youth,' I said, 'that, I believe, makes the chief difference.' 'Is there any danger of a child!' she went on, 'I ought to say "hope",' she added bitterly, 'for I'd love to have a child, your child' and she kissed me.

'When were you ill last?' I asked.

'About a fortnight ago,' she replied, 'I often thought that had something to do with it' [. . .]

A GLOSSARY OF 333 SEXUAL TERMS

This glossary defines some of those words that are not defined in the main text of the book. It contains a few slang terms but not all those listed in hapter VIII.

Accessory nipple a third or additional nipple. Also known as polythelia

Adrenaline a hormone that gets the heart pumping fast. Also called epinephrine

Adultery sex with someone to whom you are not married (playing away)

Anal sphincter the contracting muscle surrounding and closing the anus. From the Greek word meaning to squeeze or strangle

Anorgasmia the inability to have an orgasm

Anus the posterior opening of the alimentary canal (bum hole)

Artistic/musical old-fashioned code for homosexual

Asexual devoid of sexuality

Autoeroticism stimulation of one's own body for sexual gratification

Auto-fellatio performing fellatio on oneself

Bang to have sexual intercourse with

Bats for the other side a term used by straight men in pubs to categorise gay men of their acquaintance

BDSM sexual practices or activities involving bondage, discipline, sadism, masochism, or acts of domination and submission

Beaver slang term for the external female genitalia

Bestiality sex with animals

Bi bisexual

Bi-curious considering having a go at bisexuality

Bigenderism a tendency to move between masculine and feminine genders (nothing to do with big ends)

Bisexuality sexual attraction to both sexes

Blowbang a kind of cocktail party at which a lady fellates several men in a row

Blow job (BJ) fellatio (also Boris Johnson)

Blowzabella archaic term for a prostitute

Bondage sadomasochistic physical restraint

Boobs breasts

Bottom the submissive partner in a BDSM relationship (also your bum)

Breasts boobs

Buggeranto archaic term for a gentleman who is wont to pull another man's goose

Buggery anal sex (sodomy) in English law

Bum arse, backside, situpon, etc.

Burlesque a comical and earthy theatrical entertainment consisting of short turns by exotically dressed acts, and sometimes striptease

Bust the circumference of the fullest part of a woman's breasts

Buttered bun another archaic term for a prostitute. There are many of these

Call girl a prostitute you ring up first

Camp having a deliberately artificial, vulgar or affectedly humorous quality, e.g. the *Batman* TV show

Car-sex sex in a car

Carnal knowledge archaic or legal euphemism for sexual intercourse

Celibacy the unmarried state (now often used to mean chastity)

Chastity abstention from sex. The state of being chaste, especially when caught

Chastity belt locking item of underwear designed to prevent sexual intercourse

Chuff fanny

Clitoris erectile organ at the junction of the labia minora, responsive to sexual stimulation

Coitus Latinate term for sexual intercourse

Coitus interruptus contraceptive withdrawal of the penis from the vagina before ejaculation. Known in the language of the alleyways as skeeting

Come to have an orgasm

Coming out telling your mum/friends/colleagues that you are batting for the other side. A coming-out party was once a posh knees-up for debutantes. But no longer

Concupiscence a favourite biblical word for lust

Condom barrier contraceptive in the form of a kind of balloon, available from the machine in the gents'. Various flavours may now be purchased

Consummate to complete the union of a marriage by the first marital sexual intercourse

Continence abstaining from sex

Contraception deliberate prevention of conception or impregnation

Conversion therapy 'curing' gay people by 'turning them straight'

Copulation sexual intercourse

Courtesan prostitute with a rich clientele

Cowgirl face-to-face woman-on-top sex position. *See also Reverse cowgive*

Crabs slang term for pubic lice

Cross-dressing wearing the clothes of the opposite sex. Also called *transvestism*

Crotch the angle formed by the parting of your legs

Cuckold the husband of an adulteress

Cunnilingus oral stimulation of the female genitalia

Cunt a commonplace fourteenth-century word for the female genitals. Now generally regarded as unsayably offensive

Dawn boner not a female news presenter but an early-morning erection

Designer vagina cosmetic or plastic surgery to 'improve' the look and feel of the vulvo–vaginal complex or a chuff past its best. Also known as labiaplasty

Desire the libido. The urge to have sex

Diddle to stimulate a female's genitals

Dildo an object resembling a penis used for sexual stimulation

Dogging the seedy pastime of having sex with strangers in a car park or other public place while people watch from the bushes

Dominant/dom the active partner in a BDSM relationship

Domination the exercise of sexual power over a partner

Domination house a place where domination is practised, for money

Doxy floozy

Drab slatternly prostitute

Drag female clothing worn by cross-dressers and drag queens

Eat to perform oral sex on a person

Ejaculate *n.* semen, *v.* eject semen

EMBV early-morning blue-veiner. *See Dawn boner*

Endorphin a feel-good pain-reducing hormone

Erectile dysfunction (ED) the inability of a man to get or keep an erection

Erection a stiff penis

Eromenoi the boyfriend of a pederast

Eroticism the use of sexually arousing words, pictures, sounds or symbols in literature or art

Extra-marital sex sex with someone who is not your spouse. Different from extra marital sex, which is extra sex with your spouse. That hyphen is important

Fallen woman archaic term for an adulteress, a prostitute or a woman who has socially unauthorized sex

Family planning a delightful euphemism for contraception

Fanny common slang term for the female genitalia

Fellatio oral stimulation of the penis

Female ejaculation ejection of fluid by women from the paraurethral ducts during sexual excitement. A poorly understood phenomenon

Female genital mutilation partial or total removal of a girl's external genitalia for no good reason and without informed consent

Fetishism sexual desire for an object, activity or situation not generally classed as sexual

Flagellation whipping for sexual gratification

Flapper a young lady of the 1920s with short hair and unconventional ideas

Fluffer the person who gets a porn actor ready for a scene by performing a little light fellatio on him

Foreplay erotic shenanigans preceding sexual intercourse

Foreskin a fold of skin that covers the glans. Also known as the prepuce

French disease, the syphilis

French-letter a condom

Friend of Dorothy/Dorothy's friend charming *Wizard-of-Oz-*derived term for a gay man

Frigidity female sexual indifference

Fuck copulate. Frequently offensive

G-Spot, or Gräfenberg Spot, is a hypothetical zone in the front wall of the vagina alleged to produce intense orgasms when stimulated

Gamete one of the cells that join to make a human being

Gang-bang one woman, several men

Gangsuck *see Blowbang*

Gay of or relating to male homosexuality

Gender a grammatical term for a class of object. The word is now used to refer to the idea of maleness or femaleness, or as a substitute for the word sex

Gender dysphoria unhappiness with one's anatomical sex or assumed sexual identity. Also called gender identity disorder (GID)

Gender reassignment surgery the operation/s done to change the sex of a person with gender dysphoria

Genderfuck the mocking of traditional ideas of gender identity or gender roles, by, say, wearing a skirt and high heels to work when you are the man in charge of the World Bank

Genitalia/genitals the external sex organs

Gentleman's area a charming euphemism for a gentleman's covered genitalia

Glans the head of the penis. From the Latin word for an acorn. Sometimes mistakenly called the gland

Godemiche a dildo with fake testicles

Gonorrhoea a contagious inflammation of the genital mucous membrane. Also called the clap

Good-time girl coy euphemism for prostitute

Grope an old slang term, still in use, meaning to feel or fondle a person for sexual gratification (possibly in a crowded Tube train)

Gross indecency shy Victorian term for homosexuality and anything to do with it

Group sex sex with more than two people

Gynecomastia meaning woman's breasts; this is the development of breasts on a man

Hand shandy slang for an act of male masturbation

Have, or get, one's end away a locker-room term used by men to describe sexual intercourse, as in, 'If I don't get my end away soon, Mrs Pepys, I shall spend in my breeches.'

Herm a pillar surmounted by a bust, with an erect phallus protruding from halfway down. Unavailable from B&Q at the present time

Hermaphrodism having the sex organs of both sexes, or ambiguous sex organs. Now superseded by the word intersex

Heteroflexible mostly straight but sometimes a bit gay after a few beers

Heterosexual interested in sex only with the opposite sex

HIV/AIDS Human Immunodeficiency Virus and Acquired Immune Deficiency Syndrome respectively

Homosexual interested in sex only with members of the same sex

Humping slang term for sexual intercourse

Hypersexuality greatly exaggerated sexual desire and behaviour. One symptom of bipolar disorder

Ill a nineteenth- and early twentieth-century euphemism for having a period

Impotence the inability of a man to get or keep an erection. *See Erectile dysfunction*

Intersex a new word for hermaphrodism

Intimacy a very coy English legal euphemism for sex

Intromission the insertion of the penis into the vagina

Ithyphallophobia fear of the erect penis

Jackhammer *see Cowgirl*

Jap's eye ethnically offensive slang term for the urethral meatus of the penis

John Thomas one of 15 million slang words for the penis

Kink unconventional sexual taste or behaviour

Kinky 'bent'

Knockers breasts. A slang term not suitable for use in the father-of-the-bride's toast

K-Y Jelly a sexual lubricant manufactured by Johnson & Johnson

Labia majora the outer folds of the vulva. From New Latin, meaning larger lips. First known use, 1838. Think Majorca

Labia minora the inner folds of the vulva. From New Latin, meaning smaller lips. First known use, 1838. Think Minorca

Lesbian of or relating to female homosexuality

Libido sex drive

Love-handles graspable rolls of middle-age abdominal fat

Lust intense sexual desire

Mackerel archaic term for prostitute

Making whoopee having sex

Male member polite or scientific euphemism for the penis

Mammary glands informally, the breasts. More precisely, the milk-producing glands inside them

Man boobs fat on the male chest that resembles female breasts. Also known as moobs

Masochism sexual pleasure from pain and/or humiliation

Masturbation sexual stimulation of one's own genitals

Mating copulating. A term usually reserved for non-human animals but, when not, retaining a flavour of roughness

Merkin a pubic wig

Miscegenation sexual relations between a white person and a member of another ethnic group

Missionary position copulation face to face, lying down, man on top

Model delightful press euphemism for a prostitute

Moll archaic slang word for a prostitute

Mollie house eighteenth-century term for a tavern where homosexual men could meet sexual partners. An early form of gay bar

Moobs *see Man boobs*

Morning glory an early-morning erection. *See Dawn boner*

Mrs Grundy an imaginary English character, typifying respectable censoriousness

Muff slang term for the area south of a lady's abdomen. A hand warmer

Mulier equitans the 'woman riding' position

Multiple breast syndrome the presence of additional breasts.
Also known as polymastia

Narcissism self-love. (Sometimes also known as helioproctosis
or proctoheliosis, from New Latin, referring to the subject's
belief that the sun shines out of his backside)

Necrophilia erotic interest in corpses sometimes leading to
sexual intercourse with same

Nipple a protuberance on the mammary gland forming the exit
of the lactiferous ducts. Often visible under ladies' T-shirts in
cold weather

Nymphomania female compulsion to have sexual intercourse
with as many men as possible

Oestrogen general term for female steroid sex hormones
inducing oestrus

Oestrus a regular period of sexual receptivity in most female
mammals, except humans

Oldest profession, the charming euphemism for prostitution
suitable for use while offering the vicar more tea

Oral sex sexual activity involving the stimulation of a partner's
genitalia by use of the mouth, tongue etc.

Orgasm intense paroxysmal discharge of neuromuscular tensions
at the height of sexual arousal accompanied by the ejaculation of
semen in the male and by vaginal contractions in the female

Orgasmatron a white fridge-size domestic appliance in Woody
Allen's film *Sleeper* (1973) based on the orgone accumulator.
The subject enters, closing the door. After a few seconds he
emerges with smoke coming off him and a daft smile on his face

Orgone a kind of sexual and meteorological 'energy' originally
proposed in the 1930s by oddball Wilhelm Reich

Orgone accumulator a special box for catching orgone from the
atmosphere

Orgy a sex party involving many people

Osculation kissing
Oxcytocin the 'cuddle' hormone
Paedophilia sexual attraction to children. First recorded in
1905, the word comes from the Greek meaning 'child lover'
Pansexuality a sexual orientation characterized by attraction to
members of both/all sexes and 'gender identities'
Paraphilia posh name for fetish
Passive partner the sub partner in a BDSM relationship
Pearl necklace the resemblance of ejaculate on the neck of a
sexual partner to an item of posh jewellery
Pederasty love of boys. The word and the practice are from the
Greeks
Pelvic splanchnic nerves splanchnic nerves that arise from
sacral spinal nerves S2, S3, S4 to provide parasympathetic
innervation to the hindgut. I was none the wiser either
Penis male copulatory, and excretory, organ
Perversion any sexual practice or desire frowned on by the
Establishment
Phallus a representation of a penis. Not the penis itself
Pheromone a chemical secreted by animals that produces a
social effect. Manufacturers of pheromone-containing
aftershaves insist that they drive women wild. They certainly
drive their shareholders wild
Phrenology the nineteenth-century quack analysis of head-
bumps. About as sensible as homeopathy
Plethysmograph in sexual science, an instrument for
monitoring size variations in the male and female sexual organs
that result from varying blood volume
Podophilia foot fetishism
Poke rough slang term for intercourse from the male point of view
Polysexuality the attraction to several genders. Not to be
confused with pansexuality, which is the attraction to all genders
Porn abbreviation for pornography, such as books or films

intended to provoke sexual excitement

Pox, the syphilis

Premature ejaculation pouring the custard on while the pie is still cold

Prolactin pituitary hormone that stimulates milk secretion

Prophylactic disease preventative. The term is now used to mean condom

Prostate gland male gland secreting a milky-white fluid that is an ingredient of semen

Prostitution sex for money

Puberty a period of adolescence characterized in men by highly inflamed sexual desire, a squeaky/growly voice, a terrible soft moustache, bad skin and general confusion, and in women by the appearance of breasts and pubic hair

Pudenda plural form of pudendum. The external genitalia

Pudendal cleft also called the cleft of Venus, pudendal fissure, pudendal slit, urogenital cleft and vulvar slit, it is a part of the vulva, being the furrow at the base of the pubic mound where it divides to form the labia majora

Pudendal nerve entrapment also known as Alcock canal syndrome, it is a source of chronic pain and genital numbness

Pudendum *see Pudenda*

Punchable nun archaic, and charming, slang for a prostitute

Punk archaic term for a prostitute

Pussy a small, warm and furry pet

Queer either a disparaging slang term for gays or, in the field of identity politics, a radical self-description linguistically reappropriated by and for non-heteronormative persons. *Pardon?!*

Queynte a Middle English spelling of the well-known four-letter street term for the female genitalia

Quim archaic term for the female genitalia, from a Scots word meaning snugly fitting

Randy lecherous

Rape unlawful violent and forcible intercourse with an unwilling victim

Refractory period the period after ejaculation during which a man is unable to have another orgasm without going completely cross-eyed

Rent boy a male prostitute

Reproductive cycle not a bike, but the period during which various physiological changes occur in fertile women. Also called the menstrual cycle

Retifism shoe fetishism. Named after a shoe-fetishist

Reverse cowgirl woman-on-top sex position in which she faces her partner's feet

Rimming oral–anal stimulation

Ring slang term for the anus

Roger one of the galaxy of slang words meaning to have sex with. It describes the work of the active partner

Sadism causing or observing the infliction of pain or humiliation on others for sexual gratification. Named after the Marquis de Sade, who was a fan

Sapphic lesbian

Satyromania the male version of nymphomania

Schlong vulgar slang for penis. It comes from Yiddish *shlang*, literally 'snake'. First recorded use, 1969

Screw *see Roger*

Seed euphemism for semen

Semen the ejaculate

Seminal vesicles a pair of glands that secrete one of the fluids that mix to become semen

Sensate focusing a technique invented by Masters and Johnson that is said to help couples having sex problems to focus away from orgasm as the Holy Grail

Serotonin a 'happiness' chemical

Sex everyone knows what sex is but the word is sometimes also used to refer euphemistically to the male and female sexual organs. This is mainly in awful 'romantic porn'

Sex addiction *see Hypersexuality*

Sex aid/toy an object used to increase sexual pleasure, such as a dildo, vibrator or diving suit

Sex flush a female phenomenon in which pink spots develop under and on the breasts, torso, face, hands and the soles of the feet

Sex reassignment surgery (SRS) the surgical procedure/s by which the existing sexual anatomy is altered to resemble that of the opposite sex. Also known as gender reassignment surgery, genital reconstruction surgery, sex realignment surgery and sex-change operation

Sex worker a person paid to work in what is known as 'the sex industry'

Sexology the scientific study of human sexuality

Sexual arousal the mental and physical manifestations of sexual desire

Sexual congress nothing to do with the TUC, it is merely a formal-sounding euphemism for intercourse

Sexual fantasy sexually arousing mental imagery

Sexual intercourse if you don't know what this is, there's no point me telling you

Sexual inversion an archaic term for homosexuality

Sexual organ a part of the body involved in sexual reproduction in a complex organism. Informally, the penis and the vulvo–vaginal complex

Sexual orientation the way you face, sexually

Sexual potency a man's ability to perform sexually

Sexual relations a term just meaning sex to most people but tortured by President Bill Clinton till it meant who knows what

Sexually transmitted infection (STI) what was formerly called a sexually transmitted disease (STD) or longer ago, venereal disease (VD)

Shag another vulgar term meaning to have sex with

Slapper a slut, slattern or slag

Sleep together go to bed with somebody but probably not sleep

Slut disparaging term for a slovenly and promiscuous woman. First recorded use, 1402

Snog to kiss passionately. Tongues allowed

Sodomite archaic and disparaging term for a gay man

Sodomy anal or oral copulation with a member of the same or opposite sex

Spankophilia a common sexual fetish involving hairbrushes, paddles and humiliation

Sperm short for spermatozoa, the male sex cell or gamete

Spooging to spooge is to ejaculate

Spurt speed the velocity of ejected semen. Hard to measure, even with a good stopwatch and yardstick

Straight not bent

Strap-on a dildo that you put on like a parachute or rucksack

Strip poker a card game usually suggested to some girls in T-shirts by a chap who has previously put on several layers of thin clothing

Submissive/sub the passive partner in a BDSM relationship

Suck off to fellate

Supernumerary nipple *see Accessory nipple*

Swing both ways to be bisexual

Swinging the often middle-age practice of exchanging sex partners, especially spouses, for sex, sometimes as a member of a swingers' club.

Syphilis if untreated, syphilis (the pox) is a potentially deadly and long-term STI, causing a range of very unpleasant symptoms

Tart common slang for prostitute

Testes a polite but somehow awkward word for the friendlier-sounding testicles

Testicles the two male reproductive glands enclosed within the scrotum that produce spermatozoa and testosterone

Testosterone male hormone responsible for inducing and maintaining male secondary sex characteristics

Threesome sex with two partners (that is, three partners, two of whom aren't you)

Tit breast

TMS Traumatic Masturbatory Syndrome, a strange putative condition in which unusual masturbatory technique interferes with normal function

Top active sexual partner in a BDSM relationship

Trade a casual gay pick-up who is paid in money or favours or both

Transgender a term now complicated by different political meanings but including those who are not content with their anatomical sex (and assumed gender)

Transsexual a person who is unhappy with their anatomical sex and has therefore had sex reassignment surgery

Transvestism *see Cross-dressing*

Troilism three-in-a-bed sex

Trugmoldy a delicious and funny archaic slang term for prostitute

Trull archaic slang for prostitute

Trysexual a person who will try anything once

Tumescence readiness for sexual activity marked especially by vascular congestion of the sex organs

Urethra the channel that emits urine and, in the male, semen

Urethral meatus the opening of the urethra, where urine and semen exit the body.

Urologist a doctor specializing in the reproductory system of men and urinary tract medicine for both sexes

Uterus the womb

Vagina the canal leading from the uterus to the external orifice

Vanilla straight up-and-down weird-free sex

Vas deferens (plural, vasa deferentia) either of two ducts that take the semen from A to B before ejaculation

Vasodilator a drug which opens blood vessels, allowing the blood to flow more freely

Venereal disease (VD) *see Sexually transmitted infection*

Vibrator a vibrating piece of electrical apparatus now to be found in the handbags of many young women

Virgin a person who has never had sexual intercourse

Virility manly vigour

Voyeurism the practice of peering through windows, over fences and into bedrooms etc. to catch unsuspecting people engaging in sexual activity. A mainly male hobby

Vulva the external parts of the female genitalia

Wagtail archaic term for a prostitute

Wank to masturbate (mainly male). A 1940s word of unknown origin

Weasel greasing vulgar slang term for male masturbation

Wet dream ejaculation during sleep. Also known as nocturnal emission and, by the Victorians, as nocturnal pollution

Whisker biscuit ancient slang for fanny

Wife swapping the practice of couples having sex with each other's spouses. A rather hit-and-miss affair

Wife-swapping party a party where you swap your wife for someone else's

Willy juvenile slang for the penis

Womanizing a polite word for heterosexual male sex addiction

Womb fury an archaic term for female hysteria

Xenotransplantation cell, tissue or organ transplant between species, for example, sewing shavings of monkey testicle into a man's scrotum. Not for the faint-hearted

FURTHER READING

Ackerley, J. R., *My Father and Myself*, The Bodley Head, 1968.
Gripping true-life confession.

Ackerley, J. R., F. King (ed.), *My Sister and Myself: The Diaries of J. R. Ackerley*, Hutchinson & Co. Ltd, 1982. Outrageously frank journals of a gay premature-ejaculation sufferer.

Ackroyd, P., *London: The Biography*, Chatto & Windus, 2000. The chapter on sex is the one to look out for.

Alloula, M., *Colonial Harem, The*, Manchester University Press, 1987. Nineteenth-century colonial soft-porn photographs, with a political analysis.

Bloom, P., *How Pleasure Works: Why We Like What We Like*, The Bodley Head, 2010.

Carr-Gomm, P., *Brief History of Nakedness, A*, Reaktion Books Ltd, 2010. Does what it says on the tin.

Dury, G., Jones D., & Thorp, S. (eds), *Das Krapital: Roger's Profanisaurus*, Dennis Publishing, 2010. A vast dictionary of eye-watering filth from the *Viz* team.

Freud, S., *Jokes and their Relation to the Unconscious*, Pelican books, 1976. A 1976 translation of Freud's usual guesswork, originally published in 1905, about jokes this time.

Fryer, P., *Mrs Grundy: Studies in English Prudery*, Dobson Books Ltd, 1963.

Green, J., *Cassell's Dictionary of Slang*, Cassell & Co., 1998.

Green, S., *Curious History of Contraception, The*, Ebury Press, 1971.

John Lahr (ed.), *Orton Diaries, The*, Methuen, 1986. The final two years in the life of a homosexual velociraptor.

Latham, R., *Shorter Pepys: From The Diary of Samuel Pepys, The*, Bell & Hyman, 1985.

Martin, E. A. (ed.), *Oxford Concise Medical Dictionary*, Oxford University Press, 1980.

McGahan, K. *et al.*, *Joy of Sex Education, The* (booklet accompanying a two-DVD box set of British sex education films, 1917–73), British Film Institute. Booklet and films both fascinating and strange.

Sutherland, S., *Breakdown: A Personal Crisis and a Medical Dilemma*, Weidenfeld & Nicolson, 1976. How sexual jealousy sent one man bonkers.

Taylor, T., *Prehistory of Sex, The*, Fourth Estate, 1996.

Van Driel, M., *Manhood: The Rise and Fall of the Penis*, Reaktion Books Ltd, 2010. A translation of this Dutch urologist's fact-filled book, covering medical problems in some detail.

Walker, K., *Physiology of Sex, The*, Pelican Books, 1940. A euphemistic, jargon-stuffed and evasive book from a Hunterian Professor at the Royal College of Surgeons. It covers everything from 'failure in marriage' to 'the strange urge to throw ink on a woman's white dress'. Delightful short read.

INDEX

A

Abel, Alan 51
Ackerley, J. R. 218–19
Ackroyd, Peter 131
addiction, sex 217–18
adrenaline 80
adultery 10, 13–14, 15, 31,
    34, 83, 94, 149–55,
    161–4, 166, 193
agalmatophilia 147
AIDS / HIV 71, 120, 122
alcohol 214
Alexander the Great 14
Amis, Kingsley 102, 229–30
anal sex 46, 122, 249
androsterone 195, 196
anglerfish, deep-sea 1
animals 1, 4, 6, 16, 47, 48–9,
    82, 86–7, 88–91, 118,
    125–6
    see also bestiality
anorgasmia 215–16, 217
antidepressants 216
Anuszak, Chester 74

aphrodisiacs 48–9, 141–2
    see also Viagra
Apollinaire, Guillaume 225
Aranda of Australia 82
Arbuthnot, F. F. 9
Aretino, Pietro 224–5
Argyll, 11th Duchess of 149,
    159–64
Aristophanes 175
Aristotle 14
armed forces and VD 63–4
art and sex 3–4, 5, 6–7,
    10–12, 14, 15–16, 18,
    19, 23, 33, 36, 41, 43–4,
    45–6, 115, 174
Ashbee, Henry Spencer 256,
    257
Augustus, Emperor 15, 126
auto-fellatio 11
auto suck, the 181–2
Avril, Édouard-Henri 43–4

B

Baden-Powell, Lord 60–1

Barry, James 129
Bartholin the Younger, Casper 38
BDSM *see* bondage and domination
Beardsley, Aubrey 45–6
beautifulpeople.com 187
bestiality 7, 16–17, 32, 35, 46–7, 82
Bible and sex 7, 31–2, 33–5, 39–40, 119, 127
bigenderism 130
Birth Control (1917 - family planning film) 247·
bisexuality 119, 124, 126, 165–6
blow jobs *see* fellatio
Boccaccio, Giovanni 225
body language of flirtation 201–2, 203
body psychotherapy 93
body shape and sexual attraction 189–90
Bonaparte, Napoleon 40
bondage and domination 132, 140–2, 143, 233
books *see* literature, erotic; pornography; science, medicine and sex
Boothby, Bob 149, 164–9
Boy Scouts 60–1
bras 23–6
Brave New World (Aldous Huxley) 245
breasts
in ancient art 7, 23
bras 23–6
breast feeding 27, 28
cultural attitudes towards 27
evolution of 4
laws regarding 47
male breast enhancers 180
'Page 3' 27–8
during sex 20, 28
shape and size of 21–3, 26
slang terms for 111–13
brewer's droop 214
Brindley, Sir Giles Skey 221–2
British Museum 242
brothels 131–2
see also prostitution
Brown-Séquard, Charles-Édouard 89
Burns, Robert 227
Burri, Dr Andrea 123
Burton, Sir Richard Francis 9, 256, 261–2

C

Cadivec, Edith 225
cameltoe 146
Candide (Voltaire) 245
Canterbury Tales (Chaucer) 36–7

Carrington, Charles 228
cars and sex appeal 192–3
Casanova de Seingalt,
    Giacomo Girolamo
    38–9, 131, 185, 227
Cassius Dio 30
castration 103
Catholic Church and Popes
    36, 39–40, 85, 225
cave paintings 7
Cavendish, Lady Dorothy
    149, 166
celibacy 4, 34–5, 85
censorship 45, 241–6
    Fanny Hill (John Cleland)
    244, 248–9
    films 247
    Lady Chatterley's Lover 231,
    244–5
    Lolita (Vladimir Nabokov)
    234, 245–6
    Mary Whitehouse 70–1
    My Secret Life ('Walter')
    255
    The Tropic of Cancer
    (Henry Miller) 232–3
    William Shakespeare
    243–4
Cerne Abbas Giant 3–4
Chant, Laura Ormiston 45
Charcot, Jean-Martin 58
Charles II, King 38
Chartham, Dr Robert 51–2

Chaucer, Geoffrey 36–7
China 9–10, 23, 48–9, 174,
    175–6
chocolate 125–6
Christianity 33–5, 103
cigarettes 147
circumcision 32, 98
Cleland, John 44, 228, 244,
    248–9
Clinton, Bill 149–55
clitoris 38
Clone-A-Willy kits 178, 179
clothing, fetish 142
Cocksucker Blues (1972) 247
codpieces 53–4
coital cephalalgia 216
coitus reservatus 83–4
Cole, Dr Martin 69–70
Colombo, Realdo 37
Comfort, Alex 236–9
condoms 37, 64, 122, 182–5
Confessions of St Augustine 34
Confucius 9–10
contraception 37, 45, 62–3,
    100, 182–5
Cooper ligaments 21–2
Coote, Rosa 229
copulating machine 101–2
copulins 196
corsets 24, 25, 58
Corty and Guardiani sex
    studies 82, 83, 210
courtesans 10, 13–14

see also prostitutes
Crawford, Harry 127–8
Cromwell, Oliver 38
cross-dressing 127–8, 130,
  228
cunilingus 116–17
Cunningham, Professor
  Michael 200–1
Cupid 15

D
dancing 15, 131, 193–4
Darwin, Charles 5
De medicamentis (Marcellus
  Empiricus) 29
Decameron, The (Giovanni
  Boccaccio) 225
Deep Throat (1972) 246–7
Desclos, Anne 233
Diamond, Lisa 124–5
Diary of Anne Frank, The
  (Anne Frank) 245
Diderot 227
dildos 128, 145–6, 171–9,
  182
diphallia 217
'Dirty Monday' Greek festival
  177–8
dogging 136
domination *see* bondage and
  domination
Doray, Max 133–5
Doyle, Sir Arthur Conan 88–9

drag queens 128, 228
Driberg, Tom 167–8, 169
drugs 215, 216
dysfunction, sexual 210
  anorgasmia 215–16, 217
  coital cephalalgia 216
  erectile dysfunction 29–30,
    102, 210–11, 212–14,
    217, 223
  micropenis 216–17
  pain during sex 216
  partner betweenness
    210–11
  premature ejaculation
    218–19
  priapism 18, 215
  sex addiction 217–18
  sexomnia 211
  traumatic masturbatory
    syndrome 217

E
education, sex 64, 65, 69–70
Egypt, Ancient 10–12, 33,
  175
Einstein, Albert 93–4
ejaculation 75–7, 84, 115–16,
  212, 218–19
Elagabalus 30–1
Elephantis 17
Elizabeth II, Queen 25–6
Empire Theatre of Varieties
  45

Empiricus, Marcellus 29
endorphins 79
erectile dysfunction 29–30,
    102, 210–11, 212–15,
    217, 223
erections 3–4, 18, 33, 49–50,
    54, 84, 213–14, 215,
    220, 221–2, 223
Eros 14–15
erotic literature *see* literature,
    erotic
Evans-Lacey, Richard 117–18
evolution, human sexual 5–6,
    195–6
Ewart, Gavin 245
exhibitionism 143–4

F
faces and sexual attraction
    190–2, 200
Fairbairn, Sir Nicholas 120–1
Fairbanks Jr., Douglas 163
Falcon, Jonah 53
Falleni, Eugenia 128
Falloppio, Gabriello 37, 183
Fanny Hill (John Cleland) 44,
    224, 244, 248–55
fascinum 18
fellatio 7, 11, 17, 47, 116–17,
    181–2
fertility rites 4, 15
fetishism 10, 139–40
    agalmatophilia 147

BDSM 140–2, 143
cameltoe 146
exhibitionism and
    voyeurism 143–4
formicophilia 143
macrophilia 145
pegging 145–6
podophilia 140, 142, 182
smoking 147
spanking 143, 229
sploshing 146–7
trampling 142
Fifty Shades of Grey (E. L.
    James) 240
films 64, 65, 69–70, 98, 127,
    206–8, 235, 246–7
First World War 64
flagellation 228–9, 249
flappers, 1920s 61–2
Flaubert, Gustave 246
flirtatious body language 193,
    201–2, 203
Floralia festival 15
foot fetishism 140, 142, 182
foreskins 32
formicophilia 143
Frank, Anne 245
Freud, Sigmund 58–9, 101,
    140

G
G-Spots (Gräfenberg Spot)
    219–20

Gallup, Dr Gordon 199
gas masks 142, 182
gender dysphoria 129–30
gender reassignment surgery
    30, 130
genitalia, female 7, 18, 38,
    219–20
    see also orgasms
genitalia, male *see* erections;
    penises
German Weimar Republic
    63
Gheorghiu, Nicolae Adrian
    180
Girls of Radcliff Hall, The
    (G. H. Tyrwhitt-Wilson)
    232
Gladstone, W. E. 45
Glen or Glenda (1953) 127
Gräfenberg, Ernst 219
graffiti 19
Granville, Joseph Mortimer
    179
Greece, Ancient 7, 12–15, 17,
    175, 225
group sex 7, 15, 17, 117,
    135–8
Growing Up (1971 - sex
    education film) 69–70
Guo-li-zhang restaurant,
    Beijing 48–9
gynecomastia 20

H
hair, body 5
Hall, Lesley 42
Hall, Radclyffe 232, 246
hands and sex appeal 190
Harris, Frank 231, 266–7
Havelock Ellis, Henry 57,
    115
Hays Code, the 246
health benefits of sex 73, 115
Hebrew Bible 31–3, 119, 127
height and sex appeal 188
Hemingway, Gloria 130
herms and Hermes 14, 131
Hindu texts 8
Hite, Shere 104
homosexuality 35, 97,
    118–23, 139, 214–15,
    218, 249
    Alfred Kinsey's research 94,
    118–19
    ancient and historic art 10,
    12
    Ancient Greece 12–13, 14
    Bob Boothby 165–9
    conversion therapy 103
    drag queens 128
    early psychological studies
    of 56–7
    laws against 46, 67–8
    Lord Baden-Powell on 60
    Mother Clap's mollie house
    131

Old Testament Bible 31,
119
Roman attitude to 16–17,
30
Victorian erotica 228
Horace 17
hormones and sex 78–80,
190–1, 195, 196, 197
Hotten, John Camden 229
Human Sexual Response
(Masters and Johnson)
101–2
humour and sex appeal 194–5,
204
Hutchins, Revd. John 4
Huxley, Aldous 4, 245

I
I Am Curious (Yellow) (1967)
247
I Ching 9
impotence *see* erectile
dysfunction; Viagra
India, ancient 7, 8–9
insects and spider sex 86–7,
143
intercourse, sexual *see* sexual
intercourse
internet 1, 122, 132, 133,
135, 137, 187, 240
*Intimate Adventure of a London
Call Girl* (Belle de Jour)
240

Isherwood, Christopher 63

J
James, E. L. 240
jing 9
Johnson, Ben 172
Johnson, Virginia 68–9
*Joy of Sex: A Gourmet Guide to
Lovemaking* (Alex
Comfort) 236–9
Joyce, James 230–1, 246
Julia the Elder 74

K
Karma Sutra 8–9, 143, 224,
262
Keeler, Christine 156–9
Khrushchev, Nikita 186
King, Rex 96–7
Kinky Salon 136–8
Kinsey, Alfred 50, 54, 65–6,
78, 82–3, 84, 85, 94–9,
118–19
Kinsey Reports 66, 84, 85,
94–5
kissing and lips 6, 200–1
Koch, Fred C. 90
Krafft-Ebing 56

L
La Petit Mort 74–5
Lady Chatterley's Lover (D. H.
Lawrence) 231, 244–5

language, sexual 11–12,
    105–13
latex and rubber clothing 142
Lawrence, D. H. 244
laws relating to sex 31, 35,
    46–7, 67–8, 143–4,
    178–9
    see also prostitution
Le Grand Menhir Brisé 7
lesbianism 12–13, 42, 44, 83,
    123–4, 232
Lewinsky, Monica 149–55
limericks 229–30
lingerie *see* underwear
lips and sex appeal 200–1
literature, erotic
    18th century 227–8
    19th century 43–4, 228–9
    20th century 225, 229,
        230–6
    21st century 240
    ancient and early historic
        7–10, 11–12, 17, 29, 44,
        224–7, 261–6
    Fanny Hill (John Cleland)
        44, 224, 228, 244,
        248–55
    My Life and Loves (Frank
        Harris) 231, 248,
        266–71
    My Secret Life ('Walter')
        224, 228, 248, 249,
        255–61

The Perfumed Garden
    (trans. Richard. Burton)
    261–6
Lolita (Vladimir Nabokov)
    233–4, 245–6
Lupercalia festival 15

M
Macmillan, Harold 148–9,
    163, 166, 186
macrophilia 145
Madame Bovary (Gustave
    Flaubert) 246
Magnanti, Dr Brooke 240
Marcus Aurelius Antoninus
    Augustus, Emperor
    30–1
marriage and sex 8, 13–14, 18,
    31, 34, 35, 42–3, 58, 61,
    62–3, 84–5, 210–11
*Married Love or Love in
    Marriage* (Dr Marie
    Stopes) 62
masochism 97, 98, 141–2,
    228
    see also bondage and
    domination
Masters and Johnson sex
    studies 68–9, 75–7,
    99–104, 219
masturbation 35, 39, 44,
    59–60, 69, 94, 114–16,
    216

see also sex toys
McGrady, Mike 235
McLaren, Kenneth 61
Meana, Marta 125
medical science and sex *see*
    science, medicine and sex
merkins 146
Merry Gang, the 226–7
MHC (major
    histocompatibility
    complex) 196
Miller, Henry 232–3
Min fertility god 33
missionary position 35, 85–6
Money, John 139
'monkey-gland' treatments
    88–91
Motion Picture Production
    Code 246
multiple orgasms 78, 100
Murdoch, Rupert 27–8
My Life and Loves (Frank
    Harris) 231, 248,
    266–71
My Secret Life ('Walter') 224,
    228, 248, 255–61

N
Nabokov, Vladimir 234,
    245–6
Naked Came the Stranger
    (Penelope Ashe) 235
Nash, Thomas 172

newspapers 27–8, 157, 167,
    168–9, 211, 232, 234, 240
Nin, Anaïs 233
nipples 20, 22–3
Nymphia, San Francisco
    131–2
nymphomania 217

O
Oberzaucher, Elizabeth 193,
    195
Obscene Publication Act
    (1857) 15, 242
oestrogen 80
old age and sex 220–1
Onan 39–40
Oneida Community 83–4
'open' relationships 133–4
oral sex 6, 7, 11, 17, 47, 94,
    116–17
orgasms 47, 55, 73, 74–5,
    211, 216
    anorgasmia 215–16
    coitus reservatus 83–4
    female 77–8, 84, 99–101,
        212, 219
    hormones released during
        79, 80
    male 75–7, 83–4, 92, 99,
        101, 212
    Masters and Johnson
        studies 99–102
    multiple 78, 100

orgone 92–4
PGAD (persistent genital arousal disorder) 212
premature ejaculation 218–19
orgies *see* group sex
orgone accumulators 92–4
Ovid 17, 225
ovulation and sex drive 193, 195, 196, 197
oxytocin 80

P

paedophilia 96–7
'Page 3' 27–8
paraphilia *see* fetishism
'partner betweenness' 210–11
pegging 145–6
penises
    ancient and prehistoric art 3–4, 11, 14, 18–19
    circumcision 32
    phallus worship 18–19
    restaurant serving animal 48–9
    size of 3, 5, 9, 49–53, 216–17, 249
    slang terms for 108–10
    see also ejaculation; erections; orgasms
People at No. 19, The (1949 – Ministry of Health film) 65

Pepys, Samuel 172
Perfumed Garden, The (trans. by Sir Richard Burton) 224, 248, 261–6
personality and sex appeal 194
Pesotskaya, Svetlana 27
Peyronie's disease 216
PGAD (persistent genital arousal disorder) 209, 212
phallic stones and artefacts 7, 14, 18–19, 175, 242–3
Phallus in Wonderland (Gavin Ewart) 245
Pharmacopeia (Gray's) 184–5
pheromones 79, 121
photographs, Victorian 43–4
Piccolomini, Aeneas Sylvius 225
Pius II, Pope 225
place names, rude 170–1
'plasticity' sexual 16–17, 124–5
Plato 12
Plautus 17
podophilia 140, 142, 182
polygamy 8
Pompeii 15–16, 23
pornographic films 246–7
pornography *see* literature, erotic
Portnoy's Complaint (Philip Roth) 235–6

positions, sexual 8–9, 35, 44, 85–6, 237
POW charity 132
prehistoric art and artefacts 6–7, 175
premature ejaculation 218–19
priapism and Priapus 18, 215
Prince Regent (later George IV) 41
Profumo, John 149, 155–8
prolactin 80
prostitution 47, 117, 131–3, 240
  ancient cultures 10, 15, 17, 34, 131
  Victorian 42, 44–5, 146, 156
  Wolfenden report 67–8
prudery 15–16, 33, 41–3, 45–6, 70–1
  see also censorship
psychology / psychiatry and sex 44, 56–8, 58–9, 117–18, 210, 219
  see also science, medicine and sex
Psychopathia Sexualis (Krafft-Ebing) 56–7
Puritanism 38

R
Réage, Pauline 233
Regency Britain 41

Reich, Wilhelm 92–4
religions and sex 8, 10–11, 31–6, 39–40, 84–5, 103, 119, 127, 241
reproduction, sexual 4–5, 13, 18, 35, 85
restaurant, penis 48–9
Restoration Britain 38, 226
Robbins, Harold 234–5
Rochester, John Wilmot, Earl of 226
role-playing 141
Rolling Stones 247
Romans 7, 15–16, 17–18, 30, 35, 74, 117, 126, 131, 225
rubberists 142
Rude Man (Cerne Abbas Giant) 3–4

S
Sacher-Masoch, Leopold von 228
Sade, Marquis de 40–1, 225, 227
sadism see bondage and domination
Saint Augustine (of Hippo) 33–4
Saint Thomas Aquinas 34–5
Sappho of Lesbos 12, 225
scandals, sex 148–9
  Bill Clinton and Monica Lewinsky 149–55

Bob Boothby 164–9
Margaret, Duchess of Argyll
    159–64
Profumo affair 155–9
Schmid, Jeanette 130
science, medicine and sex
    Alfred Kinsey 50, 54, 65–6,
        78, 82–3, 84, 85, 94–9,
        118–19
    ancient and historic works
        29–30, 37–8, 39–40
    animal testicles and human
        potency 88–91
    flirtation and promiscuity
        193–4
    G-Spots 219–20
    health and masturbation
        115–16
    kissing and lips 200–1
    Marie Stopes 62
    Masters and Johnson 68–9,
        75–7, 99–104, 219
    research into lesbianism
        123–4
    sexual 'plasticity' 124–5
    smell and sex appeal
        195–6
    sperm count and quality
        198–9
    surveys of same-sex
        relationships 94, 118–19
    voices and sex appeal
        197–8, 199–200

Wilhelm Reich and orgone
        92–4
    see also dysfunction, sexual;
        psychology / psychiatry
        and sex
'second-skin' fetishism 142
Second World War 64–5
Selkirk, Alexander 16–17
Sellon, Edward 228
semen 9, 29, 40, 55, 76–7
'sensate focusing' 102
serotonin 80
sex crimes see laws relating to
    sex
sex toys 180–2
    dildos 128, 145–6, 171–2
    vibrators 179–80
sexology see science, medicine
    and sex
sexomnia 211
sexual attraction
    body language 201–2
    cars and status 192–3
    dance and flirtation 193–4
    dos and don'ts 203–4
    favoured physical attributes
        188–92
    kissing and lips 200–1
    personality 194–5
    smell 195–6
    voices 197–8, 199–200
sexual intercourse 72–3
    frequency of 72, 81–2

hormones 78–80
human sexual peak 73
length of 55, 82–3
numbers of partners 73–4, 81
slang terms for 106–8
see also fetishism; orgasms
Sexual Inversion (Havelock Ellis and Symonds) 57
sexually transmitted diseases 37, 39, 63–4, 71, 131, 182–3
Shakers 85
Shakespeare, William 172, 214, 225–6, 243
Sharp, Menzies 91
Shiva 18
shoe fetishism 140, 142
Simenon, Georges 74
skin and sex appeal 191–2
smell and sex appeal 195–6
smoking fetish 147
Spallanzani, Lazzaro 40
spanking 143, 229
sperm 55, 76–7, 86–7, 116, 198–9
spiders 86–7
sploshing 146–7
status and sex appeal 192
Stitz, Norma 22
stones phalluses 7, 14, 18–19, 175
Stopes, Dr Marie 62–3

Story of O, The (Pauline Réage) 233
strap-on dildos 145–6, 174
Strassman, Dr Erwin O. 22
Streetser, Thomas 184
strip clubs 131
Stryker, Kitty 132–3
Summa Theologiae by St Thomas Aquinas 34–5
supernumerary nipples 22–3
Sutor, Dr Jacobus 52–3
swear words, sexual 105–6
Swinburne, Charles Algernon 229, 256
swingers 133–5, 237
syphilis 37, 39, 63–4

T
Tale of Genji, The 10
talking dirty 11–12, 105–6
Tantric sex 134
Taoists 9
tattoos 141
Taylor, Dr George 179
television 27, 51, 70, 205
testicles 48–9, 89–90
testosterone 79–80, 90, 190–1, 195, 196, 197
theatres and sex 38, 45
therapy, sex 59–60, 93, 102, 117–18, 210, 219
threesomes 7, 135–6
Tiberius, Emperor 17

Tilley, Vesta 127
Tipton, Billy 129–30
Tissot, Samual Auguste Andre
	David 39–40
Torture Garden 139–40
trampling fetish 142
transgenderism
	(transexualism) 129–30
transplants, testicle 89–90
transvestism 127–8, 130,
	228
traumatic masturbatory
	syndrome 217
troilism 135–6
Tropic of Cancer (Henry
	Miller) 232–3
Turin Erotic Papyrus 11–12
Twister 205
Tynan, Kenneth 141, 229
Tyrwhitt-Wilson, Gerald
	Hugh, 14th Baron
	Berners 232

U
Ulysses (James Joyce) 230–1,
	246
underwear 23–5, 47, 58, 144
'upskirting' 144

V
Vassall, John 149
Vedas 8
Venus', prehistoric

Venus (Roman goddess) 18
Vestel Virgins 30
Viagra 213–14, 220, 223
vibrators 179–80
Victoria, Queen 41–2
Victorian Britain and sex
	143
	erotic art 43–4
	erotic literature 43–4,
		228–9
	prostitution 42, 44–5, 146,
		256
	prudery 15–16, 41–3, 45,
		115
voices and sex appeal 197–8,
	199–200
Voltaire 245
Voronoff, Serge 88–9, 90,
	91
voyeurism 143–4

W
'Walter' 255–6
WAM (wet and messy
	fetishism) 146–7
Well of Loneliness, The
	(Radclyffe Hall) 232,
	246
West, Dr Liz 210, 213
wet dreams 35
Whitehouse, Mary 70–1
wife-swapping 135–6
Wilde, Oscar 45, 46, 67

Wilkes, John 227
Wolfenden, John 67–8
Wood, Ed 127
Woolf, Virginia 126
work, sex *see* prostitution

Y
Yeats, W. B. 231

Z
Zervos, Skevos 90